INTO THE
WOODS

INTO THE
WOODS

The Story of a British Boxing Cult Hero

CLINTON WOODS AND MARK TURLEY

First published by Pitch Publishing, 2017

Pitch Publishing
A2 Yeoman Gate
Yeoman Way
Worthing
Sussex
BN13 3QZ
www.pitchpublishing.co.uk
info@pitchpublishing.co.uk

A CIP catalogue record is available for this book
from the British Library.

ISBN 978-1-78531-319-6

Typesetting and origination by Pitch Publishing

Printed in Great Britain by TJ International.

Contents

'Beware, beware the forest of sin.
None come out, though many go in.'

– Roald Dahl

Dedication

I WOULD like to dedicate this book to all the people who played a part in turning my life around. There are so many of them and it's not easy to pick out individuals, but it would be wrong not to mention the following by name.

Neil Port (Porty) played a huge part in my boxing career and I will remember him as long as I live. I wish he had been there to see me win the world title, but sadly that wasn't to be.

Dennis Hobson was the perfect manager for me in so many ways. We made a great team. Our journey went further than either of us expected, but I want to emphasise that it was always *our* journey.

I come from a big family. That can be a blessing and a curse! But my parents, along with all my brothers and sisters, supported me every step of the way. I always knew they were behind me and that meant so much.

My wife Natalia changed my life for the better. I've been blessed by many strokes of luck, but meeting her tops the lot.

Lastly, I would like to acknowledge my good friend and former pro boxer Thomas Bradley, tragically killed in a motorbike crash in 2011. May he rest in peace.

– Clinton Woods,
July 2017

Prologue

*'Two things only the people anxiously
desire – bread and circuses.'
– Juvenal, AD.100*

BOXING has got itself into a strange state in recent times. Mayweather v McGregor is testament to that. A sport that many thought was dying a decade ago is now booming, reportedly. Britain has a record number of world champions and the UK public are treated to blockbuster pay-per-view nights, featuring the likes of Anthony Joshua and Chris Eubank Jr. These *events*, and that is what they are, have brought the sport to a whole new audience.

Raised in the age of 24/7 connectivity, the young enthusiasts of this scene swim in a never-ending river of content. Yet boxing's ability to float in this current was never certain. As the internet era took hold, big questions were raised.

Boxing events, of course, are sporadic by nature. Fights are months in the making and can be disappointing on the night. Purists may accept this, but casual viewers? Probably not.

How then, could boxing keep the clicks coming? How could it compete with other, more immediate and accessible sports? How could superficial interest be sustained? Without the weekly cycle of match-and-analysis enjoyed by football, or the unified marketing approach of the UFC, boxing faced a problem. What do we give the fans during all the gaps between big fights?

At the highest level, it was solved by mimicking pro wrestling. Fake rivalries and artificial animosities were encouraged with social media profiles updated daily. Banter and the build-up became an event in itself.

Slick puff-pieces, contrived face-offs and 'making noise' thus provide the modern streams of engagement. As a result, the speed of a man's hands, feet and mind, or his sheer refusal to lose, have become less interesting for the youthful target audience than his behaviour on Twitter, or the clumsy vaudeville of a press conference.

Of course, boxing always had its hoopla. It is no coincidence that the first great American promoter, PT Barnum, was a circus impresario before he got involved in the fight game, but as the sport made its transition from mainstream, terrestrial TV to subscription and then pay-per-view broadcasting, as the world wide web grew to upset the media status-quo, the sheer amount of nonsense ballooned.

Among its many effects, the emergence of the internet has mired Western society in a bewildering era of *post-truth* and *fake news*. We are deluged with information daily, much of it meaningless. It is a symptom of all this that boxers now find more of a living in 'being a name' than actually winning and defending world titles.

As ever, boxing reflects the times.

Despite triumphalist press releases from promoters, repeated verbatim in newspapers, for many long-term followers this mean the sport has been debased. Flipped tables, broken bottles, sexual slurs and death-threats do not sit well with card-topping bouts that are frequently cynical mismatches. When the richest fight in history features a snappily dressed, wisecracking martial artist, making his boxing debut against a man two years retired, it's a clear sign that values have been corrupted.

For those troubled by the sport's descent, Clinton Woods represents authenticity. One of the last true fighters, his career and particularly its most successful part came right at the end of the passing age. The bout in which he won his world title, in 2005, was the very last shown by the BBC.

More than that, Woods embodied the traditional adage of 'letting fists do the talking'. For him, interviews were a conversation, nothing more. Ring-walks were a means to get from the dressing room to the ropes. PR stood for 'personal record', a best achieved in training, rather than public relations.

In a period when the old gradually gave way to the new, Clinton's meat 'n' potatoes manner stood as a rejection of everything developing around him, everything broadcasters were pushing – the 24/7 shows, the tit-for-tat, the endless *hype*.

Woods never ducked anyone and for a brief time, after beating the Jamaican Glenn Johnson in their third fight in 2006, was regarded as the genuine top man in his weight class. There are few British fighters of recent decades who can say the same.

Now happily retired, and a grandfather at 44, he is ready to tell his story. A story of how a champion is made through blood and snot, rather than razzmatazz, rankings manipulation and marketing.

There's something important in that.

Mark Turley, July 2017

Introduction

DENNIS stands beside me, chest out, chewing gum like a camel. He's muttering away. I'm not really listening. I'm inside my head, inside the ring, inside an arena, inside my home patch. Three world title challenges behind me with no wins. What did that mean?

People said I was lucky to get another, that I wasn't 'world class'. They bandy that around like it's something official.

Listen son, if can you do X, Y and Z then you're world class.

Boxing is one man against another, in a particular time and place. It happens in the moment.

It just doesn't work like that.

In the minds of those who like to watch a punch-up and believe they have some expertise, I slipped through some kind of net. Show-ponies like Calzaghe or Hamed get all the attention. Tasselled shorts, loose lips, flashy hands – bollocks to that.

'There's people here who've said you can't do it.' Dennis says in my ear, loud enough to be heard amidst the cacophony. 'That you're not good enough. Just keep that in your mind.' I nod.

And then again, slowly but more insistent, squeezing my arm on every word for emphasis.

'You – just – keep – that – in – your – mind.'

I'm bouncing on my toes, looking down at the canvas, just as a way to focus and all this stuff, the underestimations, the damning-with-faint-praise, the condescension, years and years of it, fills me right up from my boots.

'Woods is limited, but he's got heart. Best asset is his chin. Not the most talented lad, gives it everything, though.'

I'm sick of it.

The Ingles are partly to blame. Naseem Hamed, Johnny Nelson, Ryan Rhodes, all the rest. The Wincobank lot are known around the world. When you're a Sheffield fighter boxing out of a different gym, there's an assumption you must be second rate.

If I don't crack this one I'll always stay in their shadow. For forever the journos will call me a *nearly man*. They'll write that on my fucking gravestone.

The introductions begin. MC Mike Goodall can barely make himself heard. Eight thousand in the arena and my crowd are shrieking like banshees. This isn't just boxing, for them its tribal war. United or Wednesday, they're all here.

This is Sheffield.

I snort air up through my nostrils.

I am Sheffield.

'Tonight, making his fourth attempt at a world title,' Goodall says. 'From the steel city, Clinton *Wooooooods!*'

I carry on bouncing, eyes still down, while a BBC cameraman circles in front of me for a close-up. For a moment I lift my head to look down the lens, then raise my hands, still on my toes, always on my toes. That's the thing with me, the thing they never credited. I can be a mover, when I want. I'm not just chin and heart. I can be *reyt* fast.

The noise goes up a few notches, like something from a medieval battlefield. At the back of the hall comes the crashing and banging of a drum. Voices fall in with its rhythm.

Da-Da-Da-Da-Da-Da-Da-Da-Da- 'Clinton!'

The lights brighten, then dim. All I can see is the ring. The flag bearers and officials climb through the ropes and away. And that's when, for the first time, I look across.

He is there. Pacing back and forth like Tyson used to do, twitching his neck, in robe and boots of purest black.

Eighteen wins, with 14 KOs, a rising American star, with the kind of story pundits love. The pain game, the hurt business, the dark trade, pick your cliché. This ain't golf or tennis.

Rico Hoye is an ex gang-banger. As a 16-year-old, he shot a rival dead and served nine years in the state penitentiary. Now he's swapped bullets for knuckles, but the principles are the same. I'm in his way. If he wants big money, he must crush me.

The referee pulls us together in centre ring and gives his instructions. Hoye tries to stare me out. He's got the prison yard is in his eyes. He looks mean. I don't care.

The American moves back to his corner loosely, face relaxed. His manner betrays that supreme, undented confidence that only unbeaten fighters have. There is no confidence like it. You're young, the testosterone flows, everything feels taut and primed. An unbeaten fighter doesn't know he can lose.

Hoye KO'd Sergundo Mercado in a round. Mercado went the distance with all-time-great Bernard Hopkins. Before matching him for the title, the IBF made Hoye fight an eliminator against three time world title challenger Richard Hall. Hoye knocked him out in four. It was man against boy. No-one had ever beaten Hall like that.

For some reason, the IBF ordered Hoye to box another eliminator against Montell Griffin. Griffin had been the first to defeat the maestro, Roy Jones Jr, in 1997, but Hoye conquered him too. By the time he flew to England he was convinced it was his time, burning for validation.

Now he's there, the next big thing. About five feet away. And I'm looking at him.

They say he has history in his corner. His father mixed with Sumbu Kalambay, Doug DeWitt and Errol Christie in the 70s and 80s. His grandad's his coach. *Boxing Monthly* wrote: 'Hoye looked the part of a superstar in waiting during fight week'. *Boxing News* made him a heavy favourite. Their prediction read: 'Clinton facing more heartache'.

'Come on, Clinton!' shouts a voice from a few rows back.

I look down at Natalia at ringside, eyes wide, then at press row, with their pens and laptops. As far as they're concerned, I'm a Yorkshire scrapper, a skinny, white, street kid, a scally. Hoye grew up in Detroit gyms from the age of 6. He has pedigree.

My background doesn't compare.

1

1977 and a handful of shit

MAM led us through the terraces towards the steel mill. I say led us, but she didn't really. She strode on ahead, while me and two of my brothers, Heath and Todd, scurried to keep up.

Heath whimpered a bit.

'Come on!' I urged him. 'Tha'd better hurry up. We'll be late. Mam'll be cross wi thi.'

He glared at me, despite himself. Even though he was right on the edge of tears. Our Heath, always glaring.

'Hurry up thi sen,' he said, then pulled his hood over his head and broke into a half-run. Me and Todd did the same, all three of us with our flared trousers flapping around our ankles. I could have left them behind if I wanted to, but I held back.

Every Saturday we made this journey, on foot from our house near Fox Hill to Shude Lane, where the Marsh Brothers' factory was. There was such excitement in it. Saturday was payday.

We tailed along behind Mam until we got to the street behind the mill, where hundreds of work-hardened, skin-blackened men sat on steps eating their packed lunches. Rows and rows of them, like seagulls on a cliff.

If you had a photograph of that scene now it would look like a postcard from a lost age. To modern kids with their mobile phones and

X-boxes, it would seem as distant as Winston Churchill or horse-drawn carriages. But those workers, sitting there, was how Sheffield used to be. Grafters, men with families, proud men, tired men.

They were Sheffield.

Some of them smiled at Mam. She was a right looker back then. She nodded back, still striding, keeping up her pace.

Sooner or later we would find Dad sitting among them, machine dirt on his cheeks and hands, stinking of hot metal, all sulphurous and warm. How I loved that smell.

'How do?' he'd ask with a grin.

That smell always reminded me of sparklers on bonfire night. Maybe that's why I've always had a thing for fires.

We would leave him there with his corned beef and tea flask and follow Mam to the office to collect his wages. The clerk handed them over in cash, in a small brown envelope. Afterwards, we travelled into town. That money brought such *luxury*.

'You can have a can of pop and a bag of crisps each,' Mam would say, at the grocers. The three of us held on to our goodies like treasure until we boarded the bus home, then gorged ourselves on salt and sugar. That was the taste of Saturdays…

Sheffield is a big part of me, of who I am. In some ways, my story is its story too.

Known as the city of seven hills, nearly everywhere you go around here, you've got a view. As a young lad, most of my days were spent running. Mostly through woods or fields.

I was born six weeks early, with the umbilical cord coiled around my neck like a noose. You could say I came into the world fighting. Dad described getting out of the hospital alive as my first win.

I was always a skinny little wretch, with long legs and arms. As a little 'un I had shoulder-length blond hair that fell in ringlets about my shoulders. I hated it. Mam used to call me 'pony', because she said I looked like a young horse.

At four, I was out playing with a kid called JJ in the hedgerows that marked the boundary of our estate. Lowedges was renowned as a tough place and still is, but as toddlers none of that entered our minds. We would be out the back all day, digging up worms and chasing each other around the privet hedges.

I was running away from JJ, laughing my head off, when he called after me. It was plaintive. There was desperation in his voice.

'Clinton!' he hissed, with a hint of panic. 'Clinton!'

'What?'

'I've shit mi'sen!'

For reasons only a small child could know, I felt the need to verify his claim. I ran back to him and thrust my fingers past his belt, down the back of his trousers, into his pants. Sure enough, he was telling the truth.

When I pulled my hand out, it was covered in his muck. Horrified, I ran home to get cleaned up.

'Oh Clinton!' Mam said in the bathroom as she scrubbed me with soap. 'Your worst of t'lot.'

Mam was used to that sort of nonsense. She had to be, with the size of her family. There were seven of us, one for each hill of the city, all born within eight years. She even had two in the same year at school. Mandy, Julian, Adele, Shane, Heath, Clinton and Todd.

Lowedges wasn't the best place to raise a family, so Mam and Dad moved us all to the Fox Hill council area when I was four. We had a maisonette there, with its own little garden, right on the northern edge of town.

It was still no manor house, but it was ours. Us kids had to room together. My two sisters shared one bedroom, with all five boys in the other.

All the lads slept in one, big bed, with a wee bucket at the end of it. One Christmas Eve, Mam came in drunk and threw it all over us.

Behind our street sat a hill called back edge and beyond that lay miles and miles of countryside. Rolling greenery, as far as the eye could see. We would be out there all day, lost in our games, only returning for meals and sleep.

Dad's wages weren't high so Mam did what she could. While we were all at school, she caught two buses to get to a cleaning job in Topley, on the other side of town. They only paid her a few quid a week, but she still went.

From a very young age, we walked to school and back alone. Some days I'd get back before Mam and wait on the concrete steps above the bus station. When she appeared, I ran down.

'Mam, Mam!' I would hug her, help carry her bags home. Her face would crack into a smile, but an exhausted one. It's hard to explain. It might have been a look in her eyes, but somehow Mam always looked sad, even when she was smiling.

2

A boiling pot

LIKE all our neighbours and friends, we were just about surviving, but happy. Sometimes, on a Friday, when the week's money had run out, Mam would send a couple of us out to the fields to find and pick potatoes. On one occasion, I went out with Shane and we came back with turnips by mistake. They made the worst-tasting chips I ever ate.

Things changed when the Thatcher government came in. That's when the industries of the North began closing piece by piece. They said it was about economics. Dad said she wanted to crush the unions.

Whatever the cause, whole communities were left destitute. People were furious. Mines, shipyards, quarries, none of them had a place in the new future. I was six when Dad was made redundant.

The old man had been a steel worker for 25 years. He knew nothing else, but was stoic about it, signed on the dole and busied himself with his allotment. Mam found it all hard to bear.

Sometimes she would sit by herself all day, not speaking to anyone. Sometimes she came in from work with a right look, her face washed out and grey, like an old photograph of herself. She would go straight upstairs, to the bedroom, shut the door and refuse to come out.

One evening, when I was five, in one of her moods, she simply wandered off from the house and didn't come back. For three days, she was gone. We phoned the police and waited. Dad struggled to care for all us kids by himself, so I was sent to have my dinners at a bungalow on the estate, next door to the local nursery, where they offered food for children in need.

We later found out Mam walked clean out of the city and began making her way on foot along Snake Pass, a 38-mile country lane that connects Sheffield to Manchester. The 13-victim serial killer known as the 'Yorkshire Ripper' was active at the time, so for a single woman to be alone on a deserted road at night was desperately risky. She was lucky. A benevolent motorist picked her up and took her to a nearby nunnery. They kept her there until she was ready to come home. You never knew with Mam. It was like a lucky dip. She could be like that, then a couple of days later bounce in the room and be the life of the party.

Through all this, the seven of us kids stayed close and although we stuck up for each other outside, at home there was often bother. Love and hate are close relatives, I suppose.

I fought with my older sister Adele so often. Mostly, she hammered me. We would argue about what to watch on telly or who could have the last biscuit. She was so much bigger and knew how to get her own way. One time, we ended up scrapping over who could sit in the big armchair.

'I were there first!' I complained.

'Shut it!' she replied, swinging a fist into my kidneys.

'Gi' o'er!' I shouted, with tears in my eyes.

'Shut it or tha'll get another!'

'I'll tell Mam on thi!'

But Mam didn't often take my side. She complained non-stop about my temper. She said I had a pot inside me that sometimes boiled over. In the end, she had to drag me away from Adele, kicking and screaming. I got so wound up that the energy in me exploded like a chemical reaction.

I was small for my age and quiet. That's nature. But being picked on for it boiled my piss. Adele would push her luck, but always knew when she had gone too far. That time, she saw my fury and ran behind the armchair for protection. I was circling it, trying to get at her, snarling, grasping, fuming.

Mam thundered in, bearhugged me into the kitchen, laid me on the floor and sat on me. Still, I wouldn't let up. My anger, that boiling pot, frothed and bubbled. I don't know where the heat came from, its source was hidden somewhere in my chest, but the flow coursed through my mouth and limbs. I thrashed and swore.

Mam bit me. Hard. On the arm.

Shock.

I couldn't believe it. Everything left me. The pot cooled to a simmer. Its liquid pooled up in my eyes. Stillness.

'Wha'd tha do that for?' I pleaded, determined not to start blubbing. She looked right through me. Her eyes were full, too.

'I had to, pony,' she said. 'I had to. I couldn't do owt wi' ya.'

By the time I headed into junior school, the pot inside me began to bubble up there too. My first time (doesn't everyone remember their first time?) was with an African kid called Babatunde. He stood out because in the early 80s there weren't many black children at Fox Hill Juniors. That, and the fact he was fucking massive.

He called me dirty. I told him to piss off. He was big and strong and stank like a horse. He got me in a headlock. To me, his power seemed that of a grown man. I struggled, but couldn't break free.

I could easily have given up. It became hard to breathe. I could have crumpled to the ground or begged for mercy. But I didn't. The pot was boiling.

Following Mam's example, I sank my teeth into the soft flesh of his arm and bit, as hard as I could. I bit until I could taste his blood in my mouth. *The bastard, the bullying bastard.* Until I could taste his ancestors.

He screamed and released me, face open in surprise. I went at him. There was no way I would let him use his strength and weight again. Now there was room for me to move and hit. So, I swung and swung, punching and flailing. I battered him on to the playground, underneath the netball hoop. That pot had such power. It was frightening.

As I looked down at Babatunde by my feet, face on the gravel, not so full of himself, not such a bully any more, timid, whimpering, I felt a surge of triumph.

I had hurt him.

And I liked it.

That day changed my life. Word spread fast. Other kids called me 'cock o' t' school'. Suddenly, I had a reputation and reputations are funny things, like babies. When you've got one, you have to protect it. When you protect it, it grows.

Not long after Babatunde, a kid called Dominic Davison tried his luck. Davison was new and built like a tank. He had already beaten up several lads in the year and made his mark, so the ancient law of the playground pulled us together. Davison wanted to be known as top boy. To achieve that, he had to usurp me.

Whispers circulated on the yard. He was coming after me at lunchtime.

'OK,' I thought. 'Best get in first then.'

I jumped up on to the wall that circled the playing field, so I could see where he was. Once I clocked him, over by the goalposts, I wasted no time. I ran through the crowds and laid into him as soon as I reached him. It was over in about five punches. He never had a chance.

And so, Clinton Woods the fighter was born, about seven years after.

3

Santa Claus is coming to town

'WAKE up, wake up!' my big brother Shane said. I opened my eyes a crack. The air was cold and the bit of the window I could see around the curtains was still pitch black.

'Gi' o'er,' I told him. 'It's early.'

'Tha'd better get up,' Shane repeated. 'Come see if Fatha Christmas has been!'

Half asleep, I'd forgotten what day it was. His words jolted me awake.

Me, Heath and Todd were the last ones up and soon were scurrying down the stairs in our pants. A small hill of presents waited for us under the tree.

Heath opened his first. It was an Everton football kit, although I never understood why, an odd choice for a kid living in Sheffield. Todd got a pair of football boots, nice ones too. They had Kevin Keegan's name on them. My parcel was a funny shape and the biggest of the lot. I ripped the paper off and chucked it aside, not quite in disappointment, but certainly surprise. I had a pair of boxing gloves and a floor-standing punchbag.

'Why didn't I get football stuff, too?' I thought. 'I like football.'

Even if I didn't recognise what was inside me yet, Mam and Dad might have done. Despite uncertainties, I made the most of my present and set it up in a bedroom corner. It became a kind of default stress reliever.

When I came in from school, I would go and hit the bag for something to do. If there was ten minutes to kill before dinner, I would hit the bag. Energy to burn before bed? You guessed it.

It was mounted on a spring, so that when I hit it, it rebounded. Soon I got used to rocking it with the left, then catching it again with my right hand as it bounced back at me. Sometimes I'd leave it on purpose and let it come my way, then move my neck or sway from the waist to avoid it clumping me on the nose. I had no real idea, of course. As far as I was concerned I was just playing, but I was practising basic attack and defence.

Both my parents noticed how absorbed I would get, so Dad was not too surprised when I told him I wanted to go boxing. He wasn't convinced. I heard him conferring with Mam.

'He'll never mek a fighter! That's nowt on 'im. He's five stone soaking wet, if that. You watch, first time he gets 'it on't nose he'll be off.'

But he agreed to take me nonetheless. I guess he recognised how it serviced a need within me. That boiling pot wouldn't disappear, but maybe it could be channelled and used.

Just before summer holidays 1981, on a Wednesday, he tapped me on the shoulder after I got in from school.

'Come on, son,' he said. 'Me and thi have somewhere to be.'

Together we made a bus journey across town to the Hillsborough Boys Club, a Sheffield institution. A cheap, community service that had kept local lads out of trouble for decades, as well as social facilities it provided football, table tennis and boxing coaching.

Dad paid my 50p subs for the week, then led me into the back room, where boxing sessions were taken by a short, grey-haired man called Ray Gillett. Gillett had a boxer's nose, a cauliflower ear and a husky voice straight out of a Ken Loach movie, but more than anything he exuded old-school welcome. The evening class was about to get under way and about 20 boys of different ages stood around. Ray got them warming up and Dad introduced me.

'It all starts with t' feet,' Ray said as I stood there in my shorts. 'People think boxing's about punches but most important thing is feet.'

He had a line painted on the floor for us kids to practise footwork.

'Get on't line,' he said. Then he set himself for me to copy. Once I had my balance, he told me to move. Half of each session was spent on that line: up, down, up, down.

'Never cross your legs,' Ray would shout. 'Take it slow to begin with. We can worry about speed later.'

'Now, take one step, then punch. One step, punch, one step, punch. Always keep your balance.'

'Now swivel on your back foot and go sideways. Sidestep, punch, sidestep, punch. Keep your hands up.'

It was repetitive and mechanical, non-stop for 30 to 40 minutes. After that, we'd hit the bags, but even then Ray was careful. Moving on too fast was not an option.

'No combinations yet,' he would call out. 'You can't run before you can walk. Punch, then step back. Punch, step sideways. In the pocket and out again. Hands and feet, hands and feet, this is what boxing's all about.'

Ray taught us variety, but within the constraints of proper, disciplined boxing. You always kept your hands up and worked off the jab. Then, when you could, you attacked.

'Change your direction. Change your level. Change your distance,' he would shout. 'Then your opponent won't get used to what's coming.'

We did all that over and over, until our bodies performed the basics of boxing mindlessly, like clockwork toys. Ray didn't believe in gimmicks or fancy methods and he didn't try to make it *fun*. For him, boxing was boxing. It was serious stuff. The fun was doing it properly and learning it well.

The thing was, it worked. Something in it captivated me completely and in time I became one of the regular faces at the club. I never missed a session and made good friends. I felt I belonged to something.

I had been there a while when Ray spoke to my Dad at the end of training. 'He's good y'know,' he said. 'Best of t'lot in 'ere. He could even be a champion one day.'

Competitive junior fighting starts at age 11, so for three years with Ray I did nothing but train, three times a week, Mondays, Wednesdays and Fridays. After six months, Ray said I'd made enough progress to move on to sparring, which I enjoyed. I was one of the youngest in the place, but eager and lively, while top boy at the time was a long-limbed, athletic, black kid called Paul Jones. When he was 15, I was nine. The size difference was enormous.

If there was a show or a tournament and Ray was away, he would often leave Paul in charge of the other juniors. We would warm up, then Paul would shout: 'Come on, come on. Sparring lads!'

We'd gather around the ring, sharing nervous glances, knowing what was coming. Without Ray to supervise, 'sparring' meant an excuse for Paul and his little crew of mates to bash the hell out of the little ones. They'd bring us in one by one and take turns to knock us about.

They said they were toughening us up, but really it was just a lark for them, a chance to hit a live target who had no real hope of fighting back. We dreaded it.

Paul's jab seemed to extend like a trombone, reaching right across the ring to find my face, wherever I was. I couldn't keep him off. One time, he caught me in the chest so hard I thought my heart had stopped. In desperation, I grabbed and hugged him until my breath came back.

'Gi off, you little poof,' he shouted, pushing me away to dish out further pain.

Fifteen years later, Paul Jones, by then a professional with the nickname 'Silky', would beat American Verno Phillips to become the WBO light-middleweight champion of the world.

4

Things that go bump in the night

AT ten years old we moved again, from Fox Hill and all its beautiful countryside, to Waterthorpe. It was devastating. I hated it.

Our house in Waterthorpe was supposed to be a bigger place, according to the council. But as we moved our stuff in and piled the place up with boxes, I found Mam collapsed on the sitting room floor in tears.

'It's bloody tiny,' she wailed. 'I can't believe we came here. It's the worst mistake of our lives.'

The house had looked big when empty, but furniture shrank the rooms to hobbit-size. Our only tangible benefit, as kids, was that us boys had bunk beds to sleep on, rather than the massive king mattress we'd used back at Fox Hill. But the one-up, one-down situation either side of the room meant there would always be a body too many. As the two smallest, me and Todd had to share a single bed.

'There's nowt in cupboards,' Mam wailed, in one of her moods. 'I can't tek it no more. I'm going to kill meself.' Then she disappeared upstairs.

We ran to find Dad out the back.

'She's on about killing herself again, Dad,' we cried.

Dad ran in and bolted upstairs, then reappeared, red-faced, grabbing the phone, calling for help. She had got hold of a bottle of tablets and swallowed the lot. Paramedics arrived and stayed with her, trying to wake her up while we all cried our eyes out.

'Don't worry,' Dad said as they carried her out to the ambulance. 'She'll be alright in't end.'

A couple of days later, they brought her back and everything returned to normal. I never understood what was in Mam that made her do those things. Maybe she had a pot inside her too, but what was in her pot was different.

The relocation brought with it a new school placement, meaning I relinquished my position as cock o' t' school at Fox Hill to become the new boy at Waterthorpe Juniors. Waterthorpe was considered a slightly better area than Fox Hill, although to my eyes it looked like shit. Lots of little brick terraces and blocks, as if someone built it out of lego. Regardless, the kids around there had delusions of grandeur.

On my first day, battling shyness, I sat at my table nervously when a girl called Stephanie Flanagan walked past.

'What's tha' looking at?' she spat.

'Nuthin''

'Don't dare look at me, you fuckin' gypsy.'

My long hair and scruffy appearance marked me out as a target. I quickly learned the school bully was a kid called Kevin Parks. One morning I clocked him by the toilets, picking on an infant. He saw me looking and jabbed his finger at me.

'Thee keep thi nose aart,' he shouted.

I held myself back. Mam said it was a fresh start for me and I should stay out of trouble, so I did my best to keep her happy. Before long, Kevin twigged that I wouldn't retaliate. He began to take liberties.

'Gi us a quid.'

'Am skint.'

'Al not tell thee again.'

'Am skint, Kevin.'

'Fuckin' gyppo.' *Whack*

In truth, the jibes got to me. I had never been a talker. Without the status fighting gave me, him and other kids made fun of me willy-nilly.

Kevin soon got braver and began ramping up the abuse from verbal to physical. He'd cuff me around the back of the head or trip me up and laugh. Sometimes he'd kick me on the arse in the corridor, in front of all his giggling minions.

After several weeks of this, I went home fuming and frustrated. With no outlet, the pot inside me boiled and churned and gave me headaches. I told Mam what I was going through and she looked up with her sad, brown eyes.

'Clinton,' she said simply. 'For heaven's sake, hit him back, love.'

Ever the dutiful son, I found Kevin in the morning before first bell, called him a dickhead and thumped him. His eyes widened.

'Me and thi, after school.' I told him, snarling in his face.

Kevin burst straight into tears, which bewildered me a bit. What happened to the boisterous bully of the day before?

It later emerged that Kevin knew about my boxing and believed I was under an oath of some sort not to use it. Once he found that was not the case, his bottle well and truly went.

We ended up in a meeting with a couple of teachers at break time, with Kevin crying and whining and me having to promise I wouldn't punch him again. Whispers quickly travelled from kid to kid. My status was instantly changed. One right hook had made me cock o' t' school again.

I held that position without much challenge until I neared the end of my primary school career. In the top year of juniors, a lad called Damian Howe beeped on my radar. Another one who was big for his age and able to intimidate most through size alone, he built up enough bravery and bullshit to try his luck with me.

There was a football match on the field at lunchtime. My mates against his and it's not that I played roughly, but everything I did I wanted to win. I went in for a tackle, came out with the ball and Damian used his bulk to bundle me over.

'Get fucked, you fat twat!' I shouted.

He pushed me, red in the face and panting.

'After school,' he said. 'I in't scared o' thi'

'OK, ar.'

Behind the main building was a field with a stream running through it and when I arrived for my appointment with Howe, after last bell,

31

about three quarters of the school had assembled there. Teachers must have wondered what was going on. It looked like a fire drill.

'Fight, fight, fight, fight!' the crowd chanted.

I caught Damian's eye through the masses and headed for him. We came together and he wrapped his meaty arms around me, bending back from the waist, lifting me clean off the ground, squeezing my ribs like a python. As my breath failed and my lungs laboured, the familiar feeling rose inside. Howe had switched the gas on. The pot was getting hot.

As I had with Babatunde years before, I bared my teeth, bit into his arm and raked his exposed flesh all the way down his bicep. It had the desired effect. He released, momentarily stunned. That moment was all I needed.

Only half conscious of what I was doing, I laid into him, my hands a whirring blur. I must have hit him ten or 12 times in a couple of seconds. He was down and that was it. I walked home with my position as top kid secure.

By that stage, my eldest brothers Julian and Shane were old enough to go out drinking, a rite they embraced with enthusiasm. Every Friday or Saturday night, they would stagger in late, reeking of booze and laughing. Sometimes they even brought girls back. I'd lie there in the dark, listening to the sounds of smooching lips, squeaking mattresses and moans. Like all boys, I wondered when my turn for all of that would come.

One night in 1984, I lay on the top bed in the depths of night when Julian opened the door. He was always a ladies' man, our Julian.

'Clinton, Todd!' he hissed, through the darkness, beer fumes and chip fat on his breath. 'Are thi awake?'

I didn't reply. It seemed wise not to. Todd snored softly next to me.

He led a girl in by the hand. She had long blonde hair and wore a miniskirt. Julian was all over her, lips on her neck, hands on her arse. They got down on the bottom bunk opposite and went at it. After they finished, with Julian grunting on top of her, he rolled off and whispered in her ear.

'What would you do in t'mornin' if you wake up and me kid brother's got hold of your tits?'

'Fuck off, you cheeky bugger!' she replied.

I rolled over on to my back, racked with silent laughter.

We were all early starters in our family. Not long after that, Mandy moved out because she fell pregnant. She gave birth to a daughter, Jade, when she was 17 years old. Adele got pregnant too and ended up living in her bedroom with the baby, before she got a flat too.

By then, I was attending Westfield Secondary School and for me girls were assuming a different role. Rather than just an annoyance, they seemed prettier, more womanly.

And one or two caught my eye.

Round One

THE bell's gone and Hoye's come out sharp, double jab, then winging in big punches with both hands. I don't know if it's nerves but I'm finding it hard to keep up with him. I fire back a couple of jabs, which miss.

The only positive I can take from the opening exchanges is that he hasn't caught me clean. That and his power doesn't seem to be quite as mythical as everyone claimed. The way the journos went on about it, I expected his right hand to feel like being hit by a lorry, but it doesn't. You can tell he's got a bit of a dig, enough to respect, but not enough to be overawed.

He's tidy, though, tidy and smooth, and I'm thinking just to tuck up, see what he's got and take it from there. It's nearly a minute into the fight before I manage to catch him, with a right hook off the ropes. It doesn't land clean. He shrugs it off and comes after me.

From halfway, I get the timing and start catching up with him. He's coming after me and I'm holding my feet, trying to use the distance and then...

Got him!

With 30 seconds left in the round, I land a left hook as he's moving towards me. He's hurt! Hoye takes a step back for the first time and something inside me with leaps with joy. When a come-forward fighter is forced to retreat, you know it means something.

There's a bit of afters and he tags me on the bell. Poxon is incensed, screaming at the ref. I raise my fist and glower at the American as he slinks back to his corner.

I still think it's going to be a long fight, but think I've got him. I really believe I have.

'This is yours!' Richard says. 'This is yours!'

5

The art of fighting, without fighting

B Y 1984, I had been boxing for a few years and Ray was pleased with my progress. I developed an instinctive understanding of the rudiments, especially footwork and defence. That's important because when you're grounded in all that young, it never leaves you. I reckon around 14 is a cut-off point. If you haven't been taught the fundamentals of boxing by then, you can learn them, but you will never master them to the level of someone who started as a kid.

My main problem was that I was still so slight, physically. I could throw combinations and my hands were whirlwind quick, but my punches had nothing on them. I floated like a butterfly, as the Ali catchphrase goes, but stung like one too. Despite that, Ray was convinced I had talent.

'How do y'fancy gi'ing it a proper go?' he asked one evening at the end of training while he pulled my gloves off. He looked at me earnestly, as if this was some sort of big deal.

'Alright, ar,' I shrugged.

And so, the negotiations for my first boxing match were completed.

The event was a Sheffield v Bradford junior show at a community centre. The air smelt of cigarette smoke and sweat, while nerves thrummed inside me like guitar strings as I walked to the ring. In front of all those watching eyes, it was everything I could do to keep putting one foot in front of the other. I felt like a soldier, marching towards the sound of the guns. Instinct screamed at me to run back, to hide in the dressing room, to go home and forget all this madness.

I boxed a kid called Steven Hannah from Bradford Boys and wore my training shorts, which were massive, as I didn't have any others. I couldn't get hold of any boots either, so had trainers on, while the competition vest was so big it billowed around my scrawny torso like a sail. I virtually disappeared in it. The ref pulled me to one side, shaking his head, and tied it in a knot so it wouldn't flap.

As the bell went for round one, with the ring looking so small and my opponent so ready, I focused with all my powers of concentration on Ray's basics. Footwork had to be spot on, my guard tight. The junior gloves were large and cumbersome and felt like cushions wrapped around my fists.

I advanced towards Hannah. He advanced towards me, shoulders jerking up and down. I stepped away.

Ah-hah! You didn't get me that time, did you?

We carried on circling. He made a couple of forward steps. I darted to the side. Every time he moved in range, I edged backwards or sideways. Sooner or later, I'd find an opening.

Patience, Clinton, patience.

My heart thundered inside my chest. Two minutes passed like a handclap. The bell went and we headed back to our corners. Neither of us had thrown a punch.

'How're you feeling?' Ray asked.

I nodded.

'You did alreyt,' he said, raising a water bottle to my lips. 'But you're going to need to try and hit him.'

The ref agreed. A big meaty fellow, with hands like a navvy, he pulled us together at the start of the second.

'This in't country dancin', lads,' he said. 'Start punchin'.'

I shared a glance with Hannah. He looked as terrified as I did.

Realising that the moment of truth had arrived stirred an internal reaction. A small crowd was watching, mostly parents, coaches and other fighters, but a crowd nonetheless. I felt naked up there, in front of them. Naked and exposed.

I was sure they could all see my nerves. That embarrassed me.

The pot wasn't boiling exactly, but it was heating up. I went at Hannah as I had gone at Babatunde and Davison and Howe. Boxing basics went out the window and I just threw my hands, like a rapid-fire machine gun. *Rat-a-tat-a-tat.* They were tactics of sheer desperation.

About 15 seconds into the round the ref stepped in, as a trickle of blood emerged from Hannah's nose.

'That's enough!' he shouted, arm across my chest. I looked at him, flummoxed. What did he mean, enough? I only landed about four shots.

I wandered back to Ray light-headed, grinning like a loon.

'And the winner, ladies and gentlemen, in round number two, from the blue corner, Clinton Woods!'

I liked the sound of that.

With a win under my belt, I returned to the gym bouncing. I wasn't a rookie any more. I was an undefeated fighter! My second bout was booked for a big show in Sheffield, boxing a lad called Gary Swift. As I looked through the programme, I noticed other boxers on my side of the card included a couple of seniors called Dennis Hobson and Neil Port. For some reason, the names stuck in my head.

Swift turned out to be a broad-shouldered, ginger kid with a big local reputation. A lot of talk followed him and all that expectation gave him swagger. He burst into my dressing room before the fight.

'I'm fighting you!' he declared, pointing, with a malevolent grin. I smiled back meekly.

'Alreyt,' I replied. The truth was I was shitting myself, again.

Once we were in there, I found my speed enough to get me in and out, land a punch, then escape unscathed. After I discovered that worked, I did it over and over. Swift had no answer and I took a comfortable points decision.

From there, one show followed another. I built up a 12-fight unbeaten record in no time. Ray was well pleased and spoke to Dad.

'I'll stick him in t'championships,' he said. 'See how 'e goes.'

He entered me in the county's and I boxed through four rounds, winning the lot, ending up in the Yorkshire final against a kid called Paul Levi. His dad was an England squad coach and he was clear favourite, but again my speed was too much for him. He punched air for the whole fight. As a result, at just 12 years old, I became Yorkshire champion in my weight class and stood at 17-0. As boxing journeys go, it was a pretty perfect start.

They gave me nice trophy to take home. Mam and Dad stuck it on the mantelpiece, but at my age and weight, there was nowhere else I could go with it all. Ray took me aside at the club and said he believed I could beat anyone of my size in the country, but the national ABA championships were restricted to those 15 and above. I would have to bide my time.

The week after I won that first junior title, I went babysitting for my sister Mandy. She had moved on to the top floor of Westfield flats with her baby and a Scottish guy called Rab, who I didn't know. The baby was asleep and I sat in the living room, watching TV.

From outside on the estate, I heard a commotion, so put my head out of the window. Peering in both directions down the walkway, I was surprised to see my brother Shane fighting with a group of five kids. He had a big, muscular bloke backing him up and they were clearly getting the better of the situation, despite the numbers.

Shane's friend was a fearsome-looking character and whacked this lad with an enormous roundhouse punch. The kid went straight down, his head hit the ground, making an awful noise that echoed around the estate. I felt sick.

Not satisfied, the hard-case grabbed the kid by the ankles and hung him over the edge of the balcony. It was a seven-storey drop to the floor.

'No, please, no,' the kid screamed.

'I'll drop ya. We can see what pattern ya make on the ground,' the big guy yelled.

The kid started blubbing. Once he had scared the crap out of him, he lifted the lad back over.

'Now fuck off,' he said.

All five of them ran away, faces messed up, bashed and bleeding. It made quite an impression on me. Then the bruiser walked up to Mandy's flat and opened the door. Shane followed him.

'How do,' I said.

'You must be Clinton,' he replied. 'I'm Rab. I've just had some trouble with some boys outside.'

Shane grinned. I nodded.

'They cut me on the arm, the bastards.'

I looked down at the side of his arm where a two-inch gash leaked blood.

'Dinnae want the police involved, though.'

I nodded again. Shane shrugged. Rab walked into the bathroom, got a needle and thread from a cupboard, leant over the sink and sewed his own arm up.

'That's the fuckin' ticket,' he said when he finished.

I had never seen anything like it.

6

Not pulling out

TO give me a bigger challenge, Ray decided to make a fight with the county champion of the weight division above. I was still a scrawny 5½ stone, but Ray matched me with Dave 'Dynamo' Larkin, from Doncaster, who weighed an impressive 6¼ stone. The fight was to take place at the St. Patrick's club in Sheffield and everyone knew it would mean a major test of my progression as a fighter. Within our little boxing circle, there was a fair bit of talk about the fight and what it represented.

Ray burst in the changing room beforehand, as I was warming up.

'Reyt,' he declared jubilantly. 'Clinton, tha can't fuckin' miss 'im. His 'ead's the size o' Barnsley.'

It was true. Larkin had a massive head for his age and in the first round I was able to use my feet to edge it. But the dynamo had a longer reach and a bit of bite on his punches. He was a typical little Donny hard-nut, very busy, always coming forwards, always aggressive. His added size and weight soon nullified my usual tactics. After a strong opener Larkin took every round and, for the first time in my life, I lost.

Ever since the beginning of the second round of my debut, the boiling pot inside me stayed separate from my boxing, as if training and competing somehow kept it under control. But after they announced the decision and I watched the ref raise Larkin's hand, as I walked that lonely loser's walk, back through the spectators to

42

get changed, it began bubbling and churning again. I tensed up. Ray could see it in me.

'It were a good fight,' he said. 'You did well. Wha's wrong wi' thi?'

I could barely speak. The rage was choking me.

'I wanna fight him again,' I said through gritted teeth.

So started a mini-series between Dynamo Larkin and me. About a month after the first fight, we boxed again at the same venue and I beat him on points. This time I made sure he never got near me. I jabbed that big head right round the ring.

The next one happened in his home town and Larkin gave it everything in front of his Donny friends and family, but I outboxed him so easily again. With the entire crowd on his side, the ref gave him the decision anyway. The injustice sickened me. How could such a thing could be allowed to happen? 2-1 to the Dynamo.

We boxed twice more after that, with our last bout taking place in the following year's county championships. I had grown a bit by that time. His advantages had disappeared and I had way too much for him, winning both without getting out of second gear. Years later as an adult, Larkin turned pro at middleweight, won a few, lost a few, then retired into obscurity.

In the end I had 68 amateur fights, of which I lost just seven. I won the Yorkshire championships every year I entered them. Ray was genuinely excited. He told my Dad I would win pro titles and make a mark at national level.

'Just wait 'til you're 15,' he said. 'You'll make a reyt name for yi' sen.'

He might have been right, too, but as puberty began to work its mischief, my interests changed. I don't know what it is about adolescence that throws everything out of balance, but as a teenager I suddenly wanted to be as much of an idiot as I could get away with. At school, I pissed around non-stop. For the most part, teachers hated me.

As soon as the bell went at 3.30pm, me and my little crew of mates would be off to the park or Westfield shopping centre with girls. All my early fumblings were in the bushes, in a lift or a corner of the car park there. I hadn't quite lost my virginity yet, but when my luck was in I'd get a snog or a little hand-job. Before the days of internet, X-box and social media, that was our early-evening entertainment.

As I strayed further from the straight and narrow path, I had an art teacher called Miss O'Regan, who took a particular dislike to me. A prissy martinet who struggled to manage her classes, all the kids took the piss out of her and she developed a coping mechanism based on picking out the more visible ones. Of course, everyone knew about me and my boxing – the multiple regional champion. The headteacher even had me up in assembly to show off my trophies, so that put me on her radar.

We had a lesson with her before lunch one time and the whole class made pottery heads out of clay. The idea was that once they dried we could paint faces on to them to look like a character from a story. I walked to the back of the room to fetch a cutter and when I returned, a kid called Brett Nicholson had sat in my chair. He looked up at me with a fat, stupid grin.

'Fuck off,' I told him.

He wouldn't go and I couldn't be bothered to discuss it, so gave him a couple of light slaps to emphasise the need for him to move. Before either of us had twigged what was happening, Miss O'Regan flew across the room.

She grabbed me by the hair and dragged me backwards, a significant risk on her part. Having my hair pulled was my number one hate. It hurt like hell. She let go, I span around and my fist came up instinctively. It had been trained into me. I couldn't help it.

I didn't throw it but stood there for a couple of seconds with it cocked and ready before I realised what I was doing.

'Go on then, big boy,' she screamed. 'Go on, then – hit me!'

I put my fist down and stood there.

'Hit me!'

I just looked at her.

'Get out of my class,' she yelled.

I shuffled off, wandered around the school until the bell went for lunch, then realised I had left my coat in the art room. I would have to go back.

On arrival, I was relieved to find the door open and Miss O'Regan not there. All the clay heads were lined up across the front desk, wet and soft, ready to go into the kiln for painting next lesson. I grabbed my coat, then took my time to splatter each of them with a crisp jab, one by one, reducing them to little piles of mush. It was beautiful. It made me happy.

Although she knew it was me, she couldn't prove it and the next art lesson I got to eyeball her gleefully from the back of the room while she told the class of the disaster that had befallen their work.

Unsurprisingly, my best lesson was PE, although I often forgot my kit. The teachers always made as big a deal out of it as possible. On one of those occasions I was thrown into the squash courts with Andrew Drabble, an unkempt, downtrodden lad who copped a lot of flak from his peers. The sports teacher, Mr Shaw, appeared at the door and threw a couple of pairs of shorts in for us. They looked like they'd been tailored for a gorilla. Both of us could probably have fitted into one pair.

'I'm not wearing these,' I told him.

'You what?' Shaw replied, face twisted in a sneer. He was a real old-school stereotype, a proper sadistic fat-arse.

'I'm not wearing these shorts, sir. They're too big.'

He strode over, grabbed us both and banged our heads together. Drabble erupted in tears, while I stood quietly, staring at our tormentor.

That kind of scene became normal for me. It was just how school was. I had more detentions and letters home than I can remember.

Despite that, the headteacher, Mr Cross, knew and respected me as a boxer. He made time for me, often coming down to detentions to pull me out. He would take me down to the sports hall and give me exercises to do. Rope climbing, vaulting horses, all that sort of thing.

'You need to burn up some energy, lad,' he'd say. I appreciated his concern.

We had a swimming pool at the school too and he'd chuck me some trunks, make me dive in and swim lengths.

'Get out,' he'd shout. I would pull myself out on to the side and Cross would slap me on the arse.

'Now get back in. Two more lengths.'

I would do as I was told.

'Now get out.'

Another slap.

'Get back in.'

After a few repetitions of swimming and arse slapping, he'd send me to the changing rooms to shower.

'It's important to have a proper shower,' he'd say.

'Yes, sir.'

Cross would watch from the door.

'Have a good wash now, Woods. Plenty of soap. Wash your privates.'

It was a different era and I didn't think anything of it. It felt like he was taking a fatherly interest in me.

Meanwhile, heading towards my 15th birthday, my relationships with girls followed the natural course of progression. I had a steady girlfriend called Carla, one of the prettiest girls in our year, who had really lively eyes, full of fun.

One day after school, we went around to my sister Mandy's house to visit her and her baby. Mandy was busy with her little one, so me and Carla ended up getting frisky in the spare bedroom. It was all a bit underwhelming, just something to do more than anything else, but that was how I lost my virginity.

Obviously, I was well pleased with myself and bragged about it whenever possible. That winning feeling persisted for a couple of months. I had broken through! I was a man! Then Carla approached me one afternoon as I stood outside some shops finishing a can of lager. She had a blank sort of look on her face.

'What's up wi' thi?'

'I've missed two periods,' she said. 'I'm pregnant.'

Oh shit! 'Gi' o'er!' I told her, slugging back some beer. 'We only did it once!'

I walked away laughing. Whatever her game was, I didn't want to play. Getting a girl pregnant the first time you have sex? Who's ever heard of that? But she obviously meant it. She came back and tried her luck again a few days later.

'I told thi. I'm pregnant. I'll 'ave an abortion if you'll come wi' me,' she said, still with that weird, blank look on her face.

I shook my head. 'I in't goin'. How do I even know it's mine?'

So, Carla never went to the clinic and over time her belly grew. We drifted apart and I barely saw her.

Dad found out just as I was preparing to defend my county title for the last time. He knocked on the door of my bedroom.

'Don't worry, lad,' he said. 'It'll be alreyt. Just focus on t'boxing.'

Dad was scared stiff I was going to pack it in, which in truth was at the back of my mind. Like a lot of teenagers, I wanted to enjoy myself. Boozing and troublemaking had climbed my list of priorities. By then, they occupied a much higher position than training and competing.

At school, Mr. Cross heard about my situation with Carla as well. He called me up to his office.

'Sit down Clinton, lad,' he said.

'I've heard about the pickle you've got yourself into. Now listen, I know it's a good feeling when you're about to cum, we all do, but sometimes you have to think about controlling yourself.'

I squirmed uncomfortably on my seat.

'You know when you can feel it's about to happen, don't you? When you get that nice feeling?'

'Yes sir.'

'We all like that feeling, lad. But what you have to try to do is pull out. I know you feel like pushing then, pushing as deep as you can, but you have to try to pull out.'

'Yes sir.'

'Good lad. Now off you go.'

Soon after that, I pretty much stopped going to school. Aimless days were spent walking around with a mate called Mark. He was as disinterested as I was. We would head over to the train tracks and follow them, for hours and hours, and pop up in Rotherham, or even Chesterfield. Then we'd sit and have a fag, turn around and walk back.

On the way, we'd talk about all sorts. Girls, life, the future. It all seemed so big and exciting. We were young men, for fuck's sake. We could do anything.

Some days, I used to go fishing at Ford river and walk back up through Ridgeway village, a lovely area lined with big houses. There was a post office at the top of the hill to buy snacks. I would look at the huge properties and think 'fucking hell, how great would that be, to live in a place like that?' I couldn't imagine the luxury. Owning somewhere among all that space and greenery? It didn't seem like any sort of reality.

In the end, Carla gave birth to a boy and called him Kyle. I went to visit them once in the hospital. Mark went with me. The kid was cute enough, but he wasn't my problem, as far as I was concerned. Carla took the baby home. I visited a couple of times, then pretty much forgot all about it. I told Dad I was stopping boxing, too. He was heartbroken.

The truth was I was jealous of the lifestyle of my older brothers. They were working and boozing and shagging. Officially, there were only a couple of months of school left for me. As soon as that was out of the way, I wanted to live like them.

In life, you sometimes get what you wish for.

7

A right shambles

MY LAST school report read: 'We cannot comment on Clinton's progress this year as we haven't seen enough of him.' Mam showed it to me with even sadder eyes than usual, but I shrugged it off.

I didn't have the heart to tell Ray I was packing in boxing. He had invested so much passion into bringing me along and we had spent nine years together, so I told him I was going to train with the Ingles instead. It seemed more believable. Herol Graham was their headline fighter in those days and he was already mixing in world class. Perhaps if Ray thought I was staying in the game, he'd be less upset?

To keep up appearances, I did a little bit of training at the Ingle gym and had my last two amateur fights with them. As a 16-year-old I had to box as a senior, although I was still so undeveloped physically.

I won the first bout by second-round KO, despite being massively out-strengthed by my opponent. He had the better of me in the first, so at the start of the second session I steamed in and threw a load of leather. It worked.

In the other, I fought a 19-year-old Scot called Mackenzie and lost on points, but by then I'd stopped training altogether, only going through the motions. He was a hard bloke, with real man strength, while I was still a kid. The bottom line was that I couldn't be arsed. Boxing is not the game to be in with that attitude. If you climb in the ring with your mind elsewhere, you know what's likely to happen. Shortly after that one, which I decided privately was my last, Brendan Ingle stopped me in the street.

'Do you want to do some little jobs for me?' he asked. I think he saw me as directionless, needing help.

'OK, ar,' I replied.

I swept the road in front of the gym and carried boxes for him. He paid me a few pennies. Of course, I spent most of it on booze. Brendan could see my desire to box had died and it would have been a familiar story to him.

Lads fighting as juniors, then giving up and getting fat are far more common than those who stick with it. Despite all my success as a boy, Brendan would have seen me as another lost soul to add to the long, long list – a kid without the right stuff, without belief, who lacked the character for the long road. And at the time, he was right.

Of course, I quickly found out that once you left school, life without much money was pretty dull. I started to look for ways to improve my circumstances.

After a couple of drinks one night, I was walking home and went past a school where a youth club was held. Something in my head said: 'Just go and push the door, see if it's open. You never know.'

Without even thinking, I shoved the door. It slid inward easily. Inside, I found the room full of confectionery and Easter eggs, hundreds of them.

Working fast, I got a couple of wheelie bins from the yard outside and filled them up. Tubs of jellies, sweets, everything I could find. I took them home, stashed them and went back for more.

In there the second time, gathering whatever was there, I heard the door go behind me. Shitting myself, I crouched down, praying it wasn't police. A guy walked in, so instinctively, I dived on top of him.

'Gi'oer,' a voice said. It sounded familiar. 'Gerrof, ya bastard.'

I squinted through the darkness. It was my brother, Julian.

He had been in the house, seen me from an upstairs window and decided to get in on the action. Between us, we pretty much emptied the place out. But after several trips, when I got back home, I discovered all my loot had gone. Over the road, my wheelie bins lay tipped over into a little car park area. Dad appeared, face red, flecks of spit on his lips.

'You thievin' little bastard,' he shouted. I had never seen him so angry. 'Gerr' away wi' ya.'

'Fuck off,' I yelled back. My pot was boiling. All my efforts had been wasted.

Dad went inside and shut the door. He could see I was fuming. Blinded by rage I followed him and punched through the plate glass window, then put my arm in and opened the latch. Dad stood there in hallway, in front of me.

'Gerr' away,' he repeated, his voice softer.

I glowered at him.

'You fuck off, you old bastard, or I'll fuckin' kill thi,' I told him.

Dad's eyes fell. He knew he couldn't take me on. I turned my back and walked. As I made my way up the road, police arrived and parked in front of me.

'Get in the car, son,' the copper said. They drove me down to the station, gave me a talking to and kept me in a cell for about four hours. Dad had to come to pick me up. Needless to say, he wasn't happy. Our journey back home was silent and awkward.

In the aftermath, I received my first sentence and had to go to an attendance centre every Saturday for a couple of months. It was in a school building run by police where they made us march up and down the yard and do woodwork.

Pretty much as soon as I completed that sentence I got nicked again for setting fire to a stack of yellow pages in a telephone box. They gave me 200 hours of community service for that. I spent most of it gardening.

You didn't need to be a genius to see I needed to find something more permanent, work-wise, to keep me out of trouble. The authorities advised me to go on the Youth Training Scheme at the jobcentre. I was up for that.

I was fit and capable. I wasn't fussy, either. Pretty quickly, I ended up with a job at a carpet fitting company.

'That'll do,' I thought.

The firm had a long-standing contract at Middlewood, an old Victorian, red-brick mental asylum in North Sheffield, and I was assigned there. It was such an unsettling place to turn up to, like something out of a horror film, but I needed the money and something to do. You would walk into a ward and find old people squirming naked on the floor and scratching each other. Rooms stank of piss and bleach.

Halfway through my first week I stood fixing some skirting in a doorway when I saw a huge, shaggy bloke staring at me from the end of the corridor. He had long curly hair and shoulders like a yeti. I looked up, caught his eye and without a word he leapt forwards, sprinting towards me, snarling. His feet clattered on the wooden floor, hair flying all over the place. I dropped my tools and legged it in blind panic.

I told my boss what had happened. He shrugged.

'What can I do?' he asked.

The next day, I was warned by hospital staff to look out for that patient. He was, apparently, extremely violent. 'Why was he loose and unattended, then?' I thought. It would have been nice to have been forewarned in the first place.

Despite the odd moment like that, most of the inmates were passive. I reckon the majority of them were drugged up to keep them that way. One even took a shine to me and got into the habit of following me around. He had a strange, pinched face that made him look like a little troll.

'Can I sing you a song?' he'd say, in his squeaky voice, gazing up at me while I worked.

'Alright, ar.'

And off he would go, in a high-pitched warble, like something from a *Pathe* news reel.

'It's a long way to Tipperary,
It's a long way to go,
It's a long way to Tipperary,
To the sweetest girl I know!
Goodbye, Piccadilly,
Goodbye, Leicester Square,
It's a long long way to Tipperary,
But my heart's right there!'

Often while he was singing, another would show up, a tall, skinny bugger with a huge nose. He seemed to make it his business to annoy the little one.

'He's a dafty, him,' he would say, then spit on the floor. 'He's daft. He's daft. He's daft!'

'If you fuckin' spit again, you filthy bastard, I'll hammer thi,' I would tell him. I didn't like him. He was bullying my little pal.

'Fuck off, fuck off, fuck off,' he'd shout.

'Stirrup or I fuckin' will!'

He'd start screaming and running around in circles, flapping his arms. It was such an unreal place to be. In truth, there weren't enough staff and the inmates, some of whom were quite extreme cases, were often left on their own for long periods.

I finally left that job after about a year, when I walked into one room and found a naked patient with his fist up his own arse. A couple of days later, I entered another and found a woman with a horrible, twisted face, mutilating her own vagina. Those weren't the kind of images I wanted in my mind. A couple of years after I quit, they closed the place down.

At the time, my older brothers Heath and Julian worked for a local business, Artexing ceilings, a very fashionable process in the late eighties. It resulted in a patterned effect on the plaster and was regularly featured on home and lifestyle programmes on TV. That meant demand was high and work kept flying in.

I made enquiries and the company gave me a job as a labourer, paying cash in hand. I cleaned walls, scraped buckets and mixed. I truly loved it.

It gave my energies an outlet, while the *craic* with the boys kept me well entertained. We worked all over northern England, trailing here and there in the van. For the first time in my life, I felt genuinely happy. The work became so ingrained in me that sometimes I would wake up in the dead of night and find myself sitting on the edge of the bed making circular motions with my arms, as if I were stirring a bucket of plaster. I had heard of people sleepwalking. I was sleep-mixing.

I got a girlfriend called Katie and left Mum and Dad's to stay at hers. Sometimes I slept at Adele's place too. Living with parents didn't work with the sort of lifestyle I was starting to lead.

Every Thursday, we would meet the other crews at The Mill, a pub in Mosborough, south Sheffield. Tony, the boss of the company, joined us there and would give me my 70 quid for the week, which felt like a huge amount of money. Then we would all get absolutely rat-arsed. Starting there, weekends were four-night affairs, beginning Thursday and only slightly interrupted by the need to work all day on Friday. Every Monday I was skint again.

The boys from the company, along with my brothers, made for a lively crowd and a good night out would generally feature several pints, a wrap of speed and a punch-up. Chesterfield was our preferred location, although there were spots in different parts of Sheffield too.

We often went to The Shambles, another rowdy pub in Mosborough, which had a transsexual DJ called Julia Grant. Funny as hell, she used to single out people on the dance floor and make jokes about them. She became a kind of a mini-celebrity, with a BBC documentary made about her identity issues. 1988 was not a great time to be transgender. It hadn't become trendy yet.

On one of my first nights there, my mate Dave had a bit of trouble with some lads on the dance floor. He came and found me, bleeding from the nose. Of course, I felt myself heating up inside. It was coming.

We had a look around together, then headed out of the front doors, where pockets of revellers stood about smoking.

'That's him,' Dave said, pointing at a tall, muscular kid standing in the night air shirtless. He saw us looking.

'What t'fuck are tha looking at?' he snarled.

By then I was the wrong side of four pints and a couple of lines of whizz, in no mood for verbal exchanges and that pot was bubbling like mad. I strode straight over and lamped him with a right hand. He went down in a heap, but I wanted to make sure, so I got on top of him and continued cuffing him, while he struggled to stand up. He was quite a strong kid and managed to free one arm, which he used to gain leverage by pushing against my face. Barely thinking about what I was doing, I reverted to instinct and bit.

My teeth cut clean through the skin between his forefinger and thumb. He yelled and as his blood streamed down my chin, I landed a barrage of further blows and stood up. By then he was semi-conscious, babbling sideways out of ballooning lips.

Some of his companions rushed over to attend to their stricken friend, so I shot them a glance, just as a warning. My work was done and that kid's night would continue nowhere other than hospital. I shared a smile with Dave.

Another weekend, I borrowed Katie's car to go to a club called Eclipse, where Rab worked as a bouncer. I got so hammered I couldn't drive home, left the car parked outside the venue and walked back instead.

When I returned the next day to pick the car up, one of the windows had been smashed and two jackets of mine had been stolen from the back seat. I was fuming and spoke to Rab on the phone.

'I know who did it, Clinton,' he said.

'Who?'

'I'm not gonna tell ya. I'll have a word with him an' ask him to do the right thing.'

'I want mi coats and some money for t'window.'

'I'll tell 'im.'

'Give it a week.'

Seven days passed and I heard nothing, so Rab gave me the thief's name. As it turned out, he lived nearby.

I got up the next morning to see the streets covered in snow, walked around to his house and knocked on the door. I was already simmering. An old woman answered.

'Where is he?' I demanded.

'Who?'

'You know who I'm talking about.'

'He's in bed. It's only 7.30.' Then she turned and shouted up the stairs. 'Carl, get downstairs now.'

'What do you want, Mam?' a thick voice called back.

'Get down here now,' she repeated.

He appeared at the top of the stairs and started to descend, wearing only a pair of blue pants and a blank expression. His eyes widened when he saw me.

'Wha the fuck do you want?' he asked.

With my pot now on full boil, I pushed past the old lady, grabbed him and dragged him outside. She looked after us, horrified.

I had him by the throat and hauled him, kicking and struggling in his bare feet through the snow.

'Get off me, get off me,' he cried.

I pulled him around to my sister's house, opened the door and dragged him onto the stairs. Adele came out of the living room and stared at me in disbelief.

'Wha's tha' doin' with 'im?' she asked.

The kid cowered on the floor. His feet were red with cold and his pants had ridden up into the crack of his arse.

'Oh Christ, his balls are hangin' out,' she went on.

Adele turned to him. 'Tuck thi balls in. I've got a baby in't house.'

The kid did as he was told.

'Now then, ya bastard,' I shouted. 'I want me fuckin' coats. An' some money for the car.'

He was almost in tears.

'I'll gi' ya money for t'car' he pleaded. 'But I can't tell ya where coats are.'

'I said I want me fuckin' coats.'

'I can't tell ya…'

'Reyt!'

I grabbed him around the neck again and took him back out, round to my place, where the car was parked. We got a few funny looks on the way.

I shoved him into the car, locked the doors and drove downtown.

'Try and get out and I break your fuckin' leg,' I told him.

I drove the five miles down into central Sheffield. It was about 8.30am and the streets were just starting to get busy.

'Reyt,' I told him. 'Get out.'

He got out and stood shivering by the side of the road, near the university.

'I'm fuckin' leavin' ya down here unless I get me coats.'

'I can't tell ya, I can't tell ya,' he wailed, openly crying, big tears rolling down his cheeks. I put the car in first and revved it a bit.

'For the last time, who's got me coats?'

'I can't tell ya, he'll kill me, he'll kill me.'

I moved forward a couple of feet, stopped and looked back. At last he shouted out a name. I couldn't believe it. It was the kid whose hand I had bitten the previous year at Shambles.

'Where's he live, then?' I demanded. Again, he protested his ignorance and again I threatened to abandon him. He caved in and I drove him back.

I dropped the kid off outside my sister's, meaning he had the final indignity of a five-minute walk home alone, still in his pants, through the frozen streets. Then I went to find my coats. The lad recognised me as soon as I opened the door and handed them over in about 20 seconds.

To celebrate my mini-victory, I went and got my first tattoo in Crystal Peaks shopping centre with the Artexing boys – a naked woman on my forearm. When Mam saw it, she burst into tears. A couple of weeks later, I got one on the other side too, for symmetry.

A month or two after the biting incident we were walking home from Shambles again, tailing along behind some girls we had latched on to. All of us were hungry so we stopped at a chippy, where we chatted on the grass verge outside.

A lad leaned out of the chippy door, a real square-headed kid, scowling and shouting.

'Oi, Linda!' he shouted to one of the girls. 'Get the fuck in here.'

Without thinking, I shouted back.

'Fuck off, dickhead! She's wi' me.'

He came out, swaggering and swinging his shoulders, but by then I had learned it's important to take the initiative in street fights. He started speaking and my cauldron went from simmer to full heat in about two seconds. I didn't even bother letting him finish what he was saying. I hit him. He hit the deck. Job done.

His mates came bowling out of the chippy and I prepared to lay into them, too. The whole bunch of them looked fat, soft and drunk, but before I was able to get stuck in, police arrived with sirens blaring. They charged over to break up the disturbance.

As they scooped the dazed kid up off the floor, they discovered I had knocked one of his teeth out. It was almost like a comedy sketch, but the bobbies got torches from their car and spent ten minutes searching the pavement for the missing incisor, while I stood there, impassive. They never found it, gave me a telling-off and warned me to stay out of trouble. That was it.

That was always it.

8

Hay Fever

FOR the next couple of years, life continued in the same vein. In my own way I was enjoying myself, I suppose. I battered tons of kids. It wasn't even an unusual thing. Sometimes I had two, three or four different scraps in one evening.

Most of my street fights were one-punch knockouts. They say you're not supposed to use your boxing outside the ring, but as I wasn't boxing any more I figured I had free rein. It's not that I consciously set out to use boxing moves, but it was so instinctive for me I couldn't help it. A kid would step up and my feet would just find their position. I'd block whatever he threw, or dodge it, then fire back. Nighty night.

Inevitably, sometimes I took a bit myself too. I got glassed in Blackpool, resulting in a horrible gash and stitches over my left eye. Another time, some boys chased me down Mosborough High Street with baseball bats and I had to hide in a hedge. I had knives pulled on me, took a few sucker punches. Generally, though, it was pretty much one-way traffic.

The bouncers around Chesterfield and Sheffield got fed up of the sight of us. With the Woods brothers and our mates, most nights ended up with us being thrown out of somewhere. We booked taxis to take us here and there and never paid for them. We made enemies who watched us from corners with hooded eyes. It went on and on.

Shane was the worst for it. As soon as work was done and he had a taste of beer, he desperately wanted a bit of argy-bargy. His evening wasn't complete without it.

'Look Shane,' we'd say, trying to keep him happy. 'We don't wanna fight now, we've just got here. Let's have a few drinks first. We'll have a fight at end o' t'night, OK?'

It was probably a straightforward continuation, but just as I had at school, as a young adult I built a reputation. People thought of me as a rough-houser. I would walk into a pub and straight off someone would pipe up.

'Tha' were fightin' again last night then, Clinton?'

It became a part of my identity, which was weird because I thought of myself as quiet, even a bit shy. I never bothered anyone unless they started on me or one of our crowd. I guess although I didn't often start fights, I usually finished them.

None of us were using weapons, no-one was getting shot. There were disputes and scuffles but we didn't want anyone dead. Some of the kids I scrapped with even became mates afterwards, like it was all just a big, dangerous game.

For most of us, fighting in the streets was a phase of life, a part of growing up. Of course, some of us took it further than others and some found it hard to leave behind, but there was nothing forced or unnatural about it. We weren't strutting about, pretending to be hard-men or gangsters. We were just regular lads, drinking and letting off steam.

Financially, things took a turn for the better when Katie introduced me to her mum's boyfriend, a guy called Tony, who ran his own building company. In some ways, it was a shame to leave the Artexing, but he gave me a job as a plasterer. The money was great.

The extra cash made differences to my life immediately. When I saw an advert in the *Sheffield Star*, 'Car for sale, Talbot sunbeam, £50', I had to have it. I didn't have a licence but fancied a runaround.

'There's no first gear,' the bloke said when I turned up. 'It's fucked. You have to gun it and go straight to second.'

For £50, I was happy enough it had all four wheels. I handed him the money, jumped in and went to pick up Heath.

'Come for a spin,' I shouted, full of myself. 'It'll be a laugh.'

We flew around to an industrial estate and spent a happy 90 minutes doing handbrake turns and wheel-spins, until I popped both front tyres on the kerb.

'What'll you do?' Heath asked.

I shrugged. Calling a tow truck would probably cost more than the car had. It wasn't registered in my name, so the simplest thing was to abandon it. We both got out and began walking slowly away when some gypsies turned up in a van, out of nowhere. An old boy leaned out of the front window, fag dangling from his mouth.

'Are ye sellin'?' he asked. 'We'll buy it for scrap, so we will.'

I looked at Heath.

'Alright, ar. £50.'

He paid us and we wandered off to get smashed.

Katie had some money saved up and with my earnings we managed to buy a house together in Killamarsh, south Sheffield. A tiny, little rabbit warren of a place, it cost £19,999. Predictably, as soon as we moved in we started having relationship problems. I didn't hang around and we split up a few months later. Tony heard about it and asked me to come and see him.

'I'm sorry, Clinton,' he said. 'I've got to let you go. Nothing personal, just family reasons.'

That meant, at 21 years old, I found myself broke and homeless. Initially, I went back to my parents', but by then Mam had moved Dad into my old bedroom because his snoring drove her bonkers. They had a mattress in the cupboard under the stairs, so for a few weeks I slept there, like some sort of over-age, council estate Harry Potter.

That wasn't a situation you could put up with for long and with a few phone calls and trips to the council offices I managed to organise myself a small flat on the Westfield estate. It was a one-room job and I didn't bother furnishing it. All I had was a TV, a bed and some terrapins in a glass case. I worked odd jobs, warehousing, labouring, whatever I could get. Times were pretty grim. Money was scarce.

I worked through agencies and, as I had in my teens, I supplemented my income by nicking. One time, I blagged a few hundred quid's worth of fishing gear and sold it off around local pubs and bars. As soon as I got any cash, it went on booze. What else was there to spend it on?

One night, the boys and I headed up to the Blue Bell in Hackenthorpe, a lively place, with music on most evenings. It had a reputation for being somewhere to avoid if you wanted a peaceful night. For us, of course, that gave it a certain appeal.

As well as local hard-men, the Blue Bell was known to be packed with women and we all got dressed up in our best togs. Floral shirts were very fashionable and I wore a blue one that I bought from a designer shop in Rotherham.

We all filed through the door and as I made my way in, I accidentally knocked into the huge shoulders of an older guy by the entrance. He had slicked, black hair and a bit of facial damage that suggested a colourful history. Poking from the sleeves of his polo-shirt, his huge arms were like sides of beef, bigger than my legs. His eyes flashed.

'Will tha fuck off,' he snarled.

I backed away.

'Is tha fuckin' deaf? Fuck off,' he repeated. Then, looking down at my shirt, he joked: 'Tha'll gi' me hay fever!'

I might have built a name among lads my own age, but wasn't about to mix it with a massive guy who looked 30ish and ready to rip my ears off, so retreated to the bar. A quick glance over my shoulder showed he hadn't chosen to follow me. I relaxed and got a drink.

'Fuckin' 'ell,' I said to Mark, standing next to me. 'Did tha see that?' I pointed out the guy.

'That fuckin' monster nearly started on me.'

'You're best leavin' 'im alone,' Mark replied, laughing.

As we stood watching him from afar, sipping our drinks and feeling lucky he'd left me to it, the place suddenly erupted. Another punter strode through the door. This one had very unusual, penetrating eyes and wore a leather jacket. The big brute clocked him straight away and pointed at him.

'Fuck off,' he yelled. Flecks of spit flew from his mouth. 'You get the fuck out of here.'

With frightening speed, the new arrival pulled a lump hammer out of his jacket, flew at his enemy and smashed him on the head with it. The bully staggered back, paused and then launched himself, snarling. As he lunged, his attacker swung the hammer again. It connected with a sickening crunch. Blood fountained from the ruffian's head and he got pulled through a back door. Bottles rained in from all sides of the bar. People just threw whatever they had in their hands. The attacker ran off and that was it.

The fearsome character who challenged me as I entered now stood over a pool of his own blood and glass. He didn't seem so menacing then. Drinkers murmured in little groups and threw furtive glances.

We were dumbstruck. There was a feeling like something significant had just happened and even for lads like us it was a sobering scene. There was violence and then there was *violence*. What we had just witnessed was the next level up.

9

Cigarette burns

B Y my early twenties, the years of drinking and messing about meant I started putting weight on. I still felt fit and could run and scrap with the best of them, but built up a layer of flab over my torso. When I played pool and bent over to take a shot, Mark used to come and grab a handful.

'Wahey!' he'd shout. 'Tha's got bigger tits than my bird!'

I laughed it off, but in truth it bothered me. Maybe it was a touch of vanity, but at 21 I wasn't ready to see my body lapse into softness and middle age. For the first time since leaving school, I began to have feelings that maybe there was more to life than boozing and street-fighting.

Maybe that's why, on a whim, I got in touch with Carla and arranged to spend an afternoon with Kyle. He was four by then and I took him to a local park. A nice kid, he had a strange stillness about him, the opposite of me, who was always full of energy. I must admit that was the last I saw of him for a very long time. I still lacked the maturity to be anyone's dad.

One night, we were all off to a club called Xanadu in Chesterfield, had a chat beforehand and promised ourselves there would be no trouble. As usual, we got on the beers and speed. It was pink champagne that night, which was meant to be a higher class of amphetamine but was really the same stuff as usual, with a bit of food colouring in it.

Several hours into the night, I saw a lad who I knew across the dance floor and waved. I meant it as an innocent, friendly gesture, but he acknowledged me, made a face and stuck up his middle finger. By then, we had built up a lot of enemies around the area and the kid may well have been holding a grudge over some old incident that I had forgotten.

He kept his eyes on mine.

Like an idiot, I stood up and spread my arms.

'Fuckin come on then,' I yelled.

My mate Raz got in my ear.

'Oh bloody hell, what now?'

'He's gi' me the fuckin' finger.'

The kid came running across the dance floor at me, so I hit him and he went straight down. Yet another one-punch KO to add to my pub-fight record.

Within seconds, three massive bouncers pinned my arms behind my back and dragged me past the drinkers. They bundled me through a door behind the dance floor and into a backstage room.

'What's your name, son?' one of them asked.

'Fuck off.'

'You better start co-operating.'

'Oh, go fuck thi'self.'

It started with a few slaps, but when they saw I was determined to keep quiet, they absolutely hammered me. Two of them held me down while the other rained blows on my body and head. I began to feel sick.

They could see I was woozy, so the one who had been asking questions put a cigarette out on my arm to wake me up. I shrieked in pain. The other two thought that was funny and did the same thing. Then they took it in turns to try to give me dead legs, egging each other on, their huge fists adorned with sovereign rings. They were like mean kids tormenting an insect in a glass.

My internal pot boiled away throughout the ordeal, but I was helpless. As always, with no outlet for my rage, my head throbbed. Altogether, they subjected me to about ten minutes of physical torture, which felt like a lifetime, then threw me out of a back door on to the road, where police were waiting.

'You mind your fuckin' manners from now on,' the ringleader said as he closed the door. I looked back over my shoulder. That pot wasn't just boiling, it was exploding. There was no way I could let it end there.

The police took me away and chucked me in a cell. After a couple of hours, one came to see me.

'You're in trouble, lad,' he said.

'Why?'

'That boy you hit hasn't woken up yet.'

'It weren't fuckin' me, I never hit no-one.'

In the end, I was lucky. The kid regained consciousness in the middle of the night and refused to testify or give a statement. They had to let me go.

The next week we went back to Xanadu, a foolish move. I had revenge in my blood. I kept a low profile for the first hour or two and didn't even get drunk. I knew who I was waiting for.

The bar was divided into two rooms with a sort of doorway between the two and I clocked the lead bouncer moving from one area to the other. I waited for him in the doorway, head slightly bowed, staring. He met my gaze as he approached.

'Alright son?' he asked with a smile. It was as if he didn't recognise me. *Silly fucker.* I whacked him as hard as I could in the teeth. He staggered back, then came at me full of hate and fury.

We were scrapping like hell until his colleagues came to help. At least I got a few in on him. They all dragged me out the front. The queue for the venue was massive by then and the whole line of them turned to watch the show.

Again, police had been called, meaning two coppers waited on the pavement. Without speaking, one pinned my arms behind my back. As he did that, a bouncer kicked my legs away from underneath me. I fell, hard, face down on to the kerb.

'Oooh,' gasped the crowd.

One of the coppers looked over at the lead bouncer, the one I had punched in the first place.

'Go on then,' he said.

The bouncer ran in and booted me, full pelt, in the side of the head. My eye swelled up instantly. Lines danced across my vision. Not satisfied yet, he pulled me up with one hand and pushed his thumb into my damaged eye with the other. The pain was excruciating. I gritted my teeth, not wanting to cry out, with everyone looking on.

'Have that, tha' little bastard,' he said.

'He's had enough now,' replied the copper.

They scooped me up, took me away and kept me overnight, again.

'Once can be a mistake,' the custody sergeant said. 'But not twice. You haven't heard the last of this.'

I went back to my little flat in Westfield. Work had been on and off, mostly off. There was nothing to eat and the electricity had run out. I sat alone with my battered face in my freezing flat. It was probably the worst period of my life.

On the Tuesday, two letters arrived in the post. One from the police, informing me I had been charged with actual bodily harm for smashing the bouncer's teeth. I had a court date the following month. The other was handwritten. It said:

> Dear Clinton,
>
> I want you to know that you're breaking my heart. Every weekend you're going out and causing trouble. Those boys you're hanging around with aren't proper mates. You shouldn't be sticking up for them all the time. I know from your brothers what you've been doing and I'm scared. I'm scared you're going to end up in prison or dead. I worry about you in your little flat, all alone, with nothing to do but drink and fight. It's a sad life for a young man. And you deserve better. I know you've got good in you, Clinton, and I want you to show it. You could achieve so much. Just look around at where you are and ask, is this the best I can do?
>
> Love,
> Mam.

I stopped reading and put the letter down. My breath was short. I had tears on my cheeks. As she suggested, I looked around. My walls were bare apart from nails I had banged in to hang my coats on.

Mam was right. I was broke, I had been beaten up, I could go to prison and I had nothing. At the time, I couldn't even afford a bag of chips.

When my case came around a week or two later, the judge weighed my injuries against the bouncer's. He said I had probably come off worse. My eye was healing by then but still looked bad.

'The judge likes you,' my solicitor said as the court recessed. 'You'll either get three months or a spot of community service.'

It was the latter and I was relieved. It felt like I had been given a chance.

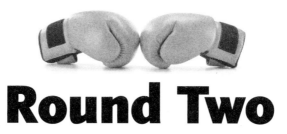

Round Two

THEY must have given Hoye a bollocking in the corner. He's come out like a looney at the start of the second. Within 15 seconds, we're exchanging combinations near the centre of the ring.

'You don't need a war,' someone shouts from ringside – sound advice. It might have been Dennis, but I can't be sure.

By this point, I've twigged that Hoye is unloading but going back in straight lines and hanging his chin out. I wait for him to throw two or three shots, bounce forwards, then unleash my own. In my mind, I'm back on the line, back with Ray – step then punch. Step then punch.

I'm using the ring, catching him with the left hook as I move. My jab is a real weapon. All the work with Mark Hobson is paying off. My timing has kicked in and when I throw it, it lands. I snap his head back. *Have that!*

Hoye hangs in there and tags me to the body repeatedly. I wonder what the judges are seeing. You never know.

'Have I lost that round?' I ask in the corner after the bell.

'No Clint.' Poxon says, feeding me water. He's nearly as fired up as I am. 'No way.'

10

Comeback

NOT long after my troubles with the bouncer, I picked up some labouring work from an agency and found myself on the piss again, at Shambles. A familiar face grinned at me from across the bar. It was Chris Longdon, a lad I knew from the years of mayhem.

'Don't you box any more?' he asked after I bought him a pint.

I shook my head.

'You're mad. You were reyt good. Why don't you go down't gym in Woodhouse and gi' it a go?'

I mulled it over for a second. It didn't seem such a terrible idea.

'Who runs it?'

'Guy called Dennis Hobson.'

The name sounded familiar. I couldn't think from where.

'It's down Stone Lane.'

'P'raps I will then, ar.'

A couple of hours and several drinks later that night, I got in yet another altercation with some lads. As usual I came out on top, but had to take a few.

Over the next couple of days, that conversation kept replaying in my mind, along with the letter from Mam. In truth, boxing was the only thing I'd been really good at. When I boxed, I won things. It would be an obvious way to get myself fit too. Maybe I could get rid of my tits?

By the Tuesday evening, after work, I found myself driving down Stone Lane, a lovely, secluded, country road, little more than a track in places, dotted with occasional buildings here and there. Popular with joggers during the day, it also had a reputation for attracting enthusiasts of dogging and other sexual fetishes at night.

The building, when I finally came across it, was little more than a shack by the side of the road and appeared way too small. As I stepped through the door, I realised that first impression was absolutely right. A small ring sat against one wall, with a few bags hanging down the side next to it. It stank of damp and mould.

A broad-shouldered, thick-armed guy with a mullet haircut stood in the middle of the canvas, taking a kid on the pads. He had his back to me, so I waited for a pause in their session before speaking up.

'How do,' I called when the opportunity presented itself.

The trainer turned. Our eyes met. Recognition flashed through my head like a floodlight.

It was the tough nut from The Blue Bell years before, the scary bastard who had threatened me. He still bore a scar on his forehead from the hammer attack as confirmation.

The last time I saw this man he had been surrounded by his own blood and broken glass. Now he glowered at me, his manner exactly the same as it had been that night, as if he was about to tell me to fuck off again.

'I'd like to box,' I said. He looked me slowly up and down. I still had a cut lip and a black eye from the weekend's punch-up.

'Hmm…' he said. 'Has tha done any before?'

'Ar, a bit.'

'Go on then.' he grunted. 'Gi' on wi' it.' Then he turned back around to continue his pad session.

I grabbed an old pair of gloves from the corner and began hitting bags. Punch followed punch, my feet worked on instinct. I felt loose and smooth. It was almost magical, like I'd never been away.

I stayed there for a couple of hours, training myself. For the whole time, the coach never spoke to me again or even looked in my direction.

The following evening, I returned. That time the trainer, whose name I discovered was Neil Port, had no words for me at all, acknowledging me only with a movement of his eyebrows. And so it went on, for a couple of weeks. Some nights the gym owner, Dennis Hobson, a local scrap metal dealer, would be in there too. He was a confident, charismatic guy, with a kind of swagger about him. He had penetrating eyes and could box a bit when he wanted as well. Sometimes he even got in the ring and sparred with the lads. His family were known in the area, bearing a reputation as people you did not want to upset. His dad drove around Sheffield in a Rolls Royce.

I felt my fitness increasing quickly. When you're young, it doesn't take long to get back in shape. People on the outside noticed and my girlfriend complimented me on the change in my physique.

Having shown commitment with a spell of solitary training, Neil slowly began to take more interest. In my third week, he allowed me into the ring for body sparring. He would sweat like a maniac. Droplets would fly off his hair as he moved around, going in my face, which I hated, but I stuck at it. By the fifth week, I sparred to the head. Other lads noticed me in there. You could hear them whispering. They saw I knew what I was doing.

It turned out the gym had been built in part of a disused steel factory where they used to make gardening tools. Dennis moved there after he started training a few kids. It had no heating and a drainage problem meant the floor flooded every time it rained. Our only luxury was a basic steam room off to the back, which Porty installed. After a bit of training, we would pile in there, chuck some water on the coals and flush out our systems, before re-emerging into the arctic air outside.

In a funny way, the place suited Neil and Dennis. It probably suited me too, in truth. At that time, none of us were the types for luxuries like air-conditioning or showers.

Porty, in particular, was an earthy, no-nonsense man's man who showed himself to be quite likeable once you got past his gruffness. Like a lot of blokes of his sort he was hard to like, but once you learned how, it stayed with you. He had an intense sense of loyalty.

Physically, he was as strong as a rhino and ate like one too. Whatever clothes he wore were always covered in smears of his most recent meal. It became a joke among the lads.

'Chips and gravy today, Porty?'

'Shurrup, you cheeky little fucker.'

He rarely smiled, every sentence he spoke contained at least two swear words and he could be the meanest bastard alive. But there was something warm, almost fatherly about him too. It wasn't just a job for him. Porty really *wanted* you to do well. After the first month or so, he got involved with my strength and conditioning. He would have me doing bodyweight exercises like pull-ups.

'Fucking one more,' he would scream, while I dangled there, arms like jelly.

'Fucking one more or you're never setting foot in this fucking gym again. I'm sick of you, you skinny, lazy little fucker. One fucking more.'

It worked. Somehow, with Neil yelling abuse in my ear, I always managed one more, no matter how many I had already done.

The gym had one professional, a shaven-headed firebrand called Robert Riley. He came bursting into the changing room one evening as I was preparing to go home.

'Oi!' he shouted, face screwed up in a sneer. 'I'm top fuckin' dog round 'ere. Tha' would do well to remember that.'

I nodded and shrugged. It meant nothing to me. Despite camaraderie and banter, there is often needle in boxing gyms, especially among sparring partners. To go from punching someone in the face to easy friendship in the space of a few minutes is not always a straightforward transition. But hierarchies didn't interest me. I had no real intention of boxing. As far as I was concerned, I was just getting fit.

The minute I walked in the next afternoon, Neil looked up from his chair and lowered his newspaper.

'Get warmed up, Clint,' he said quietly. 'Tha's sparrin' Riley.'

Riley stood in the corner, bashing the crap out of the heavy bag, sweat streaming down his face.

'A proper, hard spar to see where we're at.'

Riley had a mixed record, with a handful of wins and defeats. He had boxed for the Central Area light-middleweight title too, but was seven years my senior and had the man-strength that went with that. Even at twenty-two, I still had a gawky, adolescent physique.

I changed, came back out and warmed up. Neil sat on a stool just outside the ropes, half a smile on his face. Riley glared at me from the other corner, almost blowing steam out of his nostrils in his eagerness to get at me.

'OK lads?' Neil asked.

We both nodded.

'Time.'

Riley bolted across the ring and threw a fast three-punch combination, which I saw coming. I swayed from the waist to avoid the first two, left then right, took a side-step to dodge the third, tagged him with a jab then bounced away. That enraged him further and he came bounding after me, swinging an arching right hand that I blocked on my gloves. Despite the fact none of the punches landed, I could feel the force he was putting into them. This was supposed to be sparring, wasn't it?

The round continued in much the same way as it began. Riley pursued me. He was strong, but not that mobile for a light-middle and fighting him was like baiting an angry bear tethered to a post. He would come lunging after me from centre ring, while I moved and jabbed, circling out of his way and picking him off. You could see his frustration building.

'Time,' Neil called. We went back to our corners. Porty watched me, with a weird, fixed expression.

At the start of the second, Riley closed the distance and tried to stay on my chest. I used my elbows to deflect his shots and rocked his head back with an uppercut. As he reeled from the effects of the punch, I dug a short left hook into his ribs. He sank to the canvas.

'Time,' Neil yelled. He climbed through the ropes and helped Riley to his feet. He puffed and wheezed, face flushed, eyes blank. The spar was finished. I found out later I broke his ribs.

A few days after that, as I worked the bags, Dennis wandered over, smiling. We had barely spoken before, only a few words here and there.

'Alright Clinton?' he asked.

'Alright, ar.'

'You're doing OK, I hear. What are your plans? Why don't you give the pro game a go?'

I stopped throwing my hands and looked at him. I wanted to see if he was having a laugh. He wasn't.

'Alright,' I replied.

I had only been back in training for three months.

11

Shorts like Hagler,
fans like Hatton

DENNIS made me an appointment at the Central Area Board and sorted out my medicals. He paid for them, as well, which was nice. The whole business was completed in about a month. In my mind, I thought I could get out, have a few fights, win some, lose some and make a couple of quid. All the roustabout mates I had from pubs and bars would come to support me. I was sure of it. It would be a laugh, if nothing else.

By then, it was early November '94 and being in that pokey little gym was like training in a walk-in freezer. One evening, as I skipped in about three layers of clothing, trying to get warm, Dennis sauntered over.

'I'm doing a show at Pinegrove in a couple of weeks,' he said. 'You're on.'

'Fair enough.'

'Have you got any shorts?'

I shook my head.

'You're gonna need to sort some out.'

That night, I told my lass I was intending to box pro and would need some show shorts. The only problem was a familiar one. I was skint.

'I'll get me gran to make some,' she said.

'Oh reyt, ta.'

I went down to the Moor Market and bought the cheapest piece of material I could find, a kind of dark blue corduroy. The great middleweight champ Marvelous Marvin Hagler boxed in something similar on the telly in the 80s. I reckoned I could emulate his style. I always loved a bit of retro.

I passed the cloth on to my girl, who said she would get her gran on it straight away. I could pick up my new shorts before the fight.

When I went to collect them on the Thursday morning, I realised it might have been more sensible to enlist a professional. I held them up in front of me. They reached from my nipples to my knees.

'Oh, great, ta very much,' I said, forcing a smile. The old girl beamed with pride.

When I put them on in the venue that night, they were like three-quarter-length trousers.

'Why the fuck didn't tha say tha had no shorts?' Dennis asked in the dressing room as I warmed up.

'Come on, they're alright.'

'Fuckin' hell!'

A compact room with tiered seating, the venue held about 800 people and we sold it out without a problem. Dad shifted tons of tickets to old colleagues and acquaintances of his, soon earning himself the nickname 'Don King' because of his persistence. He would trawl the pubs of south Sheffield, punting them out for me. He enjoyed doing it, too.

A right rough-houser called Tommy, who trained on and off with Dennis, organised tons of his mates to come down. Another bruiser known as 'Knockers' got involved. He had connections to the Owls Crime Squad, the hooligan firm of Sheffield Wednesday. As I had always been a Wednesday fan, he rounded up his mob to support me too. Altogether, I moved over 500 tickets. For an unknown lad making his debut, it was a blinding start.

Dad ran into the changing room as I was warming up and gave me a pack of spearmint chewing gum for some reason.

'Good luck, lad,' he said, patting me on the back. Neither of us knew it then, but that exchange became a little ritual that would last throughout my career. I waited for my time to walk as the walls pounded with noise. It really stirred me up inside. My people were there, Sheffield people, waiting for me.

Maybe my years of trouble-making around town had some positive repercussions after all? The Clinton Woods crowd were rowdy as hell and created an electrifying atmosphere, a proper testosterone-filled cauldron. 'This is fucking boxing!' I thought as I walked through them. They howled their encouragement. My skin tingled.

Dennis found an opponent called David Proctor, a decent kid, with two wins from four fights. He came for a proper tear-up and met me in centre ring as soon as the bell rang. He fired a left, which I avoided, then swung a right over the top that clattered into my gloves. Straight away, I knew I was involved in a scrap. Proctor had no intention of lying down. But I loved that.

I kept him on the jab and stayed mobile, using the ring, using my feet. As a strategy, that worked until my oversized shorts soaked through with sweat. The spongey material absorbed everything and from the start of the second they felt like a ten-kilo weight hanging off my waist. Things might have got difficult if it had been more than a four-rounder.

Proctor got in close a few times and tried to old-man me, but I wouldn't allow it. I tied him up, pushed him off, stuck my jab in his face and bounced off to the side. In the end, I took every round.

'Your winner, ladies and gentlemen, in the blue corner Clinton Wooooods!'

What a feeling. Afterwards, a couple of hundred of us went down to Josephine's, a nightclub in the city centre, for a piss-up. Porty even got drunk with us too. He put a huge arm around my shoulders.

'This lad's gonna be British champion,' he announced. Everyone cheered, glasses in the air. I shook my head.

'Come on, don't say that,' I chided. 'It's embarrassing.'

That weekend turned into one, long drinking session, just like the old days. I even got back on the whizz. But almost as soon as I had recovered from it and wandered back into the gym, a week later, Dennis told me I was booked in again.

It wasn't a conscious thing, but from the moment I knew I was boxing, I laid off the booze and gear. I hadn't fully admitted it to myself yet, but deep inside I wanted this to work. Boxing was my only real chance to do something out of the ordinary.

My second bout saw me up against Earl Ling at the Winter Gardens in Cleethorpes, three weeks after my first. Dennis got me some proper boxing shorts, in Wednesday colours, white and blue. I left the corduroy ones in my kitchen and used them as a tea-towel.

Ling, from Norwich, fancied himself as a right hard-case, with a shaven head and lots of bluster. He had little to offer in the way of skill, though.

I used my fundamentals and was handling him comfortably until he tried to headbutt me at the start of the fifth. That old pot started boiling and I went after him, battering him against the ropes. Punch followed punch until the ref pulled us apart.

TKO. *Stick your head on that, pal.* Porty was overjoyed.

'See what you can do when you put it together,' he shouted in the dressing room. 'You're gonna be a champion.'

I winced, looking around at the other coaches and fighters.

'I told you not to say that. I don't like it,' I told him.

The fact was, despite everything, I still struggled to develop a positive mindset. I knew I should believe in myself, that confidence was important, but it wasn't a part of my character that came naturally. Throughout my early days, Porty would try and rile me up. Dennis would get in my ear, tell me to walk with a bounce, to shoot a menacing stare, but it wasn't me. I guess I just hated the idea of being fake.

In February '95, I took on Paul Clarkson in my third contest in Hull. He was a fearsome-looking character, muscular and snarling. My crippling self-doubt resurfaced. Clarkson looked too strong, too confident. There was no way I could win.

The fear I felt before first bell sickened and weakened me. It hummed through my legs and made my breath short. I looked down at the canvas rather than meet his eye. I didn't want him to know how I was feeling. I was ashamed of it.

But that fear generated something – and it taught me something too.

Fear made me fly at Clarkson as soon as the bell rang, throwing hands in a state of near panic. I caught him repeatedly. His legs went and I stopped him in about 20 seconds.

'See?' Porty was jubilant. 'You see?'

At 6-0, they put me in with a Brummie called Paul Murray, a veteran of over 100 fights, although he had only won about ten. As usual, I sold a ton of tickets and the Hillsborough Leisure Centre was jumping. The Sheffield Wednesday brass band turned up and entertained the crowd with the theme from *Dambusters* and *Rule Britannia*. Spurred on by the noise, I went out hard and put Murray down in the first with a sharp right. He stayed down until seven, climbed up, then grabbed me after the restart.

'Fucking hell!' he said in my ear. 'You're going to fucking win, what's up with you? Take it easy.'

I didn't know what he meant. His words threw me off my stride and I jabbed my way through the rest of the round. After the bell, on my stool, I asked Dennis.

'Is this fixed?'

'What are you on about?' he asked.

'Is this fight fuckin' fixed?'

'Just get out there and gi' on wi' it.'

Murray was a tough bastard and, try as I might, I couldn't put him down again or force the stoppage. After the ref raised my hand, he congratulated me and spoke again.

'There was no need to go so hard. You were always getting the win.'

'OK mate,' I told him, eyes narrow. 'OK.'

I entered the dressing room in an agitated state and demanded an explanation. Dennis and Porty shared a look and sighed.

'Murray's a journeyman.' Dennis said. 'He doesn't sell tickets. He boxes nearly every week in the away corner and makes his money by losing on points.'

Porty chimed in.

'The fight weren't fixed. That's just Murray's role.'

It bothered me, but I accepted it for what it was, a part of the business over which I had no control. I soon put it out of my mind, in the knowledge that by then my career had real momentum. I was winning and putting bums on seats. If you do those two things in boxing, people start to pay attention.

Two months after Murray, I fought on the undercard of Paul 'Silky' Jones's successful world title challenge. My old tormentor from the boys' club became WBO world light-middleweight champion, while I moved to 9-0. Most of the fans in the venue were mine and the local media lapped it up. Interesting times.

12

London

DURING those months of 1995, as everything began to take off, my brother Todd was seeing a lovely girl called Claire. They formed quite a solid relationship and he even brought her along to some of my fights. The weekend after I boxed on the Silky Jones undercard, we were drinking in a pub called The British Oak, where I noticed Claire chatting to a petite, dark-haired girl.

'Who's that?' I asked Todd.

'Some Spanish lass Claire knows,' he replied.

'Go an' ask if she'll go out wi' me,' I told him.

Todd went over on my behalf, but the Spanish girl shrugged and said she wasn't interested. Apparently, she had heard about my street scuffles and been warned I was someone to steer clear of.

During the week that followed I went on a stag night and, in typical style, got bottled, ending up with stitches. Then, the next weekend, I found myself back in the same place and saw her again. I asked Claire to put a word in for me, which seemed to do the trick. Despite my facial injury, she agreed to meet me for a date in the week. They told me her name was Natalia.

On the Wednesday night, I picked her up in my gold Ford Escort Ghia, the dream machine. No tax, no insurance, virtually no brakes either, just me behind the wheel with a smile and about ten quid in my pocket.

We went out for a drink at a pub in Gleadless. I really knew how to show a lady a good time.

The evening got off to a ropey start when she winced as she saw my tattooed forearms.

'Oh, don't worry about those,' I lied. 'I'm having knickers added to the lady and the other one removed.'

Natalia was in England doing a Business Studies degree and had just finished her first year. Her grandmother lived in Sheffield and she was staying with her. God knows what she saw in me, maybe a mixture of charm and desperation, but we hit it off. There was something a bit special about her. I knew straight away I needed that in my life.

They say sometimes opposites attract and I guess that must be true. Natalia's upbringing in the Madrid suburbs had been comfortable and cosmopolitan. She had travelled all over the world, while I had barely left Sheffield. Despite that, we began seeing each other regularly. A few months after that first date, she was staying most weekends with me at my flat. A few more months after that, she moved in.

'The first thing we'll need is some curtains and a bit of furniture,' she said.

Surprisingly, for a girl from Madrid, she loved it on the Westfield. Something happened every day around there and she found it hilarious. We could switch the telly off, sit by the window with a drink and watch the riot vans coming and going.

About a week after she moved in, a bloke was killed in the estate chippy. He was smashed in the head with a golf club by a kid from the year above me at school. Police turned up at our door to interview me about that. Welcome to Westfield, Natalia!

The local pub was just the same. Soon after, one of our neighbours, a quiet guy, got his head caved in with a baseball bat there. Apparently, he had been speaking to the wrong woman.

Meanwhile, a couple over the courtyard had some domestic problems and split up. The guy ended up putting a full suite of furniture and a coffee table on the grass outside the front door. He stayed there for about two weeks, in all weathers, no matter what. We watched one night in disbelief as the men in white coats arrived and dragged him off.

His ex-wife had him sectioned.

Another morning, we woke up hearing noises. A right fat old boot from a different neighbouring family was dragging her skinny wretch of a husband down the street by his neck. Another woman, as obese, red and angry as the first, leaned out of a first-floor window, two doors down.

'Tha can 'ave 'im,' she screamed. 'Ah shagged 'im last neet!'

The first woman looked up as she walked, still head-locking the poor bloke in her massive, meaty arms.

'Ar!' she yelled, flab bouncing with effort. 'And ah'm shaggin' 'im toneet!'

Me and Natalia literally curled up on the floor, laughing. Westfield was just that sort of place.

Natalia had only been living there a few months when the flat next door, which had been vacant since I arrived, got a new tenant. I couldn't believe what I was seeing, but our new neighbour was a patient from the asylum I used to work in.

By then, the 'care in the community' policy had caused mental hospitals to close down *en masse*, with their patients given local housing instead. The first day, she came and knocked on our door. She had big, blue watery eyes that didn't blink.

'Can thi gi' us a fiver?' she said.

'No, I in't gorrit.'

She nodded and shuffled off. Ten minutes, later she knocked again.

'Can thi gi' us a fiver?'

'Fuck off!' I replied.

We stopped answering the door after that. A couple of days later, I saw her going up and down the stairwell holding a kitchen knife, saying she wanted to kill everyone. I phoned Natalia and told her to wait at work until it was sorted. It stopped being funny then.

While all this was going on, I had two fights in the first part of 1996, winning both. That took me to 11-0 with seven stoppages and things were going far better than I ever imagined. Porty's embarrassing comments about titles became more frequent.

A friend of Dennis' called Howard Rainey started to appear in the gym. He would watch me and talk with Dennis. A big guy, an ex-heavyweight who had boxed for the Ingles in his day, he was a real thinker for a boxing man. Occasionally, he wandered over and took me on the pads. His approach was different, more philosophical than Porty and something seemed to be developing between us. I really liked him.

In March, I beat a guy called John Duckworth at the Pinegrove, a relatively easy win. Things were going so well, but during the after-fight celebrations I made one of the worst mistakes of my life. Out on the town with the boys, well oiled as usual, we moved from pub to pub. Natalia went out with some of her friends too and the idea was the two groups would meet up later on.

I got drunk enough to forget myself, which could always be dangerous, as by then I had developed a bit of local fame. We were in a place called the Roundhouse, carrying on as we usually did and a couple of drunk girls started throwing themselves at me. One draped herself around my neck, whispering things in my ear and trying to kiss me. I should have pushed her off, but didn't. Of course, sod's law, at exactly that moment Natalia walked in. I saw her and immediately my balls felt like they jumped up into my throat. She stared at me, scowled, then turned and walked straight back out again.

'Oh shit!' I cried, horrified. I peeled the groupie off and ran out. When I caught up with Natalia outside, she was absolutely fuming.

'I can't believe what you're fucking up to! You get me to move in with you then you're off around town with a bunch of tarts!'

'It's not like that,'

'I can see what it's like!'

I began to get angry with her, feeling that really, I had done nothing wrong. I was drunk and stupid. I raised my voice. Natalia stormed off.

As I fumbled for my key in the early hours of the morning, I tried to think of ways to make it up to her. Maybe I could prepare breakfast in bed? Maybe we could go out for a meal, just the two of us, the following night? I opened the door, walked in and my heart froze. All her stuff was gone. She had left me.

I was absolutely devastated and being alone that night reminded me of some of the dark times before she came along. Suddenly I realised, once and for all, exactly how much that relationship meant to me. For the next couple of days I tried calling her, but she wouldn't answer her phone. In desperation, I came up with a silly plan. I reckoned she would be staying at her grandma's house, so got a load of helium love-heart balloons and wrote messages on them.

'I'm sorry'

'I love you'

'Please forgive me' and so on.

I packed all the balloons into the boot of my car and asked my mate Gary to drive the car up to Natalia's house. The plan was he would drop me off at the bottom of the road, drive up to the house, go and knock on the door, wait for her to answer then open the boot. If she looked receptive to the whole thing, I had written a letter he could give her.

About five minutes after he drove away, I got a phonecall.

'Y'alright, Clint?' Gary said. 'Don't worry, pal, she's smiling.'

I phoned her up. This time, she took the call. The next day, I drove her to Blackpool. We sat in silence in the car all the way there, but during the day I made it clear how I felt. We got back together and I promised myself from then that I would never put that relationship at risk again. It was too important. Maybe Clinton Woods was starting to grow up.

Back in the gym, Dennis pulled me to one side and suggested I train full time with Howard.

'He's an excellent coach and he'll improve you,' he said. 'But it'll mean moving to London.'

Howard had set up a pro training stable in St Pancras, north London. The move would mean training with him Monday to Friday, then coming home for weekends. It would be a wrench to leave Natalia, but with title challenges looking likely in the near future it seemed a good idea. I asked her about it and she was brilliant.

'I want what's best for you,' she said.

Howard had already shown himself to be very technical, very focused on details. In our few sessions together in Dennis' gym, I felt he had already improved me.

'To get full length on your jab,' he said. 'You need to get your shoulder on to your chin. When you follow through with the right, turn your elbow a bit, so it comes over properly.'

All that expertise on a daily basis could well take me to the next level. Dennis organised everything and Howard set me up in a flat in Lambeth, bang on Kensington Road. Dennis gave him money to pay rent and what-not, but I don't know if he was giving him enough. The place had no electricity, so I filled it up with candles. Literally every room was covered in them. If anyone had come around, they would have thought I was a Satanist.

No electricity meant no heating so I used to have cold baths. It was pretty horrible and I spent as little time at home as possible. Not that I could do much else.

I had about £120 a week coming from a sponsor called Fullflow, but London is such an expensive city to live in and £120 didn't go far. At least I could describe myself as a full-time pro, I reasoned.

Howard lived in the same block of flats, downstairs with his girlfriend, and he gave me a lift every morning to the gym. He had a great group of fighters in there, including WBO featherweight champ Colin McMillan, British and Commonwealth light-welter champ Paul 'Scrap Iron' Ryan, cruiserweight beast Terry Dunstan, 'The Vauxhall Cavalier', who won British and European belts, British super middle champ Cornelius Carr, Commonwealth flyweight champ Francis Ampofo and middleweight Adrian Dodson.

Generally, they were a top bunch of lads. Scrap Iron Ryan didn't give a shit about anything, could run like Usain Bolt and thought nothing of jumping in the ring with men three or four weight divisions above him. McMillan was a lovely, thoughtful character while Ampofo impressed me with his physical attributes. I know it's a racial stereotype, but at 5ft 1in the 'Pocket Battleship' had the most disproportionately huge cock I had ever seen. I would glance over in the showers and the thing was hanging around his knees. I didn't know where to look.

Soon, I was sparring regularly with Dunstan, who weighed 20 pounds more than me and fought like a maniac every time he stepped through the ropes. As always, I found my movement and reach did the trick. Under Howard's tutelage, my jab came on too. It was no longer a simple annoyance for my opponents, but an effective, reliable weapon. I could place it accurately, lancing through a guard from different angles, or pop someone's head up from underneath if they had high hands. Dunstan and I boxed through hundreds of rounds like this, with him as the bull and me as the matador. He never once put me down or troubled me.

Overseeing it all, Rainey was a man of ideas and vision. He would sometimes go on strange monologues about politics or social issues that we all struggled to follow, but the training was like nothing I had experienced before. He would build his own equipment and bring it to the gym, strange contraptions he put together with balls and ropes and springs. He would make you throw punches while standing on a wobbly board, or spar with your feet tied together. Sometimes he had a rope ladder tied across the ring, from one corner post to the other, that you would have to go under and through as you shadow-boxed, to make you bob and weave.

I had grown to love training with Porty and enjoyed his spit 'n' sawdust approach. He was almost like an uncle to me, but Howard took things way beyond all that. I felt my boxing improving almost by the hour.

'That jab of yours is world class, you know that, lad?' he said to me. 'Genuinely world class.' Coming from him, I believed it too.

I would go on long solo runs up and down the Thames, crossing over at Lambeth, Tower, Waterloo, different bridges every time, then coming back. I loved pounding up and down that dirty, old river. Three times a week, Howard took all the boys to a running track at Battersea Park. Our sessions there were so competitive, but I more than held my own. I never understood why, but Morrissey, the singer, was often sitting about watching us. We all clocked on. He even wrote a song about it called 'Boxers'.

'Losing in front of your home crowd
You wished the ground would open up
And take you down…'

Cornelius Carr starred in the video and appeared on the CD cover.

At weekends, I told Natalia how things were going. She could tell I was excited and that excited her, as well as being intrigued by Howard's methods. By then, he had devised a pulley system that attached to your back as you moved around the ring, to add resistance to every movement. When you took the thing off and punched freely, you felt like a superstar.

In June, I boxed back at the Pinegrove against another journeyman, Ernie Loveridge. I felt quick and smooth and took an easy points win. Understanding more about the game, I didn't try to get him out of there. Bigger things were coming anyway. I was sure of it.

13

And the New!

AMONG Howard's boys I made it my business to train harder than anyone else. Rainey noticed that and loved it. He reported back to Dennis and between the two of them they decided to put me in for the Central Area super middleweight title. The fight was set for November '96, by which time I had been living in London for about eight months.

I was up against a kid called Craig Joseph, from Bradford. He usually boxed at light-heavy but shed three or four pounds to take me on. Other than that, I knew nothing about him.

As always at the beginning of my career, the Pinegrove was packed, steamy with sweat and deafeningly loud. Joseph had a go and was decent enough, a nice, tidy boxer but lacking a serious weapon that could have lifted him above the pack.

Sometimes, that's all it takes. A kid can be bang average, but if they have a devastating left hook, or one killer combination, they're suddenly a title winner.

Joseph just didn't quite have that special element. I was first to the punch and more aggressive, eventually beating him without too much trouble. I had height and reach on him and jabbed his head off for ten rounds.

Predictably, my first belt triggered boozy celebrations that went on until the following morning. It was great to be out all night with

Natalia and my mates. Porty was there too, having worked my corner, alongside Howard.

'This lad's going to be European champion,' Porty shouted, upping the stakes on his usual drunken boast. I shook my head and rolled my eyes, but seeing them all again made me realise how much I missed home. Sheffield was such a big part of my identity. Fullflow, my sponsor, had been talking about buying me my own gym to train in, but that was still to materialise.

Dennis had moved into a new place in Attercliffe by then, leaving the ramshackle joint on Stones Road behind. Howard was already pencilled in to be his main trainer, so that was all the encouragement I needed.

In the days after my first title win, I made the decision to leave London and return to Sheffield. It might mean a period of training with someone else while waiting for Howard to relocate, but there are only so many cold baths a man can take.

Once I got back up, Dennis recommended I train with Glyn Rhodes at the Sheffield Boxing Centre (SBC) on Burton Street in the north of the city, near Owlerton. As usual, I accepted his suggestion without too much thought. Rhodes could look after me until Rainey's reappearance.

I enjoyed Christmas with Natalia and my family, gained a bit of weight, then started training with Glyn in the new year. Life felt good at the beginning of 1997. I had found a relationship I was truly happy with, boxing had taken the edge off my teenage chaos and it seemed there were exciting times to look forward to.

At that stage, as I went for my first sessions at SBC, I fully accepted the importance of boxing in my life. During the years I left it, I had been bored. That boredom had brought no end of trouble.

Glyn's training methods weren't as innovative as Howard's. While Howard was a genuine one-off, maverick type, Glyn was simply a great guy and an honest grafter. He got me super fit and sharp in no time. Porty, of course, still lingered in the background.

Of the bunch of pros training in Rhodes's gym at the time, the top boy was none other than Silky Jones. I carried my memories of all those childhood bruisings with me, leading to some vicious spars. He was a contender at world level by then, having been stripped of his WBO belt, but winning various international and intercontinental titles. Neither of us gave an inch. We were great for each other.

In February, I stopped a kid called Rocky Shelley in the second round to go to 13-0. Shelley was meant to be a slugger who would put it on me. On the night, he walked in, square-on like a novice and I took him apart.

Two months later, I was scheduled to defend my Central Area title against Darren Littlewood, another Sheffielder.

'He's an Ingle kid,' Glyn warned. 'Could be lively.'

I arrived by myself for the weigh-in, wanting to get it out of the way quickly. Littlewood had all the boys from the gym with him. Naseem Hamed was there, by then the WBO world featherweight champ, European cruiserweight title holder Johnny Nelson, British light-middleweight champ Ryan Rhodes and several others. They all stood about, in a little posse, eyeballing me and trying to make me uncomfortable. Littlewood's dad had a reputation as a bit of a knuckler and was shouting around Sheffield about accepting bets. It turned into a massive market and loads of my crowd had money on with him, making that steamy Pinegrove atmosphere even more explosive than usual. As I walked to the ring, the noise made me giddy.

Ingle boxers all had a reputation as movers, switch-hitters and fancy-dans, but Littlewood didn't box that way at all. He was very orthodox and I was on top from the first bell. By the sixth, he was tired and I went up a gear.

We came together in centre ring. His shoulders had sagged. I could sense his growing weakness. After rocking his head back with a stiff jab, I rolled to the right, then jolted him with an uppercut. His eyes lost focus. His knees dipped.

Wasting no time, I repeated the exact same combo while he was still getting himself together. It was everything he could do to stay upright and he reeled to the side. Smelling blood, I moved to go after him but before I could land again, the ref jumped in. Easy work. I raised my hands and winked at Naz at ringside.

Following that one I had a few days during which I learned that Howard had moved into a room above Dennis' gym. I thanked Glyn, who had done everything required of him, and left to resume working with Rainey.

'It's good to be back home,' Howard told me, grinning when I saw him. One end of his apartment was like a workshop, full of bits of wood and wheels and god-knows-what. He asked me how I had been before unveiling his latest invention, a sort of skateboard with bungee cords attached to it, which you scooted backwards and forwards on for balance. I tried it out for about a minute and got off.

From there, two fights followed in quick succession against boxers with mixed records, Darren Ashton and Danny Juma. I barely had to break a sweat in either of them and won both on points. In many ways, my style was still the Gillett style. Go left, go right, duck, duck, punch. I always kept high hands.

My basics were entrenched and fighters of that level just couldn't cope with me.

The Juma fight took place in Queensferry, Wales and Natalia travelled there on a minibus with a bunch of my mates, driven by a kid called Rasdale. He was a reckless bastard at the best of times, but that night he was also off his face on a variety of illegal substances. My brother Heath got his kit off and was running up and down the bus naked, waving his cock around, as he often liked to do.

'You have to come with me on the bus on the way home,' a slightly traumatised Natalia insisted after the fight.

'Fair enough, love.'

That journey back was horrendous. Throughout the bus, the air was thick with smoke. Drunken lads were pissing in bottles, then throwing them out of the windows. Rasdale was off his tits, laughing his head off and swerving all over the road. He kept clipping the kerb without realising it, making the bus jump. Natalia gripped my arm fiercely.

'Fuckin' 'ell, tha's done it again Ras!' I shouted.

His eyes were hooded, head lolling. 'Keep thi nose out,' he bellowed back, to cheers from the other boys. We got home about three in the morning and I felt like I had aged ten years.

A month after Juma, I had another straightforward win, against Jeff Finlayson, at the Grosvenor Hotel. At the end, the ref raised my hand and the announcer went through the familiar routine.

'And your winner, ladies and gentlemen, in the blue corner, Clinton Wooooods!'

My lot went mental as usual and the MC grabbed my shoulder, which I found weird. Then Howard came over and growled something in my ear. I couldn't understand him. When the cacophony died down enough, the announcer went on.

'Now then, Clinton,' he said.

I shot Dennis a look. What was this?

'I've been given some interesting news and need to ask you a question.'

The hall went graveyard quiet, in anticipation of what he would say.

'You're now 18-0 and you've defended the Central Area belt.'

I nodded.

'Well, I can tell you, you've been offered a fight for the Commonwealth title.'

The crowd went bonkers again.

'At Wembley Arena.'

More raucous cheering.

'In 11 days' time against Mark Baker.'

I knew of Baker, a tough kid from a gypsy family in London. A former Southern Area champ, he was unbeaten in 21 and hotly tipped. It would be easily my hardest fight to date and 11 days was not much notice. There must have been a pull-out.

While these thoughts circulated, I felt the eerie silence of the hall. Every pair of eyes was on me. The announcer waved the mike under my chin. I looked at a few expectant faces at ringside. What could I do?

'Alright, ar. Why not?' I said at last.

The noise was supernatural.

14

A third of the world

AS expected, Baker turned out to be a stiff test. This wasn't prospect v journeyman, or an area-level scrap, but two unbeaten young stars from different ends of the country facing off to see who could head towards the big time. We both desperately wanted to win.

An aggressive pressure fighter who liked to tuck up, find his way into range, then throw swinging hooks capable of real damage, there was no doubt Baker meant business. For the first time in my career, I faced someone who brought a bigger crowd than me too. He was relatively local to Wembley, from Lewisham in south London, meaning one section of the arena was packed with his followers.

From the opening bell, our rhythms combined into a classic boxer v fighter match-up. One for the purists. He barrelled in, strong as a gorilla, while I fenced and used my feet. Most rounds were close.

I felt I beat him with the jab for the majority of the contest, but was never comfortable. He was always in it. With previous opponents, the fight usually reached a point when I knew it was mine, when I felt the belief go out of the other man, as if he stopped trying to win. But Baker kept believing and kept on coming.

In the tenth, he finally caught me with a massive left, which landed around my right ear. I felt as though I was underwater for a second, then resurfaced. I still had my senses, but for the rest of the round a buzzing noise echoed around my skull, as if a bee was trapped in my head. After the bell, on my stool, I began to feel sick. Waves of nausea rose from guts. To that point, it was the hardest I had been hit as a pro.

'You're on top,' Howard grunted, a hint of panic in his voice. 'Keep jabbing, stick to your boxing and....'

'... come on Clinton, work, work. Stay busy. Don't let it slip away,' interrupted Dennis.

I sat there, feeling the heat of the lights, my hair soaked with sweat. I looked down at my lap. As I lifted my head to guzzle water, I wished both of them would just shut up.

Buoyed by his moment of success, Baker came on very strong. It was all I could do to keep him off for the last couple of rounds and I was relieved when the final bell rang. In my corner, Howard and Dennis were confident I had done enough, but some in the arena thought that with home advantage, the late rally would see Baker nick it.

In the end, ref Roy Francis gave it to me by a round and a half. Porty and Dennis jumped in delight while my fans erupted in jubilation. I raised my hands to salute them, but was still a bit woozy. My head still buzzed.

They put that belt around my waist and we walked backstage. Away from the congratulations and behind the excitement, the pain in my ear intensified. I was super middleweight champion of a third of the world. But Mark Baker had done me some damage.

On returning to Sheffield I saw a doctor, who told me that Baker had perforated my eardrum. It was not something they could do much about and eventually it would heal itself, apparently. We were heading towards the Christmas break so I didn't worry too much.

With the Commonwealth title to my name, Dennis arranged a meeting with Panos Eliades, of Panix Promotions, whose headline fighter was heavyweight champ Lennox Lewis. We travelled down to meet in his London office, which had walls covered in memorabilia of Lewis' big nights. Eliades seemed decent enough and spoke about the ways he could help my career. After ten minutes or so of chatting, Lewis himself walked in, shook my hand and sat in a chair opposite.

I was dumbstruck by the man's sheer size. His hands were twice mine, his shoulders like ceiling joists. We had a photo together, which was nice. Even though I had become a pro title holder myself, I still felt starstruck in the presence of the heavyweight champion of the world.

For the first time in my career, I earned some real money. By then, I laid off the beer and whizz as much as possible, knowing it wasn't the best combination for a fighter. But soon my addictive personality led me instead towards gambling machines.

I had a mate I used to meet for coffee at the time, called John Daley. We would have a chat over a brew then head to an arcade. Most of the machines we played had a maximum jackpot of ten quid, but it soon became a habit, just feeding and feeding them with coins. Coincidentally, my favourite arcade was over the road from my bank, meaning every time I ran out of money I would go and get more.

One afternoon, early in 1998, I threw £500 away. Even John was shocked. I made sure Natalia never found out and promised myself I would have more big fights soon. I needed them.

15

The Golden Viking

1997 had been an incredible year. The Commonwealth title put me on the international map, as well as attracting interest from the media. The Sheffield papers ran stories on me. People started recognising me in the street.

The pain in my ear died away over the holiday period and I enjoyed the time off, but after New Year, as I drove to see Dennis, a billboard outside a shop caught my eye. In solid black letters about half a metre high, it said:

Boxer's Love Child!

Instinctively, I slammed the brakes on and as I climbed out of the car, a dryness coated my throat.

I went in, bought the paper, stood by the counter and read it. My sixth sense proved vindicated. The front-page splash featured a large picture of me, while the story beside it talked about Kyle, who by then was ten years old. Carla had obviously heard about my success and contacted the media.

Racked with guilt, I went home and showed the paper to Natalia. That evening, the *Sheffield Star* phoned and asked me to do an interview about it. I turned them down. I thought if ignored it, maybe the problem would just disappear. It was selfish of me. I just wanted to get back into training and crack on.

Dennis' new gym was a massive improvement on the old place, over a couple of floors, with lots of space and two rings. He had ideas to develop a high-end set-up with a group of title-winning fighters to establish himself as a leading manager and promoter. I was central to those plans.

I had been back in for about a week, enjoying the crack with Howard, using all his little gadgets and sparring with Terry Dunstan, who had followed him up.

My Christmas man-boobs and love handles were more or less conquered, when Dennis called me to his office.

'I've had a phone call from Denmark,' he said. 'You've been offered £50 a day, with accommodation and food covered, for a week's sparring with the Norwegian light-heavyweight champion Ole 'The Golden Viking' Klemetsen.'

Klemetsen was a massive celebrity all over Scandinavia and was in camp preparing to box Crawford Ashley, the European champ from Leeds. Ashley was a fearsome fighter. Most of his wins came via KO and he had been considered a contender at world level for a long time. By then, he had challenged twice for world titles, losing to top Americans Michael Nunn and Virgil Hill. The Hill fight had been pretty close too.

Dennis thought it would be good for me to get some international experience. I didn't see any reason to differ and so, within a matter of days, found myself on a rickety light aircraft flying alone to Aarhus, where Klemetsen had set himself up.

My arrival felt like a re-creation of the scene from *Rocky IV*, when Team Balboa land in the midst of the Russian winter. The airport was tiny and the weather absolutely arctic. The place was literally just a shed in a snowy field, surrounded by twinkling sea.

I was met outside the terminal by a Dane called Ivor, who identified himself as Klemetsen's trainer. He was very tanned for a Nordic, chunkily built, with tight curly hair. He drove me to my room and then invited me for something to eat at his house.

Ivor was a friendly guy and we developed a rapport quickly.

'We've watched your fights,' he said. 'We like you.'

Over a beer, he passed me a piece of paper with Klemetsen's amateur record on it. I scrolled down. Win, KO, Win, KO, Win, KO etc. Ivor explained that Klemetsen had been over to America and trained in the Kronk gym with Emanuel Steward.

He then passed me his pro record, which was much the same. I hadn't known much about Klemetsen, but it seemed he had built quite a reputation. Alone in my small room that night, I began to wonder what I had I let myself in for. The guy was obviously a banger and boxed in the weight division above me. Things could get hairy.

The Golden Viking's gym was in a sports centre at Aarhus football club. It had three rings, loads of bags and a lot of keep-fitters bouncing about using the machines. Soon Ole traipsed in, with about 20 guys following him. He had a real presence. Charisma, I guess you call it. It was almost as if he had his own personal spotlight that illuminated his presence and made him centre of attention.

A buzz built up and I watched from a bench on the side as Klemetsen got in with a Russian kid for his first spar of the day. The Russian was slightly shorter, but muscular as hell. He looked like a proper East European hard-nut, but the whole thing lasted no more than 30 seconds. They circled each other for a bit before Klemetsen stepped in and KO'd him clean with a right hand. The Russian laid flat on his back for about two minutes, legs twitching, while one of the trainers poured water on his face to revive him.

Klemetsen's dad, large framed and domineering, the boss of the training camp, jumped up in the ring.

'Get him out,' he shouted, pointing angrily, as if the Russian had failed to earn his approval.

They put a man on each limb and carried him through the ropes, like pall-bearers at a funeral.

'You! In!' he yelled at me.

I stood and walked to the ring, concentrating hard to stop my knees knocking. Klemetsen paced up and down like a caged tiger, waiting for his next victim.

Predictably, as soon as his father called time, Ole came after me with everything, throwing very heavy shots in combination. There was huge weight behind the punches. Even ones that landed on my arms hurt. This wasn't typical sparring. There was none of that 'let's go at 60 per cent and practice some moves' stuff. Klemetsen was all in. He wanted to take my head off.

I began on my bike and in the course of the first round, as he pursued me this way and that, I started to read his movements. He had a habit of pawing a left as a decoy, to manoeuvre you into position for the right. By the end of the three minutes, I saw it coming every time.

By the midpoint of the second, I was picking him off and by the third I was handling him. I wasn't doing anything flash, but it's amazing how far in boxing solid fundamentals can take you. This guy was meant to be a new superstar, at European, even world level, but solid footwork, a mobile target and a fast jab kept him more than honest. The spar finished. They looked upset. His dad gave me a flat stare.

'Tomorrow we train downstairs,' he said simply.

That night, Neil flew in to support me during the camp. Dennis had sent him. He arrived in a foul mood, cursing the bumpy flight and tiny airport.

'How do Porty?' I asked when he turned up at the door.

'The bastards lost mi fuckin case,' he replied before barging past me into the room. 'What's tha got to eat?'

The next day, we headed for the gym and went downstairs. I told Neil what to expect, that the sparring was hard and heavy, which he took in good spirits. But we were both slightly taken aback when we realised that the basement area was much smaller. Their plan soon became clear.

The ring down there was tiny. Size-wise, it was the sort of thing juniors use. They wanted to limit my movement and allow Ole to stay on top of me. As I was paid to be there, I was in no position to complain.

The spar began and again, right from the off, Klemetsen did his level best to kill me. Restricted by space, it swiftly became a full-on war. It couldn't be anything else.

He was powerful and I had to respect his right hand, but I took it as an opportunity to practise my inside fighting against an opponent of strength. He probably got the best of the early rounds but by the end I found myself tying him up, sneaking in shots of my own.

Despite that, the Norwegian camp seemed happier with how things had gone.

'Same place tomorrow,' Klemetsen's dad said. Neil muttered something about 'sly bastards' under his breath.

For the next week, we sparred in that same ring every day. Bit by bit, I learned to handle Klemetsen, even in such a confined space. I grew to enjoy boxing him on the inside. It was a great confidence booster.

Outside of the ropes, it was not such a happy time. Neil's lost luggage took a few days days to arrive and he got more and more bad tempered. Worse than that, he was a heaving, sweating lump at the best of times, but with only one set of clothes to wear, things deteriorated rapidly. Sharing a room with him was horrendous. For the first time since meeting we argued, often. Sometimes bitterly.

'Tidy your fuckin' stuff up,' I would tell him.

'Oh fuckin' shurrup,' he would say, screwing his face up, his scar twitching. 'I'm fuckin sick o thi.'

As the camp wore on and my in-ring confidence grew, Klemetsen's people became less and less happy. They wanted their boy on top. When Porty and I walked in the gym for the last day, Ole's dad produced a sort of plastic box with sleeves from somewhere.

'You wear this today,' he said. 'You're moving too much. We're preparing for Ashley. He doesn't move like that.'

Neil fumed.

'What the fuck is this?' he yelled. 'Fuckin' robot wars?'

The box was cumbersome and restrictive, enabling Klemetsen to stay on my chest and tee off. I couldn't even move my elbows properly to control him on the inside, resulting in several rounds of pain and an easy morning for him, which I guess is what they wanted.

As Neil and I were packing later, looking forward to getting out from under each other's skin, Ivor came to say goodbye.

'Please tell me one thing,' he said to Neil. 'Why is this man not a world champion?' It was the first time Porty smiled during the whole trip.

We flew home and left the Norwegians to it. When his training camp eventually concluded, Ole boxed Crawford Ashley at Alexandra Palace in London.

Klemetsen KO'd the champ with a vicious left hook in round two to take the European title. It took Ashley several minutes to recover.

16

Early retirement

IT had been an interesting experience training with Klemetsen. Norway was unused to top-level sportsmen outside of the Winter Olympics, meaning Ole was a hugely celebrated figure, the equivalent of a top Premier League footballer in the UK. He attracted all kinds of investment and sponsorship and had this massive team around him. There were people to look after his clothes, people to look after his food, there was even a guy on the payroll just to do his hair. By contrast, all I had were Dennis, Howard and Porty.

Not that I felt resentful about it. In some ways, I liked having a small team and it probably suited my character better, but I could see how there were also disadvantages. Nutrition was one clear example.

I was aware that top competitors, particularly in very physically demanding sports like boxing, invested lots of time and thought into what they put into their bodies. Yet it was never something that entered my world. Naturally slim from childhood, I ate as I pleased. Outside of camp, most of my weekends still revolved around booze.

When a fight came up, I laid off the beer and ate a bit less, if I felt it necessary, but carbohydrates and proteins, amino acids or flaxseed oil? None of that stuff occupied my mind at all. Having seen how Klemetsen's camp was run, I began to have my first thoughts about nutrition and supplements. The European champ clearly thought it worked.

After getting back to Sheffield, I was offered another week's sparring with a kid called David Starie down in Suffolk. He stood at 15-1 and was highly rated. His only defeat had come in a British title challenge against Dean Francis, who had recently stopped my old training partner Cornelius Carr.

It was a pleasant week, with competitive action. Some days Starie got the better of me, other days I was on top. When I returned to Dennis' gym at the end, he had a surprise for me.

'How did you find the sparring?'

'Alright, ar.'

'Good, 'cause Starie's your first challenger.'

The fight was set for 28 March at the Ice Arena in Hull and as usual, as soon as I knew I had a bout approaching, I slipped into business mode. Starie was potentially just as tough a fight as Baker. I would need to be at my best. As camp began, I sat one morning in the dressing rooms chatting to Terry Dunstan. He was European cruiserweight champ by then and was boxing for the IBF world title on the same show as my fight.

The card was due to be televised on Sky Box Office as the first part of a package leading up to Lennox Lewis' world heavyweight title defence against Shannon Briggs in the early hours of the morning in America. This made it a big opportunity for both of us and Dennis' stable in general. Dennis had cemented the link-up with Panos Eliades and Frank Maloney, who controlled Lewis' affairs. Through that, there was a chance to showcase my talents to a pay-per-view audience.

'So what you taking?' Terry asked.

'Eh?'

'On top of your food. You're Commonwealth champ now. You need to use all the advantages you can.'

I nodded. I had been thinking the same thing.

'What are you taking?'

'Creatine' he said. 'You take it with your meals. Just mix it up with some water. Makes you much stronger.'

'Oh right.'

'I have a bit every day. Works a treat.'

I spoke to a few of the other lads. Some of them took it as well. No one thought it would be a bad idea. I began by putting a teaspoon of the stuff in a glass of water four times a day. They call that the 'loading phase'. A week of that and your muscles are packed with it, then you can reduce to once a day. It had a potent effect almost immediately.

I've always been an energetic character, but with creatine in my system I felt supercharged. Other guys in the gym couldn't believe my training intensity as I came in off a run, sparred for half an hour, then did strength and conditioning, one after the other. Soon, I was performing better than ever before. It was as if the powder had upped my physical capacity by 20 per cent.

All of that gave me a great feeling heading into the Starie fight. I would be fitter and stronger, a new version of me. Unfortunately, creatine had other effects too.

Two days before I was due to head up to Hull for the weigh-in, Howard asked me to jump on the scales. It was just a formality. Weight management had never been an issue for me.

'They must be fuckin' broken,' I said as I stood there, looking at the reading in disbelief.

Howard asked me to get off so he could fiddle around with the machine. I did as he asked then got back on. The same numbers came up.

'A hundred and seventy fuckin' four?' he cried, bemused. 'What the fuck's goin' on with thi?'

I was a full half a stone over the super middleweight limit. I told him about the creatine and he rolled his eyes in horror.

'Most of it'll be water weight,' he said, trying to make me feel better. 'We can burn it off, don't worry.'

I knew straight away I was in trouble.

For the next two days, I starved myself and took very little liquid. All my strength and energy deserted me. I became short tempered and snappy. Natalia stayed out of my way and we ended up sleeping in separate rooms.

We weighed in the day before at a sports centre and after 48 hours of dehydration and hunger I came in bang on 12 stone. I virtually fell off the scales and Howard passed me a bottle of water.

As soon as I had enough energy, I stumbled down to the lobby, gathered all the coins I could find and started buying whatever I could from the vending machine there. Soon, I sat on the steps surrounded by chocolates, crisps and biscuits, shovelling fistfuls of junk food into my mouth.

Halfway through a bag of Minstrels, I heard footsteps, looked up and Starie walked past, on his way down the stairs with his dad. Unlike me, he appeared focused and fit. Our eyes met. He saw the desperation and hunger in mine.

I had chocolate smeared on my lips. He had a little smile on his and something wordless passed between us. It can sometimes take half a fight to work out your opponent's weaknesses, but from that moment he already knew what mine would be. He held my gaze for a few seconds and walked away.

I tried to refuel the next day by eating enormous meals. Breakfast was a massive fry-up. Lunch was a double burger and chips, followed by an early steak dinner. With no one to advise me otherwise, loading up on nutrients seemed the best approach to compensate for 48 hours of fasting.

It didn't work. I still felt weird. In fact, in some ways I felt worse. Instead of light headed and weak, I became bloated and sluggish.

The moment the bell rang, I knew it was going to be a tough night. I tried to push it to the back of my mind but my body wouldn't respond properly. My legs were heavy. My hands slow. My inner critic, the doubting side of me, went to town on it.

You've lost all your advantages, it said, as Starie circled my way. *You've lost your speed and movement.*

Despite that, for the first two rounds there was nothing in it. Pride kept me competitive, but my punches had nothing on them, as if I was a kid again. In the third, he caught me to the body and I winced, gasping for air.

He saw it. And I saw that he saw it. My midsection was so much weaker than usual.

From then on, he targeted the body. I knew he would and it's exactly what I would have done in the same situation. Not always with massive shots but constant little taps. He never gave me any recovery time. Whenever we clinched, he prodded me in the ribs with either hand. It sapped everything out of me. I was struggling.

There was no point in the fight when I found my rhythm and I knew as the last bell rang that I had lost. Even Dennis and Howard were muted. Referee John Keane scored it to Starie by four rounds. I couldn't complain and my title was gone, just four months after winning it.

To cap it all, at the top of the bill, Dunstan lost his world title challenge too. He boxed well for ten rounds, was ahead on the cards, then got absolutely poleaxed by two massive rights in the 11th. He was in a bit of a state afterwards. It was a bad night for our lot.

The dressing room was sombre and I was dejected beyond belief. The biggest TV audience of my career had just tuned in to watch my worst performance. What would they all think of me?

Dennis drove us home along the motorway and it seemed to take forever. Nobody spoke. As I stared out of the window, I decided to retire. I'd had a good journey in boxing, won the Central Area and the Commonwealth, far more than anyone expected, but I guessed I had reached my level. Losing so dismally to Starie represented the end of my run. Fair enough. These things happen. I saw no reason to carry on.

17

Twelve and a half stone

MY RETIREMENt didn't last long, although I stuck to my guns for a couple of weeks. I spoke to Natalia. She said she was happy with my decision. I don't think she believed me, though.

I began looking around for work, trying to find a plastering gig or even some labouring. Nothing came up straight away and boredom crept in. I've never been very good at relaxing. One thing led to another and two weeks after losing to Starie I walked back into the gym.

More than anything else, I missed the focus of it. Running, sparring, working out, it kept me in line, kept the pot inside me simmering away rather than boiling. I needed it. I knew it.

The creatine in my system meant my weight quickly ballooned again after Starie and I found myself walking around at over 13 stone for the first time in my life. I suppose, at 26, I may have been filling out naturally to some extent as well.

I got back in shape in no time, but still hovered just below 13 stone. As a result, I had a couple of chats with Dennis in which we began to question the wisdom of forcing myself down to super middle. He suggested I give light-heavyweight a go. As always, I replied:

'Ar, why not?'

Dennis also said he had received another phone call from Team Klemetsen. Ole's star was really on the rise and after demolishing Ashley to become European champ he had got a shot at the American Reggie Johnson for the IBF world title. Johnson was a long-established elite fighter who had previously held a middleweight world championship and defended it many times. Klemetsen would need top-class sparring to have any sort of chance.

Once again, I figured it would be good experience. What better way to set out on my light-heavyweight path than by sparring the European title holder?

This time, Klemetsen's camp was not in Scandinavia. The title fight was scheduled to take place in Italy, so to help him acclimatise to the warmer weather he was training in Anfi del Mar in Gran Canaria.

Dennis came out with me for this one, accompanied by his dad, Dennis senior, a real Sheffield character. The old man had never been out of the country before and fancied a holiday.

A car picked us up from the airport and drove us to the training base, a luxury complex overlooking the ocean, where we had a large downstairs room with a big jacuzzi at the end of the bed. Just outside our window lay a beautiful private beach hired by Klemetsen's team with a ring on it. I could barely believe what I was seeing. This was my first taste of genuine boxing glamour.

They had big signs up everywhere saying 'The Golden Viking training here'. The place thronged with women in bikinis, just standing around watching him. It was like being on a film set.

Just like last time the sparring was hard, but in our second camp I routinely got the better of him. By the second week, I got myself into such a comfort zone that I was even going out with the two Dennises and getting bladdered in the evenings. One night, after a few pints, I entered a stripping competition and won the title 'Mr Anfi del Mar'. The prize was a meal for two at a fancy restaurant. I had never earned such pleasurable money in my life.

On the tenth day, just after I finished sparring, Dennis senior grabbed hold of me,

'Clinton,' he said. 'You need to slow down in the ring, let Klemetsen get some shots in. You're damaging his confidence and they'll end up sending us home.' The old boy didn't want his holiday curtailed.

Altogether we were there for two weeks and I returned to Sheffield boosted, certain I could do something at light-heavy.

Dennis took me to a show in Hull not long after, where we sat at ringside to watch Crawford Ashley defend the British and challenge for the vacant Commonwealth title against local hero Tony Booth. Booth was a hilarious character who fought for large parts of his career as a journeyman, but had heaps of talent and went through phases of taking the game seriously. He worked doors and liked a drink, but when in the right mood could give anyone a fight. I used to bump into him sometimes on the circuit.

'You're lucky you've never fought me, Woods,' he'd say.

'Shurrup, you fat bastard, I'd fuckin' hammer thi!' I'd reply. In truth, I loved Tony Booth to bits.

Crawford, on the other hand, since his devastating loss to Klemetsen, had reignited his career with a brilliant two-round British title win over Monty Wright.

Despite the perceived difference in their calibre, for three rounds Booth gave Ashley all he could handle. If that guy had ever bothered to train properly, he could have been a top pro. Dennis turned to me before the fourth

'How do you fancy the winner?' he asked.

'Yeah, spot on, ar.'

It remained a real battle until Ashley's superior conditioning began to shine through. Always out of shape, the podgy Booth wilted in the fifth and was stopped, gasping and puffing, in round six. But none of it concerned me. I saw enough to reckon I had a chance.

Altogether, less than three months after losing my title to Starie, I found myself back in the ring against a Geordie called Peter Mason. He had a mixed record, with four defeats from nine fights. The idea was really just to see how I got on at the higher weight limit.

Rather than feeling sluggish or impeded by the extra timber, I was quicker, sharper and stronger than before. Mason couldn't live with me and retired at the beginning of the fourth. Howard was thrilled afterwards. Even Porty was impressed.

'You looked good in there, Clint,' he said as he put a towel around my shoulders.

Coming from a man who could find fault with literally anything, that was the equivalent of a love letter. Dennis figured there was no point holding me up. I had already spent years building my career at super middle, so he signed for me to fight a really hot prospect called Mark Smallwood in Manchester in November.

Two months out from the Smallwood fight, Ivor got in touch from Denmark again. This time it wasn't for sparring. He was promoting a show in Aarhus and asked Dennis to fly out and lend him a hand.

'Do you want to come wi' us?' Dennis asked.

'Alright, ar.'

Ivor met us from the airport and drove towards the fight venue. He seemed different to before, strung out and stressed.

'Right guys,' he said. 'I need you to do me a favour.'

'What's that?' Dennis asked.

'I need you to pretend that you're the top cutsmen in the UK.'

'What?'

'I need you to pretend to be a top-level cutsman,' he repeated.

'Is this a wind-up?'

'No.'

'But I've never done fucking cuts in my life.'

Ivor looked sheepish.

'Look, I've brought Meldrick Taylor over from America to box one of my lads and I haven't got a cutsman for him. He's moaning like hell and threatening to withdraw.'

'But I don't know how to do cuts!'

'It's OK,' Ivor said. 'I'll show you.'

By then Taylor, a former two-weight world champion and ring legend, was 42. He was already showing worrying signs of being punchy and had nothing to offer other than his name. Ivor walked us into Taylor's changing room.

'OK gentlemen,' he announced. 'Here's Dennis Hobson, the top cutsman in England, and his assistant, Clinton.'

The Americans went potty, high-fiving and backslapping us.

'You the man, bro, you the man!' they shouted.

When the fight rolled around I sat at ringside, laughing my bollocks off as Dennis stood nervously in the corner, holding a swab and pretending he knew what he was doing. Taylor still had some skills, bless him. The odd feint and shoulder-roll hinted at lost glory if you looked hard enough, but he was getting steadily battered by this young, aggressive Danish kid. Five rounds in, Dennis called me over.

'Clinton, Clinton,' he said. 'I need to fucking piss.' He passed me all the cuts gear as fast as he could and buggered off.

Of course, he never came back and for the second half of the fight I found myself in the same awkward position he had been in. Taylor continued to take a terrible beating and lost a wide points decision, but thankfully my services were never required.

Afterwards, Dennis reappeared and we went out for a drink with Meldrick. This was a man who had been an absolute superstar in his prime. He had his 1984 Olympic gold medal around his neck and kept bringing it into the conversation. It was almost a bit sad.

'I wear this motherfucker everywhere I go,' he told us over a beer. His hands shook. His voice was as thick as tarmac. You had to concentrate on every syllable and then still struggled to understand him half the time. One thing I knew for sure, I never wanted to end up like that.

Returning home, we had eight weeks before Smallwood. He was 15-0, very highly regarded and the idea was for a kind of unofficial eliminator. Whoever won would be in a position to challenge for domestic honours. Since beating Booth, Crawford Ashley had picked up the European title again too, meaning that everything funnelled through him.

To ascend to the next level, either myself or Smallwood would have to cross swords with Ashley.

On the night, I was almost disappointed. Despite all the hoo-haa, the Smallwood bout wasn't even hard. For two rounds it was tricky because he was tall, like me, and had a good jab, like me. That meant my default tactics didn't work, so before the third I thought: 'Right, I'll walk forward then'. As soon as I got on the front foot, he couldn't cope. I smashed him in seven one-sided rounds.

People talk about levels in boxing and, in truth, I still wasn't sure where mine was. The defeat to Starie had set me back in the minds of the public, although to me there were clear reasons for that. Other than that, every time I had come up against what was meant to be a serious domestic level test, I had prevailed. For the first time in my life, I began to speculate. How good could I be? What could I do? Those thoughts stayed with me over Christmas and beyond. I looked up at those at the top of the tree and wondered.

By then, 1998-'99, one man stood over the world light-heavyweight rankings like a demigod. Few fighters are genuinely untouchable in their era, but no one could deny the majesty of Roy Jones Junior.

At that point he held the WBC, WBA and IBF world titles, having already been champion at middleweight and super middleweight. He had dealt comfortably with legends like James Toney, Bernard Hopkins and Mike McCallum, dancing crazy circles, making faces, shuffling, shimmying and showboating, scoring knockouts from all angles with both hands. The Boxing Writers Association of America named him 'fighter of the decade'.

In January, I watched a tape of him defending his belts against a former New York cop called Richard Frazier. Jones was all showbiz. Sparkly gold robe, shorts to match. Frazier was known as a mover, like me, a boxer who liked to use the ring, but for this fight, the ring was small. So small, that the WBC had questioned its legality. Jones was a genius, but he and his team also got away with murder.

He had a hands-by-the-waist reflex-based defence, swaying around, his left cocked two feet in front of his face like a pike. In the first minute of the fight, he switched from orthodox to southpaw then back again about five times. I shook my head in amazement. Ray Gillett would have torn strips off him if he had tried that crap at Hillsborough boys.

But none of it seemed forced or artificial with Jones. He was always on balance, always twitching with a kind of manic energy. You could tell he wasn't pulling the flashy stuff out for the sake of it to impress punters or show off. It was just his style. He was like a malevolent force of nature. By the end of the first, Jones' blink-and-you-miss shots were finding their way through Frazier's guard with ease. The cop had a spell on the canvas but survived to return to his corner.

Frazier spent most of the second circling around the perimeter of the tiny ring, trying desperately to stay out of range. Jones bounced after him, somehow nonchalant and menacing at the same time, firing hooks that glanced off his gloves or whistled by his ears. Frazier had the appearance of passer-by caught in a street shoot-out, running and diving, trying to understand where the guns are, praying he doesn't catch a stray bullet. But ten seconds before the bell, he did. Blasted with a left, his night was over. Lights out.

Frazier had been ranked number one by the WBC and number three by the WBA prior to the fight. Yet Jones had wiped the floor with him without breaking sweat. I may have been above domestic level, but I wasn't silly enough to think I was in Jones' league.

Nobody was.

Round Three

POXON gives me an encouraging slap on the arse as I head out. He's always doing that. My mates rip the piss because of it.

'He's loves touching thy arse, don't he!'

I'm straight on to the jab and catch Hoye hard. I've got the timing, he hasn't.

You haven't figured that one out, have you?

He lumbers after me and throws but there is something different about him, I can sense it. It's still early days but some of the belief has gone from his movements. He is no longer throwing shots knowing he can hurt me. He is *hoping* he can.

Soon we tangle together in the middle and I'm turning him round. At close quarters, I can feel the solidity in his body has dissolved slightly. He feels softer, more malleable. I wrestle him and catch him with short punches when there's space. He breathes heavily.

Hoye doesn't want to give up and comes back at me in the last minute. But his vitality has dropped. There's another little stare-down at the bell, but his eyes have lost their cold menace. There's vulnerability there. I feel like I'm staring into his soul.

18

Clinton Woods
v Crawford
'Chilling' Ashley

**British, Commonwealth and European
light-heavyweight titles
Bowlers, Manchester
13 March 1999**

ASHLEY had been due to defend his titles in an all-Leeds affair against the hard-hitting traveller Henry Wharton. But Wharton had endured a long, hard, not-quite glorious career, mostly at super middleweight, and decided to retire instead. For that reason, Ashley's manager Frank Maloney got straight on the phone to Dennis. The two of them worked together often, and I was never one to make issues about money, so it was sorted quickly. It also made sense from a boxing point of view. My win over Smallwood pretty much made me the obvious choice.

That meant for the first time since turning pro I found myself up against a fighter genuinely thought of as world class. True, he was in the veteran category at 34, but with two title challenges already behind him Ashley was due for another, provided he got past me, which virtually everyone expected him to do. He had been in and around the top tens of the world governing bodies for a decade. I was just that gawky Sheffield lad who lost to Starie.

Maloney was talking about matching Ashley with top yank, Montell Griffin in the States. The idea was they would box an eliminator to challenge for Jones' collection of belts. That meant Crawford was just two fights away from taking on the biggest name in the game.

Again, it presented a big TV opportunity as, like before, the fight would be on Sky Box Office. Dennis loved that and got quite animated about it. His mini-alliance with Maloney and Eliades was already reaping dividends.

This time, the show at Bowlers in Manchester was used as the preliminary for the big early-morning card from Madison Square Garden. Lennox Lewis was defending three of the heavyweight belts there against Evander Holyfield, while on the UK side Ashley and I were top of the bill.

We knew Crawford could be unpredictable and we knew he could really bang. Up to that point, no one had shaken me up in a professional ring. How would I cope if that happened? Starie had given me something to think about around the abdominal area and Baker had burst my eardrum, but I had never been wobbled. Twenty-seven of Ashley's 31 wins had come inside the distance. By any reckoning, he was a major step up.

Howard got me sparring with the usual collection of lads. Day after day, I worked out with Keeton and Dunstan. He began introducing yet more gadgets to the gym and, in all honesty, it got frustrating. At times, I just wanted to skip or spar without having ropes attached to different parts of my body, while balancing with balls or posing on some sort of board with one foot. His rants about the world became a touch more bizarre too and he developed an obsession with NASA. On occasion, I worried about him slightly. I needed him as a boxing trainer, not a crackpot inventor or social theorist.

Despite that, it was a good camp. I always enjoyed the combination of Howard as lead trainer, with Porty as chief second. Grump and grumpier. They bounced off each other like some sort of music-hall comedy act.

This time there were no weight problems, but once again I found myself succumbing to dark moods in the days before the fight. Natalia kept her distance but made her feelings clear.

'You just make sure you make it up to me afterwards,' she said.

On the day, Dennis picked me up. He joked that the limo company had let him down but by the time we reached the venue, all humour had evaporated. Porty gloved me up, while Dennis and Howard paced the dressing room with obvious concern. The atmosphere was funereal. Barely anyone spoke.

Unusually for me, I had no nerves. I felt filled with energy and anticipation. Howard held the pads for me and I whacked away with a smile.

'Come on, you lot!' I shouted as the runner arrived to call us out. 'Why all the long faces?'

'Just keep him on the jab. Keep him on the jab,' Howard said as I bounced my way through the crowd. In typical fashion, my lot had started a punch-up in one of the wings. The crowd there swayed backwards and forwards, while the air filled with angry shouts, like a battleground.

'Fuckin' silly bollocks,' said Porty as the stewards piled in to sort them out. I laughed.

On the Sky commentary, Barry McGuigan summed up the thoughts of many. 'Clinton Woods is elusive, difficult to hit and he's moved up in weight, but he shouldn't have any power to cause trouble.'

Reg Gutteridge, the lead commentator, agreed with him. 'It just depends which Crawford Ashley turns up.'

Beforehand, most agreed that if he was on his game he would have too much for me and during the opening exchanges I was inclined to agree with them. Ashley came out at the first bell winging in massive shots with his upright style. He hit harder than Baker, no question.

A minute into the first and my pre-fight confidence had evaporated. That nagging voice of self-doubt returned.

You're in the wrong fucking place here. You can't live with this. This guy's gonna pulverise you.

All around, I could hear the drunken cheering of my fans. 'Clinton! Clinton!' Images of me being KO'd in front of them flashed through my mind.

Halfway through the opening session Ashley broke my nose with a sharp right. I felt the bone crunch and my eyes filled with water. That woke me up. I realised if I stayed cautious and tried to pick him off with the jab, he would eat me up. I was staying at perfect three-quarter range for him. To change things up, I started lunging forwards, applying pressure.

'How do you feel?' Howard asked between rounds.

'Alright, ar.'

'Get after 'im then,' he said.

The second started ferociously. We both caught each other with hurtful shots but as the session wore on something started to change in him. It seemed very early for him to tire. There had been rumours he was tight at the weight. Were they true?

By the end of the round, he had conceded the initiative to me. Rather than him getting off first and expecting me to counter, I was making the fight. I was dictating the rhythm. It took him by surprise and drained his conviction. From that point on, even at such an early stage, I knew I had him.

'This is a completely different Clinton Woods to the one I've seen in the past,' said analyst Jim Watt on the TV commentary, comparing my performance with the Starie fight. 'Maybe he's more comfortable at the higher weight limit.'

Watt was bang on with that observation. Whether it had been influenced by the creatine or not, my move up to light-heavy did feel like it suited me. I was stronger without losing speed or sharpness. I may not have looked the part – my arms were about half the size of Ashley's – but the power from my back and legs felt immense.

Ashley tried to wrest the momentum back with little bursts and flurries, but the flow of the fight was mine. By the fifth, he was knackered, breathing with an open mouth, slumping on his stool at the end. His knees dipped a couple of times in the seventh and I raised my hands above my head at the bell, although my shorts were stained red with nasal blood by then. I piled it on in the next and with a minute to go in the eighth, as Ashley backpedalled and flailed, his corner threw in the towel.

Time blurred. I sank to my knees. Dennis ran over and hugged me, then lifted me up. Porty cheered and roared as I wheeled around the ring. I was announced as the new champion and saluted my army of fans. The next thing I knew, Sky were interviewing me by the ring apron.

'It's the best I've ever felt in my life,' I told them simply.

Later that night, back home with Natalia and my three new belts, I felt that statement was definitely true.

19

Second to Nunn

AFTER the Ashley fight a guy called George introduced himself, saying he was my biggest fan. He was a Geordie businessman who owned property abroad and asked if I wanted to come and visit him in Cyprus. I thanked him and said I would think about it.

Dennis sat me down and told me we needed to branch out to take my career forwards. He would remain my manager but the promotional side would be handled by Frank Maloney from then on. He set up a meeting with Maloney in London and terms were agreed. In truth, I didn't like Frank. Something about him rubbed me up the wrong way. He was a horrible fucker. He spoke to boxers like shit and seemed to think he was entitled to do so.

But while we were down south, he got us ringside seats at the Docklands Arena. Herbie 'The Dancing Destroyer' Hide was defending his WBO world heavyweight title against the rising Ukrainian star Vitali Klitschko.

Klitschko hammered the Brit in two rounds. He was an absolute giant in comparison, five inches taller and about three stone heavier. How nice it would be to operate in a weight division where you beat your opponent just by out-sizing him! Klitschko didn't even have to try. It was man against boy.

My first fight promoted by Maloney saw me travel back down to the capital, to Elephant and Castle in South London, to take on a guy called Sam Leuii in defence of the Commonwealth on 10 July 1999. Leuii was the New Zealand champ and held the Oceanic title, whatever that meant, had a mixed record and bounced around between super middle and cruiserweight. Again, we were live on Sky and once again I was top of the bill, even though I was fighting miles away from home.

The middleweight contender Howard Eastman was on before me and burst through the dressing room door after stopping his opponent in the sixth. Sweat poured off him like rain.

'Finish your fight quick,' he said, looking my way, dripping. 'It's way too hot out there.'

Walking out with Dennis, Porty and Howard confirmed Eastman's observations. The hall was absolutely stifling. Apparently, the venue had wanted to leave some rear doors open to counteract the heat but the Sky crew had insisted on closing them as the streetlights affected their picture quality.

Leuii turned out to be a tough little operator, stoutly built and sturdy, but crude and easy to read. For three rounds, I boxed circles around him. Then perhaps as a result of the heat, I started to relax. A professional boxing ring is not a place to get too comfortable, no matter who you have got in front of you.

Leuii came out for the fourth like someone had stuck a chilli up his arse. He bounded after me, winging in hooks with both hands, and caught me by surprise. I was tagged with a left and circled backwards. He came after me and rocked me with a right. Fortunately, the minute's worth of flurrying seemed to wear him out. By the end of the round, he had slowed down and I started spearing him with the jab again.

Howard gave me a roasting between rounds, while a voice in the front row kept shouting: 'Just go to him Clinton! Go to him!' I looked down and saw the voice belonged to the great manager and promoter Mickey Duff, who was sitting next to Eliades at ringside.

Following the advice, I tried to return the fight to its natural rhythm and began stepping in, letting my hands go. Once again, as we passed the midpoint of the round, I got that familiar feeling. Leuii's strength, energy and heart were leaving him.

I came out hard for the sixth, put him down with a right to the head and a left to the body, then tore into him after he got up. He had nothing left and I bounced my gloves off his head until his right eye popped. Every time I made contact, blood squirted from the slashed eyelid like juice from an orange. Unsurprisingly, the ref stepped in. As a fight, I had made it harder for myself than I should have. Lesson learned.

After that one, I had a little moan at Dennis. It had been a while since I boxed in Sheffield and my hometown crowd were eager to see me now I was a three-belt champion. Dennis made a strained face, but got to work.

Soon, he lined me up to box a kid called John Lennox Lewis, from Trinidad and Tobago, in another defence of the Commonwealth. It was slated for Hillsborough Leisure Centre.

As my profile increased, the media expected more from me and I started having to do interviews or Q & As. At the pre-fight conference for this one, Lewis surprised everyone, including me, by interrupting proceedings to hold up a bible and shout: 'I am here for the glory of God and and I will prevail in the Lord's name!'

Assembled journalists tried to get him to talk about boxing, but nothing could divert the guy's attention from Christianity. He was on some sort of evangelical mission.

We were sent a video of his previous fights. He had a 9-1 record, with seven KOs, which looked decent on paper, but the tape showed bouts occurring against very meagre opponents, in places that appeared to be big straw huts.

'Wha' the fuck's that all about?' Porty asked.

I shrugged. 'No idea.'

On the night, with my fans going mental as I climbed between the ropes, Lewis bobbed around a bit and started shouting: 'God is here! Jesus is here! He is in this room!'

It was not too much of a surprise and in keeping with the character he showed until then, that he ran at me like a nutter at the first bell. Soon enough, it all followed the standard pattern.

He charged, I boxed. He got tired being moved around while eating jabs and in the end I finished him in the tenth with a four-punch combination.

Everyone seemed pleased. Number one fan George was there again and repeated his invitation to visit. I spoke to Natalia about it and we thought: 'Why not?'

Back at the gym at Attercliffe, Dennis told me he was angling me towards the WBC International title, one of the new belts that had been introduced. It was a largely meaningless trinket, but entitled you to an eliminator. At the end of that path, if everything went well, lay a fight against Jones Jr, which would be lucrative, if nothing else.

In the meantime, to keep things ticking over, he told me he had a phone call from a Polish promoter keen on raising boxing's profile in the region. They were offering about £12,000 for an established top-level European fighter to box an American trial horse called Terry Ford in Warsaw. I had seen Ford box before, in an eight-round snoozefest against Herol Graham a few years previously. The money was decent and I couldn't see how Ford could pose a real threat, so I accepted.

They put us up in a nice hotel in the city although Warsaw was a strange place at the time, still only ten years after the fall of Communism. There were streets lined with designer shops, Armani, Gucci etc and behind them would be dilapidated housing estates with blown-out windows and cars up on bricks. People looked different. They had a hardness in their faces you don't see in England.

Every night, we had dinner with other boxers from the card and we found the Eastern Europeans strangely expressionless. One night, Dennis tried to liven things up by getting a serviette with a fork on top of it to do a little magic trick. The Russians absolutely loved it and killed themselves laughing.

'I show you trick, I show you trick,' a massive heavyweight said. 'Watch, watch.'

He picked a bottle of beer off the table, placed the top of the bottle in his eye socket and opened it like that. Me and Dennis were speechless.

On the night it was a large venue and packed out, but eerily muted. Jon Penn, another light-heavyweight from Dennis' gym, was up against a local kid on the undercard and sparked him out in round one. Jon celebrated the KO wildly and we all jumped in to slap his back and cheer.

The front rows of the Warsaw crowd stared at us in shock.

'Why do you get so excited?' one of the show staff asked.

'Because he won! It was a great KO!'

'We don't understand why you behave like this.'

It was the same for my fight. As Ford and I prepared to face off, the hall was deadly silent. It felt like we were boxing in a library.

From the moment the bout started, every time I whacked him, Ford recoiled.

The crowd occasionally clapped politely and the American never got into it. In truth, he didn't want to know and I stopped him in four rounds.

Afterwards, the promoter invited us out. Howard and Porty went back to the hotel but Dennis and I accepted and ended up in an exclusive nightclub. As we walked in, the manager came over and shook our hands.

'English?' he asked. We nodded.

'Fighters?'

'Yep.'

He smiled broadly and gestured to a lift. 'You can go upstairs.'

We headed up in a polished, stainless steel elevator and found ourselves in a massive, plushly furnished room with leather settees and a huge bar. Tables and tables were lined with different varieties of vodka. Orange, plum, passion-fruit, all the flavours you could imagine. Curvy waitresses wandered around in revealing dresses.

Me and Dennis looked at each other, shrugged and started drinking. It was the nicest vodka imaginable. The stuff just slipped down. After two hours, with both of us becoming steadily more incoherent, I took Dennis outside into the street for some air. The change in atmosphere finished him and he walked round and round in circles, talking to himself.

After returning from Poland, it was back into the Christmas routine again and Natalia and I planned a trip to Cyprus to visit George. I was packing when my phone went.

'Clinton? Dennis.'

'Alright Dennis.'

'How do you fancy fighting Michael Nunn?'

'err...'

'It will make your name in America. Set up some massive nights.'

Nunn was a superstar, a former middleweight and super middle-weight world champ. A southpaw with real left-hand power, he was an athletic, mobile boxer but also a specialist in crunching body shots. I had watched him on TV beating the likes of Iran Barkley and Donald Curry.

'Panos reckons he can get him over here in April.'

'Yeah, I'm up for that.' I replied. 'Why not?'

Later that evening, as the plane took off, I sat by the window and watched the clouds spread out below me. Natalia was reading a book.

'Michael Nunn,' I thought. 'Bloody hell!'

20

This skinny boy from Sheffield

THE Cyprus trip proved to be one of the weirdest weeks of my life. George picked us up at the airport in a jeep, with a big bunch of flowers. He drove us into the mountains behind Paphos, where he had an enormous, beautiful house, and introduced us to his wife. She was a very quiet, petite woman called Susan.

'Make yourselves at home,' he said. 'I'll make us all a barbecue.'

When we finished unpacking, we went downstairs for dinner to find George drinking beers with whisky chasers. As the evening ploughed on, he got through about eight of those, a couple of bottles of wine and a few other shots of something or other. We excused ourselves and went to bed about midnight.

'He doesn't half drink,' Natalia observed.

The next day, I got up at six in the morning to go for a run and George was already sitting there by the pool with a beer in his hand. He held it up to salute me.

'Morning champ!' He said.

With alarm bells beginning to ring, the next night he took us out to a local Taverna.

Again, he drank non-stop and decided to phone the Cyprus national TV station.

All seven of the Woods kids together!

With my brother Heath in the 70s. Look what little cherubs we were!

A skinny boy from Sheffield, with his first pair of boxing gloves

Mam with all five of her sons

All the Woods boys! With my Dad and brothers

With Dennis after an early win at the Pinegrove club. Me and him made a great team.

Poster advertising my first title fight, against Darren Littlewood

About to spar at Glyn Rhodes' gym. Paul 'Silky' Jones is standing next to me.

I've just stopped Crawford Ashley as a massive underdog in 1999 to become British, European and Commonwealth champ. He broke my nose in round one.

Celebrating my underdog victory over Crawford Ashley with Dennis and Neil

Planting one on Ole 'The Golden Viking' Klemetsen in our European title fight at Wembley in April 2000

After the Arturo Rivera victory, with Tim, Denis and Neil

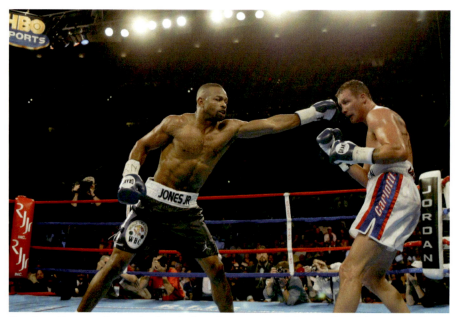

Roy Jones Jr was at his peak when he boxed me in 2002. The speed and sharpness of his punches were almost supernatural.

Jamaican Glen Johnson played a big part in my career, with three tough, close fights. Here I've connected with a right, during our final bout in 2006.

Jason DeLisle was a proper Aussie hardnut, but I beat him comfortably both times we met.

Rico Hoye came in as a big favourite in our 2005 IBF world title fight but I upset the odds again. I felt so strong and quick. It was probably the best night of my career.

After defeating Rico Hoye to become IBF world champion

Julio Gonzalez, a freakishly tough fighter and a real gentleman, too. I was very sad to learn of his death in 2012.

Antonio Tarver was such an arrogant, unpleasant man. My biggest regret is not being in the right condition to beat him.

A rare moment of success against Antonio Tarver in 2008. A disappointing night, it was the only time I walked to the ring knowing I was going to lose.

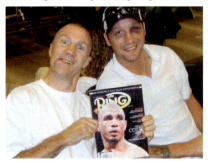

With my mate Daz Ashton and my fitness coach John Clarke, in Florida before the disastrous Antonio Tarver fight

With Glyn Rhodes after losing my last fight to Tavoris Cloud. I just felt relieved it was finally all over!

With the love of my life, Natalia

With Andy 'Spud' Woollatt, a brilliant mate of mine who used to work on boxing shows

With Danny Tyrell, one of my best mates who attended all of my fights

In my garden at Swallow Cottage. Boxing has given me a lot.

With Ray Gillett, the man who started me off in boxing

My star on the Sheffield walk of fame outside the Town Hall

My statue on the Trans-Pennine Way. I was very proud that the people of Sheffield voted for me.

The plaque that accompanies my statue

Clinton Woods

Born in Waterthorpe, Sheffield, Clinton first became interested in boxing aged seven. His subsequent fifteen-year career saw him hold British, Commonwealth, European and World titles. He was the light heavyweight world champion boxer between 2005 and 2008. He retired from boxing in 2009.

What it's all about! My wife Natalia, with my kids, Jude and Lola

My gym in the Westfield area of Sheffield

In the 'Clinton Woods boxing and fitness gym' in 2017

With my first son, Kyle. I'm very happy that he is part of my life again.

My son, Kyle, with my grand-daughter Bonnie

'We've got the European champion here,' he slurred. Soon they turned up with cameras and interviewed me for the news. I didn't mind, but George's behaviour was starting to trouble us.

The next couple of days continued in much the same way. Me and Natalia felt we needed some time away from him and decided to go to a restaurant for dinner. He saw us leaving.

'Just watch this with me for a minute,' he said before we could go.

I joined him in the lounge, where he had one of my fights on a massive flat-screen TV.

'Go on!' he screamed at the recorded footage. 'Fucking get in there, son! Knock this twat out!'

He was cheering as if it was live and I began to feel uneasy. Once I managed to get away, we went out for food and returned about midnight. As we parked and got out of the car, we could hear him shouting from inside the house.

'I don't give a fuck who's here. I ain't putting up with that bullshit.'

'No, please.' his wife whined. 'Please, please.'

Horrified, we decided to go back out for a drink and returned about three in the morning. Fortunately, everything seemed peaceful by then. The next day, all was well.

Sometime after we got back, we found out George's wife had left him. The whole thing showed me one of the pitfalls of fame. You attract all sorts of people. George had once been a lovely guy, by all accounts, but retirement had turned him into a drinker.

As the new millennium got under way, Dennis and I thought about our options. It's a funny position to be in in boxing, when you've won a few titles, got yourself world ranked but are not quite in place yet for a shot. Everyone ten or 20 places below you is snapping at your heels and calling you out, while the guys you want to get at, just above, avoid you like the plague. The last thing someone ranked number four or five wants is to box someone ranked 14 or 15. It will be a dangerous bout and if they come unstuck they slip down the list, ending up further away from championships and big paydays. As a fringe contender, you exist in a sort of limbo.

After three low-key affairs against Leuii, Lewis and Ford, I was eager for a bigger challenge – even if it did have to be a fearsome American southpaw. Instead, I found myself lined up against another nondescript opponent in the form of Juan Nelongo, an African based in Tenerife, in February. He was challenging for my European title and probably had the silliest nickname of anyone I had faced, with the words 'King Dongo' threaded into the waistband of his shorts. I thought it best not to ask what that was about.

He held the Spanish light-heavy title at the time and had a reputation as a bit of a character. At least I got my wish of fighting in front of my home crowd again. Ponds Forge was packed out and among my usual irrepressible support even some of the Sheffield Wednesday team showed up.

Dressed in a purple and gold robe, and wearing a crown, Nelongo threw sweets to the crowd on his way to the ring. His form was good but I had six inches in reach on him and the bookies made me a 1/10 favourite. Spanish boxing is not held in high regard, as a rule.

In the end, Nelongo proved himself a rugged, durable character. Powerfully built, with massive arms, the bout turned into a 12-round battle and I had to take the odd shot. He had started out as a kickboxer and, like many who come from that discipline, he was often a bit square-on. His balance wasn't the best but the guy proved himself an absolute beast. He never stopped ploughing forwards, winging long jabs and wild left hooks. After winning a comfortable unanimous decision, I was left with a cut under my right eye and some facial swelling.

The minor injuries meant I was unable to spar for a while after the fight, which wasn't ideal. As far as I knew, I was boxing Nunn in April, a fight for which I would need to be at my best, so Howard suggested I limit my impact work as much as possible. I had always been a believer in traditional methods, solid roadwork, heavy sessions in the gym, but he had visions of a new approach.

'You run too much,' he told me. 'It's bad for your knees and ankles. Hips too. You'll end up having joint trouble.'

'Come off it, Howard.'

'I want you to try this instead.'

He led me over to a corner of the gym where he had butchered a treadmill. The belt was in a vertical position and propped up against the wall, with the digital display and controls on the floor beside it.

'What you do...' he began.

I rolled my eyes.

'Is lie down with your feet facing it. Then start her up and do your jogging like that. It's completely impact free.'

His eyes were shining with a strange kind of excitement.

'OK then,' I said. 'I'll gi' it a go.'

For the next few days, I did my running sessions on Howard's lying-down treadmill. It felt unnatural and after 15 to 20 minutes of using it, my lower back began to hurt around the lumbar region. I had serious doubts about where all this was going.

The facial damage from Nelongo had more or less healed when Dennis told me that Nunn would not be ready to come over for April. There were some issues to be worked through in the negotiations. I shrugged.

'But listen,' he said. 'I've got another big one.'

'OK.'

'What's the biggest fight for you in Europe right now?'

The Pole Dariusz Michalczewski held the WBO title at the time, the only one of the four major belts not worn by Jones. Was it him?

'Other than that, then,' Dennis replied.

I thought about it. There was a German, Rocchigiani, who had held various titles at various times and another called Ulrich who was on the way up. France's top boy, Mohammed Siluvangi, had lost a narrow points decision to Crawford Ashley in '98. Beyond that, all the really big names were over the Atlantic. Then, suddenly, it hit me.

'No!'

Dennis laughed.

'I've had his old man on the phone, giving it all that. You know what he's like. Despite everything that happened in sparring, he reckons with 10oz gloves, you've got no chance.'

Since losing on points to Reggie Johnson and suffering another blip two fights later against the Nigerian Peter Oboh, Ole Klemetsen had racked up eight wins inside the distance, including a TKO victory over former super middleweight world champ Thulani 'Sugarboy' Malinga. That one had been for a minor belt, the IBA world championship, but had whetted his appetite. The Golden Viking had his eyes on bigger prizes. He wanted his old European title back.

Set for 29 April on a Sky show at Wembley Arena, Woods v Klemetsen was chief support to Robert McCracken's world middleweight title shot against American Keith Holmes. It would firmly establish Europe's dominant light-heavyweight.

Both of us had stopped Crawford Ashley and both of us were knocking loudly on the door of world honours. As soon as it was agreed, I felt supremely confident. In both our camps, I had handled him – and he had to know that as well as I did.

Training started in earnest with all the usual sparring partners, along with cruiserweights Lee 'He's No Baby' Swaby and Mark Hobson. I found a rhythm quickly, which is one of the main advantages of fighting on a regular basis. Ring rust has no time to settle.

On the other side, some of the Ingle boxers helped out in Klemetsen's camp. Plenty in Sheffield didn't like that and all sorts of insults were thrown around. They saw it as disloyal but it never bothered me for a second.

Two weeks from fight night and we headed down to London for the press conference. It was great to see Ole's lot again, especially Ivor.

'I watched you beat Ashley,' he told me. 'Brilliant performance.'

With us all sat there at the top table, the introductions were made and it was thrown open to questions from the floor. One of the newspaper reporters asked Klemetsen how confident he was, a silly question. What boxer will tell you he's worried he might lose? Ole's dad grabbed the mike.

'Let me answer that,' he shouted, enjoying his moment. 'Ole wins for sure. There's no way he can lose to this skinny boy from Sheffield!'

I looked at Dennis and laughed. I actually liked the line, in some ways. Maybe that could be my new nickname?

With the media stuff out of the way, as before on the bigger occasions, I felt tension creep in prior to the fight. Natalia got fed up. We drove down to London for the weigh-in and we slept in separate hotel rooms. It had nothing to do with the old boxing wisdom of avoiding sex before a contest, although that was something I believed in, but was just because she couldn't stand to be around me.

'I'll see you afterwards,' she said.

'Fair enough.'

The day of the fight arrived quickly. I stuffed myself with food, as usual, and Dad popped into the changing room to give me some gum for the 28th time.

'Good luck, lad, give me a love,' he said, kissing me on the cheek.

I thought about what I needed to do, sharing words with Howard and Porty. No shitty music. I hated that before a contest, all the blaring rap and rubbish people used to play. If it was my choice, there would be a bit of Matt Monro or Dean Martin on.

Yet once the ringwalk began, all anxiety left me. I felt no nerves at all. Ole was in there waiting for me. As I neared, I watched him bouncing around, his dad and Ivor behind him. He looked fired up and in good shape, but the simple fact was I knew I was better than him. His only chance was to catch me with a big one and bomb me out, but by that point in my career I had total confidence in my chin too. I had weathered storms against big, tough men and my self-doubt had subsided.

Sure enough, Klemetsen waded straight in. His dad probably pumped him up, maybe told him how no one could take his power, that he could walk straight through me. I let Ole tee off, kept turning him, spinning away, then picked moments to fire back. By the halfway point of the first, he was cut under the left eye.

'Go on, Clinton!' I heard Porty roar.

Over the opening rounds, the pattern remained the same as Ole tried to solve the conundrum of my defence. I was a touch taller than him, had a slightly longer reach, kept high hands and moved my feet and head constantly. Klemetsen winged in hooks and tried to knock my block off. He rarely connected. Still, he had centre ring and was the aggressor, which caught the eye of some at ringside.

Halfway through the third, Ian Darke on the Sky commentary summed it all up: 'If Clinton Woods loses this fight, he will have already achieved more than he ever dreamed of.'

It was exactly the sort of statement the media always made about me. I couldn't hear him, but provided a perfect response nonetheless. Just as the last words of that sentence left Darke's mouth, I caught Klemetsen with a right hook, shook him, then drove him back across the ring with a three-punch combo.

By the fourth, Ole was cut over both eyes. By the fifth, I was turning the screw, trying to apply intelligent pressure. The last thing I wanted was to go after him wildly and leave myself open, so kept picking away, chipping at his exterior. With every passing minute, I felt him weaken.

At the start of the eighth, his energy had dipped enough for me to take a chance. *Come on, let's do this!* I closed the distance and threw a left hook. *Have that!* The next thing I knew, I was on the floor.

Ole had thrown his own left at the same time as mine and his had landed a fraction of a second earlier. The impact of the punch sent me straight on to my back. My legs came up over my head and as I let them fall back to the floor and bounced to my feet, relief washed over me. My vision and mind were completely clear. I turned my back and walked slowly towards my corner. Dennis, Neil and Howard looked up at me between the ropes with pleading eyes.

'Fuckin' hell!' I said through my gumshield.

Neil grinned.

The ref administered a standing eight and Klemetsen came at me as if he'd just had a line of whizz. I got back on my boxing, kept him off and within 30 seconds, he ran out of steam. I felt him go completely. His tank was empty.

I began to pile it on. Klemetsen had no answer. A minute after I had been on my arse, I had Ole backed on to the ropes and reeling all over the place. His corner were frantic. I bashed him up pretty nicely and that film star face was turning into a bit of a mess.

In the ninth, he was running on fumes and I knew it. I put it on him and it was just target practice. Nothing came back. I had been knocking him from one side of the ring to the other for about 30 seconds when I rocked his head back with an uppercut. Eyes glazed, Klemetsen sank backwards and sat on the middle rope with a blank expression. The ref dived between us to stop me from battering a helpless target.

I wheeled away, lost in that beautiful moment of complete satisfaction. There's nothing better than defeating a tough opponent. Howard kissed my cheek. Dennis grabbed me from behind.

'Not bad for a skinny boy,' he said in my ear.

Ole's father consoled him in his corner. I went over, gave him a hug.

'That's the way it goes,' I said with a shrug. 'It wasn't your night.'

Afterwards, I went to his changing room to shake hands, offer condolences and ask him if he wanted to go out for a drink, but when I walked in he looked at me with hatred.

'Your gloves,' Klemetsen snarled. 'You had something in your gloves. Look at my face.'

He was clearly disappointed, but I couldn't believe what I was hearing. I stared at him for a second, shook my head, then walked back out without saying a word.

Natalia and I celebrated on our own, with a few drinks and a bit of dinner in the hotel on room service. With the money I had gathered by then, we were finally able to move off the Westfield and bought a house in the Ridgeway village area. My more recent international-level fights had earned me five-figure purses. I hadn't become a rich man, by any means, but boxing was finally starting to pay some dividends.

21

Howard's Way

IN the week's rest after Klemetsen, I got a few more phone calls from Dennis. He was very keen to set up the Nunn fight and threw the date of 15 July at me. 'And by the way,' he said. 'We're going to have to relinquish the European.'

As far as I was concerned, that didn't make much sense. I had just proven myself the undisputed no.1 light-heavyweight in Europe and was proud of it. Why give it up?

But Dennis explained that having ascended into the top ten of the WBC, the onus was now on picking opponents to protect and advance that ranking, rather than defending titles – modern boxing. All the governing bodies seem to do things to promote their own interests, rather than the sport in general. The fight with Nunn was going to be for the WBC International title and would effectively act as an eliminator for the world. Meanwhile, at the top of the pile, Roy Jones was rapidly running out of opponents. Nobody could live with him.

Ten days after stopping Klemetsen, I went back to the gym and Howard lumbered over with a wide smile.

'Great performance last week,' he rasped. 'We can really push on now.'

'Thanks, yeah.'

'But listen, we've got to think long term. From now on, I want you to stop running.'

'What?'

'No more running in your training. You just use my machines instead.'

'What're you on about? I run every day. I always have and look Howard, no offence, but I hate that fuckin' machine. It does my back in.'

'None of the top boxers run these days, you know.'

I shook my head.

'Come on, you're talking out your arse. Of course they do. What about Lennox Lewis? There's videos of him running on TV.'

Howard screwed his face up.

'Lewis?' he replied. 'He in't a top boxer!'

At the time, Lennox was the WBC and IBF heavyweight champion and had just relinquished the WBA. He was universally recognised as undisputed world champ and most pundits placed him on the all- time list with Ali, Louis and Dempsey. But Howard had a strange light in his eyes.

'Never has been,' he repeated, staring and squinting. 'Waste of space.' That was when I first began to think he was genuinely losing the plot.

One thing I knew for sure was that I was not prepared to stop running. It was something I actually enjoyed, as well as being great for fitness. Later that day, I had a word with Dennis.

'I'm not comfortable with what Howard's getting me to do.'

'What d'you mean?'

'All t'new methods and gadgets. It's doing my head in. I think I need a change.'

'But he's got you some great wins, Clint. And the next one's Nunn.'

Dennis was right, as usual. To that point, all the best nights of my career had come through Howard. I still rated him as a coach, but sometimes gut feeling conquers logic.

'I know, ar.' I said. 'I know.'

As training camp began, I tried to put my doubts to the back of my mind. They sorted me out a heavyweight called Scott Lansdowne for sparring and I tried to make the best of it although the truth was the situation was far from ideal. One thing my time in pro boxing had taught me was the value of quality sparring. Going full pelt with guys like Terry Dunstan and Klemetsen in the past had really set me up for good performances.

Nunn was 6ft 1in, long and lean, nimble and a lovely mover. Technically, he would be my most challenging opponent. Lansdowne, on the other hand, was 5ft 10ins in height and roughly the same distance across. A lovely bloke, he was about as graceful as a double decker bus and had never even won an area title. The only thing the two of them had in common was that they were both southpaws.

The sparring was easy. Too easy. Lansdowne would lumber after me like a creature out of *Lord of the Rings* and I would just box his head off. I usually kept my head down and got on with things, but after a couple of weeks I spoke up.

'How is sparring this kid going to prepare me for Nunn?'

'He's the only southpaw we could get,' Dennis replied.

'It's great sparring, great sparring,' Howard enthused. I looked at Dennis and rolled my eyes.

Once again, the scheduled show was a massive one, on Sky Box Office, featuring Lennox Lewis top of the bill against the South African Francois Botha. Unable to pull out, I ploughed on through my pre-fight training with a feeling of apprehension. Two weeks before the fight, the posters arrived and Porty put one up in the gym.

'Former middleweight and super middleweight world champion,' it said. 'Michael *Second To* Nunn'.

The old bugbear of self-doubt reared up and consumed me. My camp had been nowhere near good enough. There was no way I could beat somebody of Nunn's calibre with such poor preparation.

Five days before fight-night, we were due to travel down to London for the press conference. Interest was obviously focused on the heavyweights, but a buzz had built around the Nunn fight too. With the Starie disappointment two years behind me and a string of wins since, some of the pundits were beginning to talk about my future prospects.

I was in the passenger seat of Dennis' car on the M1 when his phone rang. His face dropped and I knew immediately that something was wrong. My ears pricked up.

'Fuck!' he shouted when the call finished, slamming his palm on the steering wheel. 'He's not fucking coming.'

'Who?'

'Nunn. They wouldn't let him fly because of his criminal record. He's stuck in the States. The fight's off.'

'Oh shit,' I said, unconvincingly, while inside I cheered like a madman. What a relief!

Rather than cancel altogether, Dennis found a last-minute opponent in Greg Scott Briggs, a trial horse cruiserweight from Chesterfield. That meant I was able to relax for my last few days of training. I didn't even need to worry about making weight any more. I ate as I pleased and came in nine pounds heavy at 184. Briggs was 193. It would be a public workout, nothing more.

With the tension gone, I was able to enjoy my stay in London a bit more than I usually would have. I had a couple of late nights and even had a glass of wine with dinner the night before.

The arena was full and noisy. As usual, Sheffield turned out in force to support me. The one thing I could always count on was those noisy bastards. Porty was busy wrapping my hands in the dressing room when a photographer came in.

'Quick snap please, Clinton?' he asked.

I stood and put my hands up, in the classic boxer's pose. He smiled and pinged off a couple of photos.

'Thanks very much,' he gushed, leaving me shaking my head and dabbing at my face. I don't know if I failed to blink at the right time, but somehow the flash stayed in my eye. I winked and grimaced but couldn't shake it off. Over the next few minutes, it developed into a migraine.

'The last thing I need,' I thought, but didn't tell a soul.

By the time I reached the ring my head pounded and my vision was split. Nausea spread up from my guts.

Briggs was a big lump, if nothing else. He could tell I wasn't right and had a good go in the first. After the opening two rounds, Dennis tore into me in the corner.

'What the bloody hell are you doing? You're supposed to be world class and this plodder's making you look bad!'

By the third, my vision cleared and I got him out of there quickly. Fast hands, rat-a-tat, game over. Years later, he was interviewed by a newspaper and claimed he 'wobbled' me in the early stages. He's allowed his bit of reflected glory, I suppose, but it wasn't true. He never hurt me, not really.

Regardless of any of that, for the viewing public my performance had been poor and I knew it. I was in danger of stagnating. I stewed on it, then phoned Dennis after we got back home.

'Me and Howard,' I said simply. 'I think we're done.'

22

All roads lead to Jones

MAKING the final break with Rainey seemed like an easy thing to do at the time. As usual, Dennis managed it for me, meaning I avoided the awkward situation of having to tell him to his face. When I mulled the whole thing over, I did have mixed feelings. There was no question that Howard improved me as a boxer. In many ways, he was the best coach I ever had. I just felt the relationship had grown stale. The changeover also caused a slight delay in my career.

I got back into training with Neil, who was his usual charming self.

'Tha's a filthy, fat bastard,' he told me on the first day back. I was carrying a couple of weeks' worth of chips and beer around my waist. 'You need to train all that blubber off.'

I was happy working with Neil. I always had been, but Dennis still felt I needed a more prominent, guiding figure, someone to be my chief coach. He wanted a man with profile and a track record. Someone worthy of training a top contender. Months crawled past with no fight dates. After a while, I started going out with the boys and getting hammered at weekends again. Old habits can be hard to break.

Altogether it was six months before I fought again, in March 2001. This time it was for the much-vaunted WBC International belt. Again, the original idea was that I would box Nunn, but when the inevitable happened and he dropped out, Dennis finally gave up on that one. He tried to get another ranked American, a guy called Rodney Moore, over instead but that fell through too. In the end, he managed to get a bout with former British super middleweight champ Ali Forbes sanctioned instead.

Strangely enough, Ivor ended up coming over from Norway to run my corner. He arrived a couple of weeks before the fight and took me through some stuff in the gym.

Despite liking Ivor, I found his training amateurish. He preferred that very upright European style, which might have suited Ole but wasn't my way. I always preferred to stay mobile and move my head. Ray had drummed all that so far into my brain I couldn't ever forget it.

On the night, Porty still did most of the talking, or growling as it usually was with him. Forbes proved himself a tough guy and really put it all out there, as expected, but he had just turned 40 and his best days were in the past.

He was the sort of opponent I could have stopped early if I'd had a bit more devil in the right hand, but murderous power was never one of my attributes. I boxed him and boxed him, stayed on top throughout and eventually wore him down in the tenth.

Afterwards, Ivor went home and we took stock. With the international title in my possession, that win placed me as the number three light-heavyweight contender with the WBC. Dennis and Panos still had their sights firmly set on a bout with Jones. Beating Nunn would have guaranteed that, but without the big-name scalp we would have to do it the old-fashioned way.

Between them, my management team organised a final eliminator against the WBC's number one, a Ugandan boxing out of Italy called Yawe Davis. After suffering some early defeats, Davis built an impressive record, including a second-round TKO win over Manchester's Carl 'The Cat' Thompson. When the fight was signed, Davis was Italian champ and had picked up the European belt I relinquished.

We agreed that the Ivor experiment wasn't worth repeating and Dennis drafted in Ian Allcock as my new coach. Originally from Nottingham, Allcock had worked with my old mate Silky Jones for a while, as well as top heavyweights Scott Welch and Herbie Hide. I liked him straight away. He was a proper tough bastard, like Porty, and trained me hard. He would even come out running with me, which none of my other coaches had ever done.

Ian had this amazing personal confidence about himself too. You could be in a café having a cup of tea with him, a pretty girl would walk in and within a minute he had gone over and got her phone number. It's not that he was a particularly handsome man, he just possessed some kind of innate charisma. Immediately, he lifted the atmosphere. Training felt like real training again.

Yet just as Nunn had before, Davis pulled out, two weeks before fight night, with an injury. Dennis spoke to the media and told them he thought I was cursed. How could I get to the top level when fights with top fighters kept falling through? Instead, I ended up boxing a journeyman called Paul Bonson, who turned up for the pay packet and ran away from me for the whole six rounds. It was a pointless evening, but that's the way it can go when you take on last-minute replacements.

Fortunately, Davis' injury healed quickly, he proved himself an honourable man and we were able to rearrange for September at Ponds Forge. In camp for this one, a new body appeared in the gym. Blonde haired, tall, with an unusual angular face, Richard Poxon became an enthusiastic, energetic presence in the team, working with some of the less established fighters. I didn't realise it then, but he would play a big part in my future.

Training with Ian was gruelling again. There was no let-up. He loved his high-intensity, high-volume sessions. Every day I went home shattered.

In fight week, Davis arrived full of quiet, brooding confidence, having smashed Coventry's Neil Simpson in three rounds in his last outing. He seemed a solemn but rugged character, with an unreadable face. At the press conference, he was even less vocal than me, which was unusual. Besides his strength and toughness, the main concern was that he boxed southpaw. I hated boxing southpaws, but the stakes were high. As far as the WBC were concerned, this was the two best light-heavyweight contenders facing off.

Dennis billed it as 'the fight for the right' and as soon as the opening bell rang, I could tell Davis had a bit of class about him. He was rock solid and wasted nothing. If there was no opening, he didn't throw. If he threw a punch, it was accurate. He wasn't a tricky southpaw, but the angles his shots came from made life difficult.

I quickly twigged I had to stay sharp and watch my balance. The most important thing was to keep my left foot outside of his right to avoid getting drawn on to the left hand. Davis had 25 inside-the-distance wins and the last thing I wanted was to turn it into a battle between his power and my chin.

Despite that, throughout the fight I found him easy to hit. I was first to the punch all night long, but could not put a dent in the guy. It was like hitting a statue. At the finish, I had small cuts over both eyes and felt like I had been run over. On the other hand, Davis looked exactly the same as when we started. Dennis brimmed with confidence, though.

'You've done it!' He said. 'You outworked him.' He tried to hoist me on to his shoulders, got me off the ground, couldn't manage and gave up. Meanwhile, commentators at ringside hailed it as one of the fights of the year.

'Took it by a country mile,' Ian said, towelling me off. In the end, they were both right. I picked up a wide unanimous decision and found myself in pole position to box Jones.

To celebrate, I bought a BMW with a personalised number-plate: WBC 1.

23

They're gonna love you, man!

DESPITE beating Davis in September 2001 and all the talk of Jones coming over to London, or maybe one of the football stadia in Sheffield, the wheels of business turned slowly. Davis bashed my face up a bit and I needed time to heal, so I spent a fair while at home and got stuck into some DIY. The new place needed a lot of work.

It was about two weeks after the fight when my phone went as I was putting some shelves up.

'How do, Clint. It's Dennis.'

'How do.'

'Can you come to my place on Sunday for a meeting? There's an American guy flying over from Top Rank promotions to see us.'

'Course I can, ar.'

That sounded promising. Top Rank were the biggest American promotional company at the time and represented Jones Jr. Dennis lived nearby, on the lovely country road I used to admire as a kid, which was now just around the corner from me. I walked there and arrived on Sunday afternoon to find him chatting away to a large, boisterous character who introduced himself as Brad Jacobs.

Jacobs had a nest of gingery curls on his head and a moustache of similar colour. He jumped up as soon as I walked in.

'Hey, you must be Clinton. It's great to meet you, man. We're so excited about you.'

'Oh reyt, ta.'

'The American public are really gonna love you!' he went on. 'I mean L-O-V-E! They wanna hear about your drinking and your street-fighting. It's a great story!'

HBO pay-per-view was proposed. That would mean a million dollar purse for me. Up to that point, the most I had been paid for a fight was about £25,000. I smiled and nodded. Internally, I thought it sounded too good to be true. The guy was a typical American bullshitter. He had to be.

The three of us talked for over an hour and it seemed there was a willingness on both sides to make the fight. Before he left, Jacobs invited us over to watch Jones' next bout, against the Australian Glen Kelly in Miami, in February.

I kept myself ticking over in the gym and while negotiations for the Jones fight went on, I stayed inactive. Dennis had spoken at length to Eliades and they didn't want me to risk the big one by signing for lesser fights, which could end up as banana skins. We talked about possible venues, Sheffield Arena, even Hillsborough football stadium. Jones was the biggest star in world boxing and bringing him to England would be a big deal for sports fans.

'Flight's booked for Wednesday,' Dennis said on the phone before the Jones vs Kelly bout. 'Get yourself a nice suit.'

I picked up a lovely blue Hugo Boss number and we flew over, enjoyed the bars of Miami for a couple of days, then headed to the venue. A few people recognised me there, which was nice. I had a chat with Kevin Kelley, the former featherweight world champ who had boxed a right ding-dong with Naseem Hamed.

When Jones appeared, we took our seats at ringside to enjoy the spectacle, which soon became a one-man show, as usual. By the end of the first, I already knew the Australian had no chance. He had one advantage – size.

Every other variable – speed, skill, movement, brain – was with Jones. Jones did his usual virtuoso act, wobbling his shoulders, feinting this way and that. Kelly just lumbered around after him with his hands up, taking shots.

Jones did as he pleased and dominated, utterly. Kelly went down in the sixth from a right to the guts. In the seventh, the American put his hands behind his back and stood in front of his opponent, swaying his chin left to right, goading him to take a shot. The instant the challenger opened his body to throw, Jones swung a right hook from the seat of his pants that caught Kelly on the ear and turned his legs to spaghetti. It was an incredible bit of boxing. Dennis and I pissed ourselves laughing. In my heart, I still didn't believe I could beat Roy Jones, but I knew I would do better than Glen Kelly.

At the press conference afterwards, Jones sat at the centre of the top table like an emperor, with about 20 microphones in front of him. He wittered on with the throng of journalists hanging on his every word. He explained that he'd just finished recording his album, thanked God and then his manager. Then for some reason he started shouting: 'I'm the pound-for-pound man around here! Pensacola in the house, Pensacola in the house!'

One of the journalists asked who he would fight next and threw a few names out. A guy called Antonio Tarver was being touted around. I had never heard of him. The middleweight champion Bernard Hopkins' name was mentioned, but Jones was dismissive. He had already beaten him in the lower division.

'Why would I fight Hopkins?' he snorted. 'He got nothing new.'

Dennis grabbed me by the arm.

'Get up!' he said in my ear. 'Get up!'

I looked at him.

'You what?'

'Fuckin' gerrup!'

I stood up, feeling like a naughty boy in a school assembly. Dennis did too.

'Roy!' Dennis shouted. Jones looked over.

'When are you gonna fight my man?'

Jones smiled. It must have been prearranged. 'Come on up,' he said.

I started walking, self-consciously. 'Oh fucking hell,' I thought.

When I reached the stage, he did his best regal pout and yelled: 'Who the hell are you?'

'I'm Clinton Woods, from England,' I replied.

'Hmm…' Jones seemed to think it over for a few seconds. 'So tell all the people here why should I fight you?'

'I'm the number one contender,' I said simply. 'I've been at the top of the rankings for years. I beat Yawe Davis. You should fight me next.' I wasn't quite on Jones' level when it came to brash, fight talk.

The champ eyeballed me for a bit, just for added theatre. Then he opened his eyes wide and looked down at the pressmen with their pens and dictaphones poised.

'Everybody!' he announced. 'This will be my next fight!'

We took a few questions. Dennis gave them all a couple of quotes. When the press conference finished, we walked out of the arena on to the street, pleased with our performance.

'See,' Dennis said. 'Weren't too bad, was it?'

'No,' I admitted reluctantly. 'I suppose not.'

'There's our hotel, there,' Dennis said, pointing at the towering Hilton in the mid-distance. 'Let's walk.'

'OK,' I said. It seemed like a good idea at the time.

Still suited and booted, we began our stroll through the unknown streets of Miami. Before long, the splendour of the arena was replaced with alleyways and shabby apartment blocks. Groups of young men loitered around. We came to an intersection of streets, either side of which stretched a patch of wasteland. On one side sat a badly burned sofa, dumped and abandoned, on the other a rusted basketball hoop.

'Fuckin' ell,' Dennis said. 'It's worse than Westfield.'

'Ar,' I laughed. ''tis ar.'

The next thing we knew, there was a huge guy walking behind us. And when I say huge, I mean like seven feet tall and built like an HMS Frigate. He was so close I could feel his breath on my neck.

'Yo!' he shouted suddenly.

'For fuck's sake,' I thought.

'Gimme some fuckin' money,' he demanded.

'Look, we en't got nowt' I told him. His eyes lit up as he realised we were foreign.

'I want some fuckin' dollars!' he repeated. I began to prepare myself. It was looking likely I would have to fight this guy. I just hoped he wasn't armed.

Out of nowhere, a car screamed to a halt on the intersection next to us. It was full of black guys. I breathed in sharply. This was not looking good. The front side window came down slowly and the driver looked out at us. He had hooded eyes and wore a white bandana.

'Are you OK, guys?' he asked.

I looked at Dennis.

'Not bad, ar,' Dennis said.

'Hey Dee,' the driver called out. The big guy behind us stopped walking. 'Let 'em be, man.'

'I ain't doin shit,' Dee protested. The driver looked at him with authority.

'I said, let 'em be.'

Dee nodded his head and started walking sideways, across the scrub towards the burnt sofa. The driver nodded at us and drove away.

As the car sped off, I looked over and saw Dee turn around and head back towards us.

'Oh shit,' I said. 'He's fuckin' comin' back.'

Instinctively, Dennis and I upped our pace. We reached the end of the wasteland and turned a corner, dodged either side of a lamppost in a weird position and marched on. From behind us came the sound of footsteps. Dee was running to catch us up.

Still at least ten minutes from the hotel, we looked around, hoping to see a way out of the situation. A mangy cat crossed the street in front of us.

Clang! Came a noise from behind.

'What the hell?' asked Dennis.

We turned around to see Dee's enormous form prostrate on the ground. He had hurtled around the corner, ran straight into the lamppost and knocked himself out.

We cracked up laughing.

'We'd best fuckin' leg it,' I said to Dennis. 'When that fucker wakes up, he'll think we did it!' Dennis agreed and we jogged back to the hotel, savouring our lucky escape.

The following day, we returned to England full of hope. Eliades continued his grand talk about a stadium event in the UK. The way he saw it, I could become a national star, like Hamed or Ricky Hatton.

'Any news?' I would say, day to day in the gym. Every time the answer was no or just a shake of the head. After a while, I stopped asking. Eventually, a month or so after Jones agreed to fight me, Dennis walked out of his office looking serious.

He said: 'Look, Clint, we're still working on the Jones fight. Panos is sure it'll happen, but I think we should probably get you out in the meantime. It's already five months since you were in the ring.'

My heart sank a bit. If the negotiations were taking that long, maybe the whole thing was just talk.

'Alreyt,' I said.

Dennis set up a keep-busy fight with a guy called Clint Johnson at the York Hall in London. He was a nothing opponent but at least the venue was a positive. York Hall has a special place in British boxing folklore and I always wanted to box there.

Johnson looked the part, no question. As we stood in the ring and they pulled off his blue T-shirt, I had to do a double-take. The guy was like a cartoon superhero. He had muscles in places where I didn't even have places. Fortunately, though, boxing is not and never has been a Mr. Universe contest.

As it turned out, Johnson was fairly clueless and I stopped him in three rounds without even having to try.

Again, we went back into a sort of limbo. Everything was geared around waiting for Jones. Ian and Porty kept me ticking over and we hung on. It was a strange time. I was training, but not too hard to avoid injury. I was trying to behave myself, in terms of booze and food, but had nothing to aim for regarding a specific date. I got a bit tetchy and people around me noticed it.

'You still not heard anything?' Natalia asked. It was a warm evening and we sat outside in the garden.

'I in't heard nowt.'

I could see it bothered her too. 'I'm sure Dennis'll sort it soon.'

I don't know if it was some kind of female magic, but the next day I walked in the gym. Dennis stood over by the ring, talking to Ian and Porty, with a big, self-satisfied grin on his face. It was early June.

'Guess what?' he asked as he saw me coming.

'Go on.'

'Sorted!'

I dropped my bag.

'You're jokin'?'

'No. 7 September, in America.'

It turned out the delay had been caused by Eliades trying to fashion a deal to bring Jones to the UK. Initially he had been keen on the idea, but his people resisted it throughout the negotiations. The bout had instead been fixed for the Rose Garden in Portland, Oregon, which raised a few eyebrows in our gym.

Jones was a Florida native, so a bout in Oregon did not make a huge amount of sense. Sure, he was a massive star and could fill a venue anywhere in the States, but the obvious choice outside of Miami would have been to take it to Vegas. One of the big casinos would have been ideal.

The troubling fact that kept coming up in conversation was that Oregon was the only state without compulsory drug testing. Was that why Jones' team wanted to box there? We shrugged our shoulders. There was no point letting it play on our minds.

We had three months to prepare and Ian immediately ramped everything up a notch. For him, supreme fitness was key to everything. He would come and pick me up first thing in the morning to go running. We would head out into the countryside and hit it hard.

On the straight, flat sections, Allcock was like lightning, but I could always claw him back on the hills. The competitive element between us added an extra edge to the runs and six or seven-mile sessions, done at very high intensity, became the norm.

After that, it would be home for a bit of breakfast, maybe an hour's rest, then into the gym for bags, pads, sparring and circuits. Ian would stretch me every day and told my sparring partners to go full pelt. The boys from the gym did their best to keep me on my toes. No special sparring was brought in.

'To be honest,' Porty said in a quiet moment. 'There's no one they could get who'd box like Jones anyway.'

For ten solid weeks, I adhered to Allcock's brutal regime. Hard runs, hard sparring, hard everything.

'You'll be in the shape of your fuckin' life,' he told me.

Two weeks before fight-night we flew out to the States, initially just the two of us. I slept on the plane over, which was unusual for me, and

Ian had to wake me when we arrived. It felt like someone had glued my eyes together.

We had single rooms booked at the local Hilton and when the hotel found out who I was and more importantly who I was fighting, they tried to move me to a top-floor penthouse for no extra charge. I went up with them and looked at it. It was massive, with its own pool table and plate glass window, but I turned it down. It made me uncomfortable.

'I preferred the other one,' I said simply.

Back in my little room, I laid down and put the TV on. As if it were fated, Jones was giving an interview about our fight.

'The ring is my shop,' he said. 'And let me tell y'all about my shop. You bring me an engine, I'm gonna break it down. I don't care if it's a Volvo, a Yugo, a Mercedes, a Bentley, a Hummer, I don't care what it is. Bring me the engine, I'm gonna dismantle it, that's my job.'

Even I had a little laugh. Ian and I set up camp in Portland in a local gym. They were great to us and very friendly. I sparred a couple of neighbourhood lads and a kid from London called Andrew Lowe. The first day or two, it all went well enough. I felt OK, but as the fight drew closer, a strangeness came over me.

Instead of tuning up, becoming sharper, my body slowed down. My back and legs felt weak. I could tell my punches were lacking force. Seven days before the biggest fight of my life and my face broke out in cold sores.

Dennis and Porty arrived. They had only been in town five minutes when they kicked off an almighty row.

'Look at fuckin' state o' 'im!' Neil screamed at Ian in the hotel bar. 'He looks like a fuckin' corpse!'

Dennis yelled that I had over-trained. 'He's meant to be fuckin' peakin'!'

Allcock tried to defend himself, saying I must have picked up a virus or something, but the two of them were livid.

'You stop fuckin' runnin' now,' Neil insisted.

For the whole of the remaining time in America, I kept finding Porty in corners muttering away under his breath about my condition and how amateurish the training had been. Once or twice I asked him about it and he looked at me with a sort of sadness.

'You're fightin' best fighter in't world' was all he would say.

The atmosphere was poisonous and I began to feel homesick. Fantasies played out in my head of sneaking away from the gym, getting a plane and going home. Natalia arrived a couple of days before the fight and helped cheer me up.

As the night approached, I was offered $20,000 to advertise a company called SBCBET.com. They wanted to give me a temporary tattoo of their logo on my back. The night before the fight, a freaky guy full of piercings came to my hotel room to do the work. It took about 40 minutes, probably the easiest money I've ever made.

Despite the money on the table – and my overall purse for the Jones fight was close on one million dollars – on the night, backstage at the Rose Garden, my dressing room had all the atmosphere of a morgue. They gave us a big room all to ourselves, as befits the challenger for the undisputed world title, but the wide-open spaces made the emotional distance between my team members seem even worse. Porty and Dennis paced at separate ends, while Ian wrapped my hands. Even he was silent, his usual confidence destroyed by all the in-fighting.

I tried to gee them up.

'Fuckin' 'ell lads, come on!' But I was fighting a losing battle. Any spirit or optimism had drained away.

Unbelievably, about 200 of my fans made the expensive journey to the States. It was the first time most of my brothers had been abroad and they made their presence felt as I emerged first. Michael Buffer stood waiting under the lights in a black tuxedo. I paused at the entrance for a moment and took it in.

'Be proud,' I told myself. 'Be proud. Look how far you've come.' Strangely I had no nerves again, none whatsoever. At that moment, on the American commentary, Larry Merchant described me as a 'lunch-bucket prize-fighter'. Oblivious, I sucked up some air, put a big grin on my face and resolved to enjoy the experience, no matter what.

24.

Roy Jones Jr v Clinton Woods

**Rose Garden, Portland, Oregon, USA
7 September 2002
WBC, WBA & IBF light-heavyweight
world championship**

BUFFER did his thing, the ring cleared and the bell went.
Right, fuck you lot, I'm having this. I went right out and took centre ring. I threw a couple of jabs at Jones' hands, just to give him something to worry about, pushed him on to the ropes with straightforward aggression and unloaded a volley of shots that bounced off his arms and ribs. As starts go, it was decent. Jones peeled off the ropes to my right, so I turned with him and followed his movement with a right hook. It didn't land properly, glancing off the side of his head, but I just wanted him to know I was keeping up.

BANG!

Out of nowhere, a left flashed through my guard on to the bridge of my nose.

Where did that come from? He hadn't even set his feet yet.

Before I'd finished thinking, another one landed. The guy wasn't just quick, he was a mutant, like something out of a movie.

By the end of the first minute, the fight had settled into a rhythm of me pursuing this force of nature, even tagging him occasionally, but being met with bewildering, arching shots that seemed to come from nowhere. None of them were especially hurtful but I rarely saw them coming.

At the start of the second, Jones found another gear. Maybe he got himself warmed up. His hands were busy, constantly in my face, peppering jabs, lancing uppercuts, while his feet jittered around like Sammy Davis Jr.

I could be in trouble here.

I came back into it, pushed him back, maybe even won round two on points, but bang on the bell he caught me with another hook and my knees dipped.

'Are y'alright?' Porty asked as I slumped on my stool. He looked worried.

'Alright, ar.'

My last good round was the third. I made it my business to discomfort him, got on his chest and boxed him in corners, on the inside. His right eye began to swell. The crowd were loving it. No one had taken it to Jones like that for years. It was close and hard. Then, on the bell, he caught me again.

This time, a trademark left hook crashed into my side. In a flash, everything left me. All the weakness and failings from the end of my training camp came back. I sagged. I gasped in pain. Head bowed, the walk back to my stool seemed so long. Dennis stood in the corner shouting at the referee,

'Low blow! Low blow!'

'It weren't fuckin' low,' I said in his ear.

A ringside doctor came over and put his hand on my torso.

'You've broken a rib,' he said.

I shook my head.

'I'm alright, I'm alright.'

I stood for the fourth and knew what was coming. *OK, you've lost this, just make the most of it.*

From there, Jones came after me. He brought the heat. Fighters know when fighters are hurt and he could sense it the way hyenas identify a lame antelope. I did my best to fend off his blazing combos

155

and even threw an Ali shuffle at one point, just for a laugh, but it all became a question of when, not if.

He cut me right between the eyes, an unusual spot. God knows how he managed that. Blood trickled down the middle of my face and into my mouth.

He started jigging about, playing possum in front of me, daring me to hit him.

You piss-taking bastard.

I would have loved to have jumped in, even put the nut on him if necessary, but I couldn't leave my abdomen exposed. I was in too much pain. Jones saw me protecting it and opened up to the head.

Between rounds, my team seemed lost and panicky, like blokes with buckets and towels on the deck of a sinking cruise liner. Dennis gave me water while they looked from one to the other hopelessly. In the end, Ian piped up.

'Jab,' he said. 'Try to establish your jab.'

I nodded. But three minutes later, before the sixth round, he had changed his tune.

'Forget boxing,' he said simply. I didn't really know how to interpret that.

The end came halfway through the sixth when Dennis chucked in the towel. I couldn't complain. Jones was all over me. I was killing myself just to survive. At my best, I believe I would have got to the end of the fight, but not that night.

More than anything else, this was the fact that bothered me as I walked back to my dressing room. I was gutted to have been stopped. Even on top form, for me to have beaten Jones would have needed a major slice of luck, but I always thought I would at least take him 12. I knew that as a result, all those commentators who loved to write me off would fill their boots.

Dennis paid for all of us to eat out at one of the best restaurants in Portland. We sat around a huge table, my Dad, my brothers, Natalia and our friends, over massive platters of seafood and meat. The mood amongst us all was good, surprisingly. I wasn't too badly hurt, although I had an impressive-looking black eye. It was a great payday.

Ian Allcock was notable for his absence, but it was a funny night, because next to the restaurant was a transvestite bar. Groups of cross-dressers wandered in occasionally to eat. The lads found it hilarious.

'Look, there's another one!'

'Come on, if you were pissed enough, would you have a go on that?'

It made me chuckle, but I noticed Porty staring at the lads with disgust.

'Less of that,' he said. 'There's ladies here.' For such a combative guy, he had some strange sensibilities. Between words, he shovelled food into his gob like it was a competition.

Regardless, with the help of a huge meal, a few jokes and more than a few beers, I soon forgot all about Roy Jones Jr.

25

The city of brotherly love

I T was no surprise really, but after everything that went on in the build-up to Jones, I never worked with Allcock again. In truth, I barely saw him. He was on the same flight as me, then after we landed I shook his hand, said goodbye and he walked off, straight out of my life. At that moment I wasn't aware, but Dennis had given him the boot.

I was slightly disappointed with how the money worked out after such a big fight. Despite the overall purse being so high, my share ended up only a fraction of that. Hobson and Eliades both took sizeable slices and all manner of expenses were deducted. It was hard not to feel a little dejected by it. Added to that, my contract with Panos came to an end.

I had failed on the big stage and was now back to being managed and promoted only by Dennis. As with my previous defeat, I told Natalia and anyone else listening that I was retiring. She didn't take me seriously. And of course, she was right not to.

Just as I had before, I thought about other ways to earn a living, plastering, maybe a spot of gardening work, while I waited for my rib to heal. In the meantime, Dennis phoned now and then. Although Jones had beaten me comprehensively and there was no getting away from that, options were presenting themselves. The world title picture was opening up in an interesting way.

The WBO belt had been held for eight years by the Pole Dariusz Michalczewski, who by the end of 2002 was starting to show signs of fading. Jones, meanwhile, had announced plans to move up to heavyweight to try to make history, against the WBA title holder John Ruiz. As a result, he would be relinquishing his collection of light-heavyweight belts to do so.

Details of Jones' exact plans were unclear. Some said he would retire if he won the heavyweight title, others that he would then shed the excess weight to return to light-heavy. We didn't bother ourselves with it too much, but it did raise questions about how exactly he intended to gain and then lose 20 pounds of muscle in the space of a year. The bottom line is it's impossible for the human body to do that naturally. Perhaps there *had* been more to his choice of venue than met the eye.

After a month or so away, I found myself turning up at the gym again. A bit of casual pad work with Porty and Poxon began turning into more serious training until Dennis told me he was lining me up for a bout with Rodney Moore in January. I hadn't officially announced a comeback, but I think Dennis knew if he offered me a fight I would take it.

Just like Nunn before him, Moore failed to show at the second time of asking and I ended up boxing a fat middleweight from Argentina called Sergio Beaz instead. I suppose it was nice to shake the rust off, but in truth I'd had sparring sessions that were tougher than that fight. Beaz didn't see the end of the third.

Not long after that, back in the gym, I was skipping by the mirrors when I heard deep, thunderous laughter coming from Dennis' office. Seconds later, he opened the door and walked out smiling, followed by a hulking black guy. As usual, arrangements had been made of which I was totally unaware.

'Clint,' Dennis said, 'Meet Tim. He'll be working with you from now on.'

'How do,' I said.

'Terrible' Tim Witherspoon had two spells as world heavyweight champion and shared rings with the likes of Larry Holmes, Greg Page and Frank Bruno. For a period during the 1980s, he had been one of the biggest names in the sport.

'What the hell is he doing in Sheffield?' I thought.

We began going through some bits together and it soon became clear why Dennis had picked him. Tim's approach was pretty much the polar opposite of Ian's. Where Ian would work me and work me, then work me some more, Witherspoon was much more laid back.

'Defence is all about instinct,' he would say. He encouraged me to drop my left hand, as he used to do.

'The jab's quicker if you bring it up from the waist.'

Sometimes, at the end of a session, Dennis or Porty would whisper in my ear: 'Don't worry about that, Clint. You keep your hands up.'

Witherspoon was also mad-keen on overhand rights, a punch I hadn't thrown much before because it can leave you open. He encouraged me to chuck it over in sparring.

'Only use it when your opponent's on the ropes,' he said. I began to see how it could be an effective weapon.

Tim's attitude was that everything centred around boxing work. In terms of strength and conditioning, I was virtually left to get on with it myself. His own career had sometimes seen him criticised for lack of fitness and I suppose as a heavyweight you can get away with it, but that really came across in his approach to coaching.

Outside the gym, it took him no time to become a local character. He loved a drink and developed a passion for British beer, although he couldn't hold it at all. By the end of the second pint, he would invariably end up singing at the top of his lungs, wherever we were. He had a decent voice, to be fair. We tried to get him on the after-dinner circuit, so he would earn a few quid, but Tim would just get hammered and make a fool of himself.

Bizarrely, while in the UK, he also developed an irrational fear of badgers, which I never understood. Sometimes we would jog together around Rother Valley park.

'Man, is there badgers here?' he would say, eyes wide with fear.

'What are you on about?'

'I've heard about them, they're vicious, man, they're vicious.'

Other than the booze, Tim's main weakness was a bit of female company and before long he became intimately acquainted with all the massage parlours in the area.

There were times he failed to turn up for training on time. We all knew where he was.

In my first bout under Witherspoon's tutelage, I took on the Mexican and WBC Continental Americas champion Arturo Rivera in Reading. He was a rough, ugly, hungry-looking bastard, with a reputation as a power puncher. Tim came running in the dressing room before the fight.

'I've just met your opponent, man!' he said, excited like a little boy. 'It's no problem man, no problem!'

'Why?' I asked.

'I just felt his hands. They're soft!'

I looked at him for a moment, unsure if he was on a wind-up.

'He's got soft hands! Soft hands!' he repeated with glee. 'Soft hands, he can't punch! Soft hands!'

'Alreyt mate, cheers,' I replied.

My stablemate, the cruiserweight Mark Krence, was in the room with me and found it hilarious. Whenever Krence saw Tim from that day on, he would whisper in my ear 'soft hands, soft hands!' in an American accent. We laughed our heads off.

In the end Witherspoon was proved right, though. He was ecstatic when I stopped Rivera in round two with an overhand right.

'Chip off the old block!' he said.

By the time I beat Rivera, Roy Jones had collected the WBA heavyweight belt, easily beating John Ruiz by unanimous decision. He then began the unlikely process of returning to light-heavyweight. None of us knew it at that stage, but that was the peak of his career. Soon, he would be on the slide.

All the talk was about him facing the new kid on the block, Antonio Tarver, a southpaw who outpointed Montell Griffin to become WBC and IBF light-heavyweight champ. To keep things as complicated as possible, which is so often the case in boxing, soon after winning the belts Tarver relinquished the IBF title. They were pressuring him to face their mandatory challenger rather than Jones. But at that time, Jones was still the money fight.

With several cards already thrown in the air, later that year age caught up with Dariusz Michalczewski and he lost the WBO belt in his umpteenth defence to a rugged Mexican called Julio Cesar Gonzalez. As often happens, when either defeat or politics cause longstanding champions like Jones and Michalczewski to lose titles, the scene entered a period of flux. Besides the names already mentioned, a roughhousing Australian called Jason DeLisle, Jamaican warhorse Glen Johnson and myself were very much in the mix at the top end of the rankings. While most pundits still saw Jones as the genuine number one, the picture had been blown wide open.

Dennis worked like a demon behind the scenes to engineer something. Frequently, I would walk past his office and hear him yelling down the phone.

'What do you mean he's not a big enough draw? He's the number two contender!'

'I don't give a shit about that! My man is the best light-heavy other than Jones!'

Eventually, he gained some traction with the IBF. As their belt was now vacant again, a bout looked likely for their title, but first I would have to get past a character called Demetrius Jenkins, a wild but vulnerable banger from Detroit.

For this one, Tim decided he needed me to go out to the States to train. As we built up to my second world title tilt, he wanted complete focus. Adaptable as always, I agreed. Mark Krence agreed to come with me for company and, in April 2003, I flew into Philadelphia International Airport.

We were met at arrivals and taken to the area we would be staying, which was absolutely beautiful. Forty minutes' drive from the centre of Philadelphia, it was a kind of gated community for ex-military personnel. We had a spacious house, surrounded by parkland, dotted with communal spas. You couldn't have dreamed of a better spot.

We had a couple of days to settle in before starting camp at the famous James Shuler memorial gym on Brooklyn St, in an area known as Drexel.

James Shuler had been a top US amateur who built a record of 22-0 as a pro, becoming American middleweight champ, before running into Thomas Hearns. A week after losing to the 'Hitman', he was killed in a motorcycle accident. His friend, Percy Custus, opened the gym in tribute and it became recognised as one of the top gyms in the USA. Tim wasn't based there, but it was one of his preferred spots for training.

Witherspoon called me on my second day.

'Now listen, Clinton,' he said, 'All my best wins came after I chopped wood. If I chopped wood, I knocked them out. So I want you to do it too.'

'OK.'

'We start training at the gym tomorrow.'

I had a hire car for use while I was there, so we arranged that I would pick Tim up on the way into town. It was a strange drive for a kid from Sheffield. Krencey and I drove past the famous 'Rocky' steps at the Museum of Modern Art and Tim arranged for us to pick him up on a particular corner. For the whole time I stayed in America with Witherspoon, he never wanted me to see where he lived. It wasn't until later I figured out why.

When we neared the area where the gym was located, Tim turned to me.

'Stop the car,' he said. 'We need to swap seats. You don't wanna drive around this area.'

'What d'you mean?'

'You'll see.'

We let Tim drive and before long were headed through the most deprived neighbourhood I had ever seen in my life. Even though I grew up on and around Sheffield council estates, what I saw in West Philly was the next level. Some buildings were burnt out. Piles of rubbish lay in the streets. Among the people on the pavements were a number who looked barely human, skeletally thin, yellow eyed.

'Junkies,' Tim explained.

'Crack and meth are big problems around here. Tearing the city apart.'

People had put sofas by the road and guys would be lounging on them, drinking and smoking in the middle of the street. The gym itself was set beside an intersection, over the road from a vacant lot and next door to a youth club.

'Are you ready boys?' Tim asked as he parked.

I looked at Krencey.

'Let's have it.'

We walked into the small space and were confronted with a typical boxing club scene, a ring, some bags and pads. The only thing that marked it as different to previous gyms I had known was that every face in the building was black. Every face that is, except myself and Mark. Tim put his hands in the air as we stood awkwardly by the door.

'Everybody!' he shouted. 'We got Clinton Woods here, people! He fought Roy Jones!'

I felt so embarrassed. A few heads turned to look my way, a few eyebrows were raised, mostly with barely disguised contempt.

'He's got money for sparring,' Witherspoon went on. Suddenly a rumble of interest built up around the room.

'Tim,' I said in his ear. 'Don't fuckin' say that about money. They'll think I'm a right Bertie-big-balls.'

'Just give 'em a few dollars man, it's fine, it's fine.'

The first guy to step up was a young super middleweight called Yusaf Mack. He really looked the part. His body was ripped to shreds and he had perfected a convincing ghetto-scowl that suggested he harboured serious intentions. He stood in the ring and started banging his chest.

'I'm the champ!' he yelled. 'I'm the champ!'

I looked at Krencey beside me.

'Fuckin' hell,' Mark said. 'What's wrong with him? It's only a spar.'

Tim called time and Mack came at me, pulling out every trick in the book. He feinted left and right, flashed his jab out, danced around. For the first minute, it was like being back in with Jones.

'Fuck that honky up!' other guys in the gym shouted.

'Yeah Yusaf, kill that white motherfucker!'

By the end of the round, he began chucking in massive right hooks. The bastard was actually trying to get me out of there. I wasn't having that.

From the start of the second I decided to stop playing, stepped forwards and stuck it on him. Once I got on the front foot, he couldn't live with me and soon I was backing him into corners. After the third, he waved his arms in a gesture of surrender and got out of the ring. He'd had enough.

When we left the gym that first day, Tim explained he had friends in Philadelphia who were property developers. They cleared plots of land for building and would ensure they left felled trees for me.

Soon, on a regular basis, I was driving around to different parts of Philly to chop wood and despite all his crazy talk, I found Tim was right. It did have positive effects. My back and shoulders became strong like never before. Even my forearms gained solidity. If I was sparring and blocked shots on my arms, it felt like little fleas touching me. It seemed the old methods really were the best.

Over the first weeks I sparred frequently with Mack, but with time it became less and less competitive. It always went the same way. He would begin full of swagger and mouth but as soon as I hit him with a decent shot, he would crumble and start to backpedal, then eventually jump out. Some spars only lasted a round.

It's funny how the boxing scene can seem so tiny and faces crop up in different places. Years later, Mack would end up getting KO'd by Carl Froch in a challenge for his super middleweight world title in Nottingham. After that, he was implicated in an increasingly bizarre series of stories. At first, he starred in a gay porn film, then made a clutch of media appearances in which he professed his love for transsexuals.

That made me think. It showed the hidden depths that can exist within people. Nothing could have been further from the brash, macho image he portrayed in the gym.

Another frequent Shuler gym sparring partner was Steve 'USS' Cunningham, who would later have two spells as world cruiserweight champion. Cunningham was a good fighter and a bigger man than me. It was always competitive between us and I liked Steve. He never got involved in insults or name-calling.

The only one who hurt me was a heavyweight called Larry Robinson. At first, I told Tim I didn't want to mess about sparring with heavyweights, but Tim was keen. Robinson and I had several non-eventful spars, where I just moved and boxed. One day, however, he must have turned up in a bad mood.

Tim told us to go at 50 per cent, which is one of those things that trainers always say to fighters but often gets ignored. Robinson fronted up with a right face on and went all in from the beginning. He caught me with a massive swing and for a moment I saw stars. My head cleared quickly and that old pot, which boxing usually kept on a steady simmer, went to full boil in a second.

I flew at the big guy in a rage. Within seconds of the spar starting, it had turned into a ferocious toe-to-toe brawl. Every cell in my body was focused on crushing him. Panicking, Witherspoon jumped in the ring, pulled us apart and got between us.

'Get out!' I screamed. 'Get the fuck out!' It took me a few minutes to calm down.

In the strange way that these things can work in boxing, Larry and I became good friends after that and we never sparred again. He had a bit of power, Robinson, but not much else. I don't think he ever went on to do much.

By then, a month or so into my stay, I had earned the respect of the guys in the gym. They saw that I meant it and, like all fighters, in the end they appreciated that. All the racial tensions and anger slowly ebbed away. Because they saw how aggressive I could be in sparring, they started calling me 'English Marciano', which I absolutely loved.

After my spell in the ring, I would go on the bags.

'That'll do for today,' Tim would say.

'No, Tim, it won't.'

I would make him do pads with me. After that, usually when he had enough, I would do some circuits. Press-ups, chin-ups, abdominal exercises, I made it my business to be as fit as I could be.

To introduce a bit more variety, Tim got other guys involved. Eddie 'Fast Hands' Chambers began turning up at the gym, who I hated sparring with. He was a big guy and his shots weren't especially hurtful, but as the nickname suggests his hands were like lightning. He was a real tricky bastard.

One time, Witherspoon drove me out, over the Walt Whitman bridge, to a place called Trenton, New Jersey, where I sparred with a world-ranked super middleweight called Kabary Salem. He was OK, but I still got the better of him. The following year, Salem challenged Joe Calzaghe for the world title, putting the Welsh wizard down in the fourth round before losing on points.

Throughout that training camp, I got to know Tim well. I loved him really, he was a genuine, humble man, but his situation saddened me. He had one real friend, an old man called Leo. Other than that, he had plenty of associates but they were only people who used him. Tim had earned some decent money in his career, but problems with the taxman, his former promoter (the notorious Don King) and his family had sucked it all up. The guy led a pretty bleak existence.

166

I paid him a weekly allowance and got to know a few of the people around him. They told me that in his pomp in the mid-eighties, he used to hand money out to people in the neighbourhood. Like a lot of former champions, he had been married and lived in a big house. But when he lost his titles and the money dried up, his wife left him and the house was sold.

People said he would walk into a nightclub with fistfuls of notes and pass them around. While I was with him, I even saw him doing it in the gym. He would give away the little I gave him for living expenses to guys who asked.

'Tim, mate, what're you doin? That's all you've got to live on,' I'd say.

'It's OK, man,' he'd reply with a smile. 'It's only a few dollars.'

I struggled to understand how he could do it to himself. He must have realised how far he had fallen. Halfway through the week, he would often come back to me, looking sheepish.

'I need some more money, Clint. My kids are starving.'

Some people, it seemed, could just be too kind for their own good.

Round Four

HOYE has a little go again at the start of the fourth, but I fend everything off and come back at him. Even when he attacks, I feel like I'm in control.

I keep turning and tagging him and the frustration is clear in his movements. Halfway through the round, he's warned for hitting me low. Thirty seconds later, he does it again. The ref shouts 'stop boxing!'

I stand in the neutral corner watching and Hoye's face is a picture. He hasn't won a round yet and now he's having a point deducted. He rolls his eyes. His shoulders sag. He looks demoralised.

We come back together and I feel so comfortable. I roll around, throw an uppercut and step out. Every shot he throws seems to whistle past my head. It's not that I'm consciously dodging them, it's just one of those nights where it all works. The newspapermen and pundits can say what they like.

Nearly man, my arse.

I'm on fire.

26

The (very) nearly man

2003-4 saw a lot of change in the light-heavyweight division. In early June, we returned to England for the scheduled bout with dangerous fringe contender Demetrius Jenkins. For last-minute preparation, I continued chopping wood for a farmer called Mr Bradley, on the outskirts of Sheffield.

Jenkins gave me a decent fight at a packed Ponds Forge and forced me to respect his power, but I stopped him in the seventh. Once again, the punch that won it was an overhand right. Despite his easy-going approach, Tim's training seemed to be reaping benefits.

We had a little after-party at the Hilton and Tim loved the craic drinking with all my brothers and mates. Once we all had a few, the boys got me up on stage with a mike to sing the old Tom Jones song *Delilah*. I don't know why. At that point, I felt good about myself again. Three stoppage wins since Jones, the last two against decent opponents, had put me right back in the mix.

Beating Jenkins so comfortably saw me installed at the top of the IBF rankings and news soon came through that I could box for the vacant title. Dennis sat me down and told me he had managed to broker a TV deal with the BBC. He gave me a list of three names: Glen Johnson, Rodney Moore or Jason DeLisle. As the number one contender, I was apparently able to choose who I wanted to box for the belt. I didn't have a strong opinion, so picked Johnson.

The fight was set for 7 November 2003 at Hillsborough Leisure Centre, while the following day, in Vegas, Jones would meet Tarver for the WBC and WBA belts. At the time, the talk was of the two winners meeting in a unification, an idea that thrilled me. Besides the possibility of being able to call myself a world champ, I desperately hoped one day to have another crack at Jones, if only to prove I could take him and his bag of tricks to the final bell.

Again, it was lovely to come home and spend some time with Natalia. The house looked great, but on top of that, whenever I was away from Sheffield I realised how madly I missed it. There's something about the city and its people that I value so highly. America was full of fakers, guys like Yusaf Mack talking the talk and strutting around, but not backing it up. Everyone you spoke to over there was going to be champion of this and top man of that and making millions before they were 30. The Sheffield culture has always been the total opposite. It's so refreshing. People are friendly and humble and don't try to pretend to be what they're not. That's why I love it and always will.

To train for Johnson, I went back to Philly but on arrival for my first day back at Shuler's, I was unable to get in. Police had cordoned the road off. A gunfight had seen three men shot dead on the pavement outside the gym. Meanwhile, a few shops in the neighbourhood had been looted and had their windows smashed. It was another reminder of the contrast with home.

After ten days, Porty came out to keep me company. He seemed even gruffer and harder to please than usual.

'I can only stay for a week,' he told me. 'I've gorra get back for work.' I found it strange that he put himself on such a tight schedule. What was the point in just coming for a week? It wasn't like him, but I didn't argue. He came down to Shuler's every day and in the evenings made it clear, as only he could, that he wasn't happy with my training.

'Tim's slack as fuck,' he would say. 'You're not fuckin' fit enough.'

After he left, I thought little more about it. Porty would always be Porty. During the 12-week training camp, I sparred a lot with Cunningham, did the usual bits and pieces then flew back to Britain in confident mood. I told Natalia I knew I would win. It was nailed on.

I would be too quick for Johnson and wear him down. He was already nearing his 35th birthday and, unlike me, had a long, tough career behind him, having turned pro as a middleweight in 1993. Our bout would be his 50th fight, but only my 37th.

One thing about Johnson that I appreciated was his humility. At all the press engagements during fight week, he was respectful and decent. I shook his hand and wished him luck. He did the same to me. There was no needle or grief. That's the way it should be, in my opinion. It might not be what the TV people want, but ultimately we're sportsmen in there, not circus clowns.

Despite all Neil's misgivings, as I bounced towards the ring to the sounds of 'This is England' by The Clash, I felt decent and focused. Tim walked ahead of me, shouting his head off. For once, he couldn't be heard. The place was rammed with my screaming fans.

Once the ring cleared and the bell rang, I have to admit that Glen Johnson shocked me. He came out for the first in full-on attack mode, swaying and bending from the waist, firing in hooks. He was immensely strong and although his shots weren't sharp or concussive, they were heavy in a thudding way.

For the first two, Johnson charged at me and I fended him off. In the third, his pace slowed just enough for me to start imposing myself. I began catching him to the body and with hooks to the head. Tim got excited in the corner.

'Give it to him, baby! Give it to him!'

From there, it turned into a to-and-fro battle. Most rounds were close. Johnson got back on top in the seventh, while in other sessions I pushed him back.

As he tired in the middle rounds, Johnson's corner threw water on their man to revive him. It splashed all over the canvas and in the eighth both of us slipped over in centre ring. Referee Ian John-Lewis had to pause the action and wipe it up with a towel.

Johnson had obviously watched the Jones fight and deduced that I was vulnerable to the body. That was a mistake on his part. He whacked away down there all night, but never hurt me.

I could feel him weakening and right at the end of the tenth I caught him with a right. His knees dipped. We knew it was close, but he was definitely feeling the pace. In the final round, after Tim and Dennis implored me to go at him, I began to break him up. I hurt him with a combo halfway through the session then tagged him repeatedly as he came after me. In the end, I put him down with a rapid-fire series of punches in the middle of the ring.

To my horror, obviously remembering what had happened earlier in the fight, ref John-Lewis called a slip and let Johnson off. I couldn't believe it. If that was a slip, it was one that came on the end of about seven top-class shots. Johnson had just been handed a massive reprieve.

After 12 rounds of tight action, the bout was scored a draw and I found myself in a low mood at the press conference afterwards. Johnson was convinced he had been robbed in a home-town decision, which I didn't think was fair. Typically, the media seemed to agree with him. If John-Lewis had counted the knockdown in round 12, it could all have been a very different story.

Everyone went for drinks afterwards at the Hilton but I wasn't much interested. I sat quietly in the corner of a side room with Natalia and hardly touched my beer. As far as I was concerned, there was nothing to celebrate. I hadn't won and I hadn't become world champion. All I had done was cement my status as one of the top contenders by battling out a gritty draw with one of the other top contenders. My career was no further along than it had been before the fight.

Natalia told me not to worry about it, that she was proud of me no matter what. I could still get another chance and our life together was going well, even if my boxing dreams hadn't materialised. Then out of nowhere, my mate Darren ran over to the table.

'Fuckin' 'ell, Clint' he said. 'Porty just had Tim in a headlock over t'bar.'

By the time I got over there, the scene had calmed down. Neil and Tim had both left. I found out later that Neil's temper boiled over at Tim's relaxed training methods. He had started an almighty argument with him, then assaulted him. Porty was convinced I would have won if Tim's regime had been stricter.

That proved to be the end of my working relationship with Tim Witherspoon. He flew back to the States a few days later. I guess Dennis must have agreed with Porty's assessment. More than anything, to me the whole episode said something about Neil Port, that he could manhandle a former world heavyweight champion like that.

The same weekend, over the pond in Nevada, a noticeably slower and tired-looking Roy Jones eeked out a very tight split decision points win over Tarver. The crowd in the arena were incensed and chanted 'Bullshit, bullshit!' when the verdict was announced. As happens with this sort of stuff in boxing, controversy attracts attention and immediately there were calls for both bouts to be rematched. All four of us, regarded as the top light-heavies in the world, would live to fight another day.

27

Third time unlucky

WHEN there's clamour in the press and money on the table, things can get done surprisingly quickly. Whereas my first and second world title shots had been years in the making, the third happened almost straight away. I barely had a couple of days rest at home before Dennis was on the phone. The Johnson rematch had been set up – 6 February at Ponds Forge.

'Who's training me?' I asked.

'Reckon we'll stick with Porty for this one.'

It was probably the sensible thing to do. With only three months until the fight, training would need to start more or less immediately and there was no time to investigate options.

Despite that, I couldn't help but feel sorry for Tim. I even worried for him a bit. All the whoring and boozing looked like it was taking its toll. He hadn't looked well and the thought of him returning, alone, to his little flat in the projects saddened me. I had invested the money I cleared from the Jones fight. Natalia had made me do that. Without her looking out for me, I knew I could have ended up the same way as Tim. It happens to a lot of fighters.

As always, Porty and I just got on with it.

'I'm not having you slacking off this time,' he said. We started training at Hobson's new gym, on the Gleadless estate. It's pretty rough around there but still represented a step up from South Philly.

Dennis called the new place the Fight Academy. He had made himself a few quid from boxing by then and was able to pay £48,000 for the building and a fair bit more to fit it out. There were two rings upstairs and a forest of punch-bags, with weights machines and massage rooms on the ground floor. It was a decent place, professional standard.

The timing of the fight meant that Christmas 2003 was basically a write-off. I had to train and go out on runs in the bitter Yorkshire winter. To help with preparations, Dennis arranged for Porty and I to fly to Tenerife in December.

A lot of people thought the Johnson rematch might be my last chance, so I wanted to get it right. The idea was that heat and altitude would increase my fitness, something we thought was needed after a year of training with Tim.

I had a couple of drinks with Porty on the plane over and we joked around as always, but he seemed a bit distracted, as if his mind kept wandering off. Towards the end of the flight he said: 'We'll see how tha goes wi' this one, but I think I might need a break from boxing.'

There was a faraway look in his eyes.

'You got 'owt else you want to do?'

Suddenly, he looked deadly serious again.

'No, just fed up wi' it.'

We were staying in a town called Los Abrigos, a beautiful, peaceful setting near the beach and only a short drive from the boxing gym in Santa Cruz. Everything began as normal, morning runs along the coast, then back to the apartment for a bit of breakfast. After that, we could maybe have a couple of hours to relax in the sun before heading to the gym for sparring and circuits. Fortunately, we each had our own bedroom, so avoided the minefield of living in each other's pockets, as had happened in the past.

It became a surprisingly happy and relaxed camp. Porty worked me hard, as always, and his manner in the gym remained as old-school and uncompromising as ever. But there was no tension and we felt completely at ease in other's company. By that point, we had worked together for ten years. He could be a right animal at times and very intimidating for strangers, but I reckoned I knew that old bastard inside out.

About four days into the camp, after a great run and a massive bowl of porridge, I sat with Neil on a couple of sun loungers out by the pool. I was reading a book about Jeffrey Dahmer, the serial killer. I'm fascinated by crime books and they are virtually the only things I read. Neil was quizzing me about what Dahmer had done and why and getting quite irate about some of it.

'Dunno why you want to read that shit,' he said.

As I replied to him and tried to calm him down, something caught my eye. I did a double-take to confirm, but it was undeniably there. I peered down through my sunglasses in disbelief. *What the hell?* Porty had a small tattoo of a butterfly on his ankle.

It seemed so out of character, not just because it was such a delicate, feminine design on this huge lump of a bloke, but also because he was always slating me for my tattoos. He told me so often how he thought they looked cheap.

I burst out laughing. 'How can th'ave a go at me for my tattoos when tha's got that on thi leg!' I pointed at it. 'It's the sort'a thing mi sister would get!'

He screwed his face up. 'Shurrup, you cheeky fucker,' he said. 'You know Mam's just died. It's a memory of mother. She loved butterflies.'

I felt like a right bastard and apologised, making a mental note not to mention it again. But a few days later, in a similar situation, it suddenly struck me that all his body hair had disappeared. Neil had been a real hairy bugger for as long as I had known him, all over his chest and back.

'Where's all your hair gone?' I asked. 'You almost look human!'

Again, he didn't see the funny side. In fact, he looked a bit down. I wasn't used to seeing Porty like that.

'I've always been ashamed of that bloody hair,' he said. 'I've had the piss taken out of me for years. I decided to get rid o' it.'

His tone of voice made me feel like I should leave it. I had never thought of Neil as the sensitive type before – generally he just flattened anyone who pissed him off – but I was starting to see a new side to him. It was strange and made me feel I didn't know him as well as I thought.

We carried on working and I felt myself getting sharper and sharper. The best time in my first fight with Johnson had been the last three rounds and I wanted to put myself in a position to really turn the screw in the rematch. If he was going to start to gas out, I would bring the heat.

I finished a quick, crisp session on the pads.

'You're lookin' reyt sharp, Clint,' Porty said. Compliments from Neil were a rare thing and really meant something.

He had got a decent sweat on himself and his hair was dripping. He pulled his hand out of the mitt and rubbed his face with his meaty fingers. Momentarily, my breath caught in my throat. I could not believe what I was seeing. His fingernails were streaked with pink nail varnish.

It looked like he'd scratched it off in a hurry, but there was enough there for it to be obvious.

'Neil?' I asked. 'As tha' painted thy nails? What's going on wi' that?'

He snapped, eyes flashing. 'Shurrup, you silly cunt.' There was real anger in his voice. 'My missus put that on me for a laugh before we came out here. I can't get it off.'

'I never noticed it before.'

'You weren't looking then, were ya?'

On our last day in Tenerife, at lunchtime, he dribbled food all down his front. Typical Neil, such a caveman. As he wiped up the mess from his chin with a tissue, I noticed he was wearing a women's necklace, thin and dainty, with a heart-shaped pendant. He saw me looking.

'Don't say a fucking word. It were me mother's,' he growled. I knew better than to challenge Neil in a mood.

Throughout the three weeks in Tenerife, I felt strong. The warm weather suited me, but once I got back to England, away from the sun and all that vitamin D, training became an odd struggle. At 32, I wasn't sure if it was age catching up with me, but I began feeling deeply, deeply fatigued after each session.

As January turned into February and fight night drew ever closer, the feeling grew. If I was at the gym and sat down between exercises, I would find myself nodding on the chair, drifting off to sleep. Every morning was an ordeal to drag myself out of bed. That was unusual for me. I always had bags of energy. I battled through, as always, and 6 February rolled around before I knew what had hit me.

Backstage at Ponds Forge, the feeling was inescapable. I had heard of guys like Lennox Lewis being so relaxed in the dressing room that they snoozed before their ringwalk, but that had never been my style. Yet that night, it was exactly how I felt. Even the thunderous reception from the Sheffield public couldn't stir me up. There was no point moaning, but I knew something was wrong.

Johnson came at me just as he had the first time, but I didn't have the energy to fend him off. In the second round, he caught me repeatedly with heavy right hands, while I backpedalled and clung on. It was going to be a long night.

There was no snap in my punches at all. I felt listless and lifeless. After round four, I gave Neil my honest assessment. 'I'm fucked,' I told him. 'There's nothing in me.'

Boxing has a way of teaching you different things about yourself at different times. Whatever was wrong was probably going to stop me winning the fight, I knew that. Firing on all cylinders, I had a decent chance against Johnson, but running on empty? No way. He was too tough, too good and too determined for that.

Despite that, something inside refused to let me quit. The hall was full of people, Sheffield people, who had paid good money to come out and support me. Some of them had followed me for years. Among them were a few who had been to every fight I had. My Dad was down there at ringside, full of pride at how far his son had come. What would they all think of me if I refused to get off my stool? If I got Dennis or Porty to chuck the towel in?

Again, just like the first fight, Johnson started to tire in the later rounds, but this time I lacked the strength to capitalise. The fight ground on towards its inevitable conclusion, with both of us slowly draining our last resources of strength.

'Come on!' Porty said to me before the last. 'Everything is on this round. All of it, all ten years of your career.' I didn't respond and just gazed past him across the ring. More than anything, I yearned for it to be over.

Those words stayed in my head as I walked out for the 12th. 'All ten years of your career.' This felt like a destination, of sorts.

Like the two or three before it, the last round was scrappy and neither of us landed much. The bell rang and Neil came over and picked me up, just for the sake of it. We all knew, really. I was so tired I was barely able to raise my hand to salute the fans.

All three judges gave it to him. I had no complaints, congratulated him and left the ring.

On the way, I decided that was it. I was done with boxing. For definite this time.

The dressing room was funereal. Dennis and Poxon sat in silence. So did I. After a while Neil got up, put his hand on my shoulder and said: 'That's it, Clint. I'm off. You won't see me no more. Don't ring me, don't come around, that's it.' He nodded at the others and walked out.

'What's up wi' 'im?' I asked.

No one answered.

Right then, I didn't really want to see any of them.

28

Bye bye Roy

I TOOK a bit of a pasting from Johnson and, although pleased I saw the fight through to the end, I had some serious healing to do. Over the next couple of days, I considered my options.

I had vacated the British, European and Commonwealth belts to go for the world, so was no longer a champion of anything. The idea of coming back in at domestic level and building myself up again didn't hold much appeal. Game over.

There was still a fair bit of work to do on the house, so I got stuck into that. I figured I could buy a van and start up a little firm. Hard graft had never been something I shied away from and I felt sure I could build a good life without fighting.

Almost since my career began, my one constant had been my relationship with Natalia and it seemed like the right sort of time to make things official with her. She had stuck by me for so long and improved my life no end. A week after losing to Johnson, I took her out to a Chinese restaurant called Zing Va and gave her a ring. She looked at it, put it on and said: 'So are you asking me to marry you or what?'

I explained that it was a leap year and women could propose to men in leap years. She gave me a look.

'That's not gonna happen, Clint.'

So, I bit the bullet.

'I suppose I am then, ar.'

We had champagne and talked about our hopes for the future. We both wanted a few kids. On the way back home, in the car, all loved up, she turned to me and asked.

'So have you definitely stopped fighting?'

'I think so.'

She gave me a cute but knowing smile, as if she was party to some secret information.

'I don't reckon that's true, you know,' she said in that endearing mixture of Spanish and Yorkshire accents she had developed. The words rang in my ears all the way home.

Over the weeks that followed, I kept turning the fight over in my mind. I couldn't help it. Whenever I had a quiet moment, and I had a few of those, I would find myself thinking about it. As a fighter, you know in your guts. You might say things for the cameras or the papers, but inside yourself you know. And I knew I could beat Glen Johnson.

I watched the fight back a thousand times and I always came back to the same thing. I had been so weary. After five rounds, I was exhausted.

I still hung in there with one of the very best light-heavies in the world, but after the midway point of the fight I didn't have the energy to sustain any pressure. It's not like I had a glaring defect to correct, a weak chin or slow hands. I had all the tools. I just had to be fit enough to use them.

Inevitably, after a month or so without boxing, I began to miss it again and ended up back at the gym. Dennis was pleased to see me and asked how things were going. I assured him I had no intention of getting back in the ring. I just wanted to keep fit. He accepted that with good grace and left me to it. I would turn up most mornings, do a little workout, then leave.

One day, Poxon wandered over. I had often seen him working with pros like Mark Brooks and Femi Fehitola.

'How do, Clinton,' he said. 'Fancy a go on't pads?'

I didn't see any harm in working out with him.

'Why not?'

He stood in front of me.

'Come on then, jab.'

Whack!

'Double jab, right hook.'

Whack, whack, whack!
'Jab, straight right, left to the body'
Whack, whack, whack!

Richard was not a guy with much of a track record, unlike previous coaches I had worked with, like Rainey, Rhodes or Witherspoon, but he had a kind of energy about him. His background was all a bit mysterious and no one was sure where he popped up from. Regardless, he managed to make the pad session enjoyable while also being a vigorous workout. I got a buzz out of training that I hadn't felt for a long time.

'Fancy another go tomorrow?' he asked at the end.

'Alright, ar, why not?'

A couple of weeks passed during which I worked out with Poxon every day. The sessions got better and better. I loved working with him and it soon became obvious to everyone, including myself, that once again, retirement would not happen just yet.

Yes, I had lost to Johnson and, yes, my performance in the second fight had been far worse than the first, but he wasn't out of my league, as Jones had been when I boxed him. I had a chat with Dennis in his office.

'So what do you think went wrong?' he asked. 'Was it training with Porty?'

'It weren't that,' I shook my head. 'Neil worked me hard, much harder than Tim. I just din't feel reyt.'

'What d'you mean?'

'I were tired all'time.'

'When?'

'For a few weeks before t'fight. Every time I sat down, I felt like falling asleep.'

Dennis shook his head.

'Why din't you say owt?'

'Din't want to be any bother.'

'Well listen, the Yanks are still keen on you. I get phone calls all the time. If you fancy gi'ing it another go, it could work.'

We agreed between us that if we were going to have another crack at it, we needed to make sure things were done properly. By then, I was closing in on my 33rd birthday and while that's not old for a light-heavyweight in the modern era, especially one who started late, like me, it was unlikely I had years and years left in me. The old school of boxing training – morning runs, bit of gym work, dieting to make weight – was being replaced at the top level by a more scientific approach. Guys I was mixing with were using nutritionists, massage therapists, even psychologists or hypnotists. During my career to that point, I had only Dennis, Porty and whichever head coach had been around.

The first step was to find out what had been wrong with me. Dennis sent me to see a doctor, who did some blood tests. He discovered I had an iron deficiency and as a result I started taking B12 injections. I had to administer them myself, at home, directly into the quadriceps muscle in my upper leg. The first few times I did it, it took me hours, sitting in a chair with my trousers around my ankles, poking at myself with the syringe and wincing. I always hated needles. Natalia had to do it for me once or twice, but the effect was immediate. My energy levels shot up. Before long, I felt fitter and stronger than ever before.

The doctor also advised that the likely cause of the iron deficiency had been poor diet. My exacting training regime made demands on my body that my food intake was not compensating for. For the first time since turning pro, we took on a nutritionist, John Clarke, who also managed my weight and circuit training.

'No gravies,' he told me. 'No sauces. Don't eat microwave stuff. Drink water as if it's your job. No more snacking on rubbish, neither. If you're peckish, eat a handful of nuts.'

John was a competition body-builder and ensured my portion sizes were right, that I got enough protein, all that stuff. He really knew what he was doing and the benefits were obvious.

In May, things were shaken up when Tarver KO'd Jones in round two of their rematch. Many people assumed it was a blip and the imperious Jones of the past would reappear, but in reality, he was done. Tarver assumed the position of *de facto* world number one.

I got fully into working with Richard and with John's help soon began to feel sharper and stronger than ever before. Poxon was not necessarily as technical as someone like Rainey and I couldn't put my finger on one thing he taught me which stood out, like Witherspoon's overhand right, but something about the partnership felt positive. He was even slightly younger than me, but that didn't bother me.

I heard whispers in the shadows. 'Who does that Poxon think he is? He's got no boxing background. He can't train someone at world-class level.' But I liked the way things were going.

He got me working on the line again, just as Ray Gillett had all those years before, and Richard was always in the gym. Sometimes I wondered if he ever left. He would be there when I arrived and still waiting around after I finished. He never once let me down.

Poxon's approach was super organised and he showed me training notes where he had planned what we would do, weeks in advance. You could tell it really mattered to him. He wanted everything to work as much as I did.

I talked things over with Dennis. He was convinced there were still possibilities with the IBF. My two fights with Johnson were close enough to sustain my ranking in the top ten, although I had dropped a few places. It might take a couple of wins, he thought, but we could get back into position to challenge relatively quickly. Johnson was due to defend against Jones in September, while a banger from Detroit called Rico Hoye, a former American champion, had grabbed everybody's attention by KOing Richard Hall in an eliminator. Hall had been a world-class operator for a number of years. Experts began tipping Hoye as the new kid on the block, the man to clean up the mess left by Jones and Michalczewski's defeats. He was promptly installed as number one contender.

Dennis managed to fix me a fight with Jason DeLisle, the Australian and pan-Pacific champion. Set for October, it would give the winner the official number two contender spot. If I could beat him, it meant I would be second in the queue to take on the Jones/Johnson winner. We knew very little about DeLisle, apart from the fact he appeared a typical Aussie hardcase, with a sort of bleached blond mullet haircut and a nose that looked like it had been broken in half.

The more time that passed with the new training regime, the better I felt. It was visible on my body too. I had never had a fantastic physique, not compared to some fighters, but my muscle definition and size had both increased.

John had me on a heavy resistance programme for 12 weeks, with the weights gradually coming down as we neared the fight. He controlled my running too, sending me out on the hills four or five days a week, doing seven-milers. At the same time Richard kept me sharp with pad work, sparring and other boxing dills. I felt transformed. I had been a professional fighter for a decade but it was the first time I had a truly professional set-up around me.

The wedding went great. We held it at Aston Hall, a posh hotel to the east of the city. Natalia and I had a short honeymoon in the Lake District, nothing more than a long weekend really. She was fine with it and understood. She knew what she was getting herself into. You can't marry a boxer and expect a normal life. I had an important fight in two months and couldn't afford two weeks off.

A month out from my date with DeLisle, Rico Hoye beat Montell Griffin, another top American, to cement his growing reputation. The following week, Jones took on Glen Johnson in Memphis for the IBF belt the Jamaican won against me. Virtually every pundit expected Jones to put on a show and razzle-dazzle Johnson, but he was somebody else by then, no longer the Roy they remembered. From the beginning, he looked laboured and off the pace, again.

Johnson outfought him throughout and was comfortably ahead heading into the last quarter of the bout. In the ninth, he unleashed one of those thudding, almost clumsy-looking right crosses I knew only too well. Those shots had real blunt force. It caught Jones on the temple and completely poleaxed him. Fight over, Jones was out cold before he even hit the floor.

As the once untouchable Roy Jones Jr lay on the canvas for nearly ten minutes, it felt like end-of-an-era stuff. As well as taking the sheen off his speed and reflexes, it seemed the journey up to heavyweight and back had also robbed him of his punch resistance. Two consecutive heavy KO losses left him looking a shadow of his old self.

In truth, I felt a bit sorry for him. I had been privileged to box him while he was still at his peak and nobody likes seeing an all-time great being humiliated. Regardless, it meant it was now between Johnson and Tarver for the position of true champion.

By the time 24 October rolled around, I still knew very little about DeLisle, but one thing I was sure of was that I had had the best training camp of my life. The fight was at the Octagon centre in Sheffield, a fairly small venue packed from wall to wall, as always, with my fans. The atmosphere was cacophonous.

'He's going to come at you hard,' Dennis said before the start of round one. 'That's what he does.'

The bell rang and true to form he charged like a bull. He was all front foot and hooks. I jabbed and circled, trying to keep him off, but two minutes in he caught me with a left and put me down. I didn't see it coming. I hit the deck pretty hard and the room went quiet.

So you're on the floor, are you? What happened there? You didn't even see it, did you? Maybe you're getting old, mate. It happens to fighters. They say they can get old overnight. They say you can get old in the ring. Look at Jones. Maybe you've had it. Maybe you should have packed it in.

I climbed up and the ref gave me a standing eight count. DeLisle was literally stamping his feet on the ground and snorting, getting ready to charge. When the ref waved box on, he came bounding towards me like a headcase, sensing the kill. I shot out a firm jab right from the shoulder, Howard Rainey style, really putting my hips into it, perfectly timed, straight on to his nose. It broke his momentum and forced him to take a sideways step, giving me a chance to move to his left, buying a bit of time. I knew from that point on I'd be OK.

I rode out the rest of the round and they calmed me down in the corner. Poxon was good at that. He spoke clearly and well. I still knew what I was doing. I wasn't groggy.

From round two I took over. I was too good for him, too strong as well. I wobbled him with an uppercut in the fifth and put him down with a right hook in round seven. He hit the boards heavily and I was surprised he got up. After that, he faded badly. The longer the fight went on, the more I controlled it.

'It's in the bag,' Richard said before he sent me out for the 12th. 'Just keep picking him off and you've won by a mile.'

There was no fatigue this time, no lack of energy. I kept on him, jabbing, catching him with hooks as he came to clinch, beating him up on the inside. Halfway through the round, I trapped him in a corner and laid into him with both hands. He was gone by then and it was just target practice. Four or five hooks rocked his head back one after the other and the referee, Roy Francis, screamed 'Stop boxing!' and jumped between us. I'd battered him. In truth, the fight hadn't even been close.

We enjoyed the win in the dressing room afterwards with the boys, but there was no big celebration. Getting a stoppage win over DeLisle was great and showed I still belonged at the right end of the top ten, but it hadn't brought me anything I hadn't had before. I was now officially the number two contender to champion Glen Johnson, who I had boxed twice and failed to beat. I went home, had a bit of time off with Natalia, then waited for news from Dennis.

A couple of weeks later, it came. Boxing politics can be such a maze of riddles and it threw us a surprise. Johnson had been mandated by the IBF to fight Hoye, his number one contender, but had turned the fight down. Instead, he signed for a big-money match-up with Tarver, to see who was 'the man'. As a result, the IBF had stripped him of their title.

Bizarrely, Tarver relinquished the WBA and WBC titles for similar reasons, meaning by then he only held the lightly regarded IBO version. As a result, the two men regarded as the best light-heavyweights in the world would be boxing for a nothing belt that no one took seriously, while the three major titles all lay vacant. Sugar Ray Robinson would have been turning in his grave.

On this occasion, though, the awful mess of modern boxing worked in my favour. Normal practice in these circumstances, we were told, was to match the number one and number two contenders for the vacant championship. That meant me versus Hoye for the IBF in the first few months of 2005.

Of course, I accepted the fight, although Hoye had a fearsome reputation and I'd been keying myself up for a trilogy night against Johnson. Pretty much everyone said I couldn't win, that Hoye was the coming star, that I would be KO'd early and end up retiring. I didn't really care. I had been the underdog for every major fight of my career.

Dennis went into purse bid negotiations like a man possessed. He said he would do whatever was necessary to make the fight in England. In the USA, I would have to knock Hoye out to win.

His tenacity and commitment got us what we wanted and the fight was booked for 4 March at the Magna Centre in Rotherham, a 4,000-seater local venue. The BBC remained in our corner, too. The national broadcaster was turning its back on boxing, but we had worked together well in the past. The Hoye fight was due to be their last-ever televised show. If it was going to be my final contest, at least I would go out in style.

29

A Penny for your thoughts

THE way I dealt with DeLisle was a great vindication of my new training set-up. It filled me with confidence that I had made the right decision in coming back. Working with Richard and John took me up a notch from the days of Witherspoon or Porty.

Despite that, thoughts of Neil often played on my mind. Training without his blunt, surly presence seemed strange, no matter how well it was going. I had heard nothing from him since he walked out of the Ponds Forge dressing room in February. Dennis had not seen him either. What was he up to? Was he OK? There were lots of naughty Sheffield boys with a grudge against Neil. Anything could have happened.

A day or two after I received confirmation of the Hoye fight, I realised it was Porty's birthday. Of course, he had said not to contact him, but it's not so easy to forget ten years of friendship. 'Screw it!' I thought and phoned him, off the cuff.

'Neil!' I said, when he picked up.

He spoke quietly and strangely. There was no warmth in his tone. 'I told thi not to ring me.'

I ignored him.

'Where's tha been? Are y'alreyt?'

'Alreyt'

'But it's thi birthday, in't it? What's tha doin toneet?'

'Nowt. I'm in't house.'

He sounded depressed.

'Reyt, I'm comin' o'er.'

I didn't give him a chance to protest, ended the call and drove straight there. Neil lived alone and had done for a few years, his ex-wife and two sons around the corner. When I arrived, he opened the door straight away. He had been in the hall, waiting. He looked stressed, tired and miserable.

'What's up wi' thi?' I asked. He shrugged.

'Come on,' I told him. 'We're goin' for a curry.'

He hesitated for a moment, then something seemed to occur to him. He nodded slowly. 'Alreyt.'

Neil always loved an Indian meal, but he struggled to relax as we sat down to order. He kept looking around, left and right, like he was worried who was about. I tried talking to him but he was too distracted.

It was more than obvious he was in trouble.

'Look, Neil,' I said. 'Summat's up 'ere. I don't care what trouble you're in. I'll help thi out, mate.'

After the waiter walked off, he gathered himself, looked me in the eye and said: 'OK, Clint. It's like this. I've got summat important to tell thi.'

'Alreyt,' I replied, nearly whispering.

'Not 'ere, though. Come on, we're goin.'

We hadn't even touched the food, but he was insistent. We went back out and got in the car. There were a few moments of silence. He had such an odd look on his face.

'Clinton,' he said. He was breathing noisily. His words came in gasps. 'Ever – since – I – was – a – little – lad - I - always - knew – I – was – supposed – to – be...'

I waited. It felt like a long time.

'...a woman,' he said at last.

What the fuck?

He stopped for a few seconds and sucked in some air, as if it all had been a great effort to say. His hands were shaking.

'It's summat inside me. As a little'un, I often dressed as a girl, whenever I could.' There was another pause. 'As an adult too.'

If it hadn't been for the look on his face, I would have thought he was taking the piss.

'Anyway, I've been down to a clinic in London an' 'ad it all checked out. I'm starting hormones. Look…'

He pulled a piece of paper out of his pocket.

'…I've even gorra certificate to say I'm allowed to use the women's toilet.'

Maybe it was nerves, but a little laugh escaped my mouth unintentionally.

'It in't fuckin' funny,' he shouted.

There was a short silence. I wasn't sure what to say. It had rapidly turned into the most awkward conversation of my life.

'Would you like to meet Penny?' he said, finally.

'Eh?'

'Does thi want to meet Penny?' he repeated. There was a kind of eagerness in his eyes.

'Penny?'

He looked down. 'Penny Fletcher, it's my other name.'

I wasn't sure that I did want to meet Penny, but it seemed like Neil really needed it.

'OK, mate.'

'When and where?'

I thought about it. It would have to be somewhere where no one would see me. My mind raced.

'I'll meet you at the Little Chef at the bottom of Manor, tomorrow at half past nine.'

He seemed relieved.

'OK,' he smiled. 'It's a date.'

I went straight home and told Natalia what was going on. Her first response was the same as mine, that it was a wind-up, until I convinced her otherwise.

'It can't be true,' she said. 'Neil? My God! No way! I never would have thought it in a million years.'

The following evening, I arrived early to prepare myself. I hoped to enter unrecognised and find a quiet corner to hide away in. Typically, the moment I walked in, the first person I saw was a girl I went to school with. She worked there as a waitress.

'Look love,' I told her. 'Don't get the wrong idea, alreyt? But I'm meeting a bloke dressed as a woman.'

This had the potential to be very embarrassing for me. I was a pretty big name in the area and if it ended up in the papers it would be mortifying. Fortunately, she saw the funny side, laughed her head off and promised to keep it to herself.

So, I sat and waited. And waited. It seemed to take forever. I actually felt nervous, like before walking to the ring. I had no idea what to expect.

After about 20 minutes, Neil appeared. It was a good job I got there early to settle myself down because I had never seen anything like it. He looked absolutely horrendous, like something out of a bad comedy programme.

He had skin-tight, women's trousers on and you could see his cock and balls clearly outlined in the material. On his upper body, he wore a lacy blouse with his massive arms sticking out of the top. He teetered on his heels and there was a two-inch thick layer of make-up on his face. He clocked me and gave a little wave.

'What's tha think then?' he asked, sauntering over, swinging his hips, trying to be feminine.

I pointed at his groin, covering my eyes. 'Tha needs to do something about that, mate!'

Instantly, he turned back into the old Neil, scowled at me and bellowed: 'Shurrup, you silly cunt.'

'Look, Neil...,' I began

He interrupted me. 'Don't call me Neil, I'm Penny.' He was talking like a woman again. 'So what's tha think, Clinton? How do I look?'

It was breaking my heart a little bit. He obviously wasn't well, in his body or his mind.

'Neil... I mean, Penny, I don't know what to say.' Out of the corner of my eye, I saw the chef peering out of the kitchen door laughing his nuts off. 'They're gonna fucking hammer thi, mate.'

Anger flashed on his face and again he turned back into his old self.

'Who is? No cunt can fuckin' tell me what to do!'

It felt like talking to two different people, as if he were a split personality and the different sides of him were wrestling with each other. He was obviously going through a kind of breakdown.

He's not well. He's your mate and he's not well.

I offered him a drink and he asked for wine. After a while, he ordered salad. Neil never ate salad.

He calmed a bit after that and I tried to have a normal conversation, but it was so hard to look at him. His lipstick was all over the place and his wig was wonky. He kept putting his hands in front of his face while talking, as if he didn't want to be scrutinised. He told me he'd been dressing like this for years and going out to gay bars in Manchester and Liverpool. After his visit to the clinic in London, he took lessons to teach him how to speak and move like a woman.

'You know what,' he said. 'If I were on a night out, you could be stood right next to me and you wouldn't know who I was.'

'I fucking would, Neil... Penny.'

'I was in a place in Huddersfield last week, getting lots of admiring looks.'

'Has tha got a bloke, then?' I asked. He flinched.

'No, no, I in't interested in blokes. I just wanna be who I am.'

'Fair enough,' I said.

He looked down and then back up again. Maybe it was the make-up, but he suddenly looked so miserable, like one of those clowns with tears painted on their cheeks.

'Does thi still want to see me, Clinton?' he asked. 'I'll understand if tha don't.'

'Of course I fucking do,' I replied. 'Tha's my mate and always will be.'

We finished our drinks and said goodbye. I watched him totter over to his car on his heels. His shoulders and back were still enormous. What an unbelievably strange night it had been. It took me a couple of days to get it out of my mind. It was a real effort to refocus on boxing.

In December, Johnson beat Tarver in Los Angeles on a split decision, making him the clear number one light-heavyweight in the world, although he only had a mickey-mouse title. That gave me added confidence, looking forward to the Hoye fight in March.

Johnson, by all accounts, was now *the man*. We had fought a draw and a split decision. In the first fight, I had him all over the place in the

12th. I knew my new training regime with Poxon and Clark meant I was better. If Glencoffe Johnson was the best, I really wasn't far behind.

With my training camp due to start in the new year, I was able to relax and enjoy the festive period. About a week before Christmas Day, I went out for a few drinks with my brothers and suggested going up to the Burleigh Arms, Neil's local. He was likely to be in there and I wanted to buy him a drink, to see how he was. I had told them about him so they knew what to expect.

As soon as we walked in, we saw him. He was sitting on his own in the corner, dressed as Penny, with a little sherry glass. He had these massive, meaty hands and this tiny glass. It looked almost comical, but also very sad. Everyone was ignoring him.

My brother Julian bounded straight over to his table, pulled in a stool, sat in front of him and said: 'Fuckin' hell, that's the best I've ever seen you look!' Neil, or Penny, raised his head and just came alive. He was so glad of the company. Before long, he was laughing and joking with us all. It was truly uplifting to see him like that.

He was smaller than the last time we'd met. His course of hormones had begun and he was preparing for the operation. His muscles were disappearing and his face looked softer. No amount of make-up could disguise his scars, though.

We had a real laugh with him for a couple of hours and I left feeling positive about it. Neil seemed to genuinely enjoy himself. Seeing him happy as Penny made me think maybe he could make a new life for himself, maybe this could all work out for him somehow. Maybe I hadn't lost him.

The next morning, I got a phone-call.

After we left, someone approached Neil in the pub and told him his ex-wife had been going around the area calling him a 'pervert in dresses.' Enraged, he had left the pub just after us, made his way home and got changed. Dressed as a man, he then went around to his ex-wife's house to confront her.

When he arrived she was out, and instead he got into an awful row with his two sons. He lost his temper, put his youngest in a headlock while threatening to kill their mother. A vicious fight ensued and he was stabbed four times by Neil Jr, his eldest.

My coach and friend for the last ten years was dead.

30

Woods v Hoye

Vacant IBF light-heavyweight world championship
Magna Centre, Rotherham
4 March 2005

NEIL'S death was a shock to all of us and really took some thinking about. Here was a man who had prided himself, his whole life, on being a hard bastard, deciding to undergo a sex change at the age of 40. Both Natalia and my Mam, who knew him well, were totally baffled. There was no way he would ever have physically passed himself off as a woman, no matter what feelings he had inside or hormones he took. His build and character were as masculine as you could possibly get.

His marriage had broken down but he had stayed close to his sons, as far as we knew. So, for it all to finish the way it did was beyond tragic. None of it made much sense to any of us.

Dennis was particularly cut up about it. He had known Porty longer than I had, although like me he had no clue about his private life. That was one of the biggest mysteries, that this man, who we all felt we knew so well, lived another, completely opposite life and kept it secret for so long. I made myself feel better by saying that at least he had one happy night as Penny before he died, but it was scant consolation.

It helped that I had the Hoye fight on the horizon. With training camp due to kick in in January and this really being my last chance, I slipped into a state of concentration quickly. Dennis sent me some DVDs of Hoye to watch at home. He was an intimidating specimen, 6ft 3ins, with a long reach, ironing out everybody they had put in front him. A few of his early-career finishes had been genuine one-punch knockouts. He whacked them and left them twitching on the floor.

In his distance fights, he had shown impressive boxing skills and a lovely, long jab. His reach was bigger than mine. I scrutinised him for weaknesses, but none occurred. Hoye had a flowing, relaxed style, was smooth going forwards or backwards and could obviously bang. The old habit of doubting myself, as I always had in my younger days, crept back in.

You can't beat this guy. Look at him. He's too good for you.

Poxon got me sparring with British and Commonwealth cruiserweight champion Mark Hobson, which was brilliant sparring. Hobson was taller than Hoye but had a similar reach and I had to get used to slipping the jab before delivering my own. Neil Dawson, another cruiser, helped out when Hobson got tired.

In terms of health and condition, the training for the Hoye fight was absolutely perfect. No illnesses, no problems, no arguments or tension in team. It was as solid a 12-week camp as you could hope for. With John's help, I felt my body hardening up. I was super strong.

Two weeks from fight night, Natalia told me she was pregnant. We kept it to ourselves, but it served as an added motivation. It was all proper, grown-up stuff now. I was boxing for a world title for the fourth time and about to become a father again. This time, unlike the first time, I was determined to do that right, too.

Myself and Hoye were called to do some media work, all the usual stuff. They made us stand nose to nose for the cameras at a press conference at the Hilton, typical pantomime. He had a history of gang involvement and even killed a man once, but when we met he never acted like a typical brash American, nothing like the guys I had known in Philly.

He had massive square shoulders and unblinking eyes. He was very quiet, with a calmness about him, as if he knew he was tough and had no need to act up.

At the weigh-in the night before, I had my first cause for real optimism. With John guiding my diet I had no doubts, jumped on the scales and weighed in a pound under the limit. Hoye got on, frowned deeply and came in two and a half pounds over.

Two and a half pounds is a fair lump to shift so they gave him a couple of hours. After riding a stationary bike, probably a bit of sauna time and three visits to the scales he made it, half a pound inside. The fight was on, but knowing how much he struggled gave me a little edge. I knew from experience that battling with weight could take a lot from a fighter.

I slept at home, as I preferred to do. Hotels are always so impersonal. Dennis tried to book me a room somewhere and even Natalia said it might be a good idea, but I enjoyed the security of being at home. The house was all finished by then and we had turned it into a really nice place with an extension.

I woke up early, had a granola breakfast and pottered about. The granola was John's influence showing itself already. In the old days, once I had weighed in, I would scoff. Fight day morning would have been a full English with all the trimmings. There was no way John would let me get away with that.

'That's bonkers,' he said when I told him about my old habits. 'You went through all that training and dieting, then bloated yourself like that the day of the fight? I'm surprised you ever won anything!'

Of course, there were nerves, but not in a negative way. I believe very strongly that you need some nerves. I'm not one of these spiritual fighters who go on about some mysterious warrior code, but psychology definitely plays a big part in boxing. If you're too nervous, you'll freeze. If you're not nervous enough, you'll start slowly. To spectators it probably looks like much the same thing, but internally it's all very different. I watched some TV and tried to relax.

About an hour before I was due to leave, I tried to force a plate of wholemeal pasta down for some pre-fight carbohydrate loading. Apprehension in my throat and the pit of my stomach kept making me retch. Natalia sat with me, talking softly, trying to keep me calm.

Late afternoon, I drove to the venue myself, with Natalia in the passenger seat. We didn't speak. I was lost in my thoughts and she in hers. For my part, I knew if I lost this one, it was all over. There was no way I could fail in four world title shots and continue to have a career at the top level. I was lucky to still be there as it was. I also knew that dropping back down in class and maybe boxing for the British title again didn't interest me. As far as Clinton Woods the fighter was concerned, this was shit or bust.

For her part, I reckon she just wanted it to be over. Natalia hated it when I boxed. Every time I told her I was retiring, it gave her a glimmer of hope, although I don't think she ever truly believed.

We entered the venue. It was empty. Most of my crowd were still in the pub. She kissed me then went off to her ringside seat. I knew exactly what she would do – stay there for the whole fight without looking up. That was her way of coping with the situation.

She always said she wanted to be there in case *something* happened and whenever she said the word *something* like that, she always emphasised it. We both knew what she meant, although we never elaborated. Boxing rings are dangerous places.

Although she wanted to be at my fights for that reason, she could never bring herself to actually watch. Sometimes I would look down between rounds and she would be there in the first row, staring at the floor, like an aeroplane passenger during an emergency landing. It was as if the answer to all life's questions was somewhere between her feet.

After kissing her goodbye, I made my way to the changing room. Dennis, Richard and John were already there, buzzing about. They had music on. My sort of music, old-time stuff, none of that noisy, shouty rap that so many fighters seem to like. I put on my boots and placed a four-leaf clover Natalia gave me in Spain inside my sock. As soon as I started limbering up, I knew it was going to be a good night. I felt amazing. I had never been so sharp, so powerful. I felt like I could demolish houses with my fists.

As my time neared, through the walls, I heard the noise of the crowd cheering the undercard. In the main support bout, a young cruiserweight called David Haye knocked out Glen Kelly in two rounds. The same Glen Kelly I watched box Roy Jones in Miami.

Dad came in with his chewing gum, as always. He kissed my cheek.

'You know what that is, don't you, son?'

I winked at him.

'Thanks Dad.'

When the runner opened the door and shouted 'Five minutes to ring-walk', I was hammering the pads so fast I barely noticed.

'That's enough,' Dennis said. 'Don't tire yourself out in here.'

The doors opened and we walked through. The noise that met us was unbelievable. My support filled the majority of the building and screamed like Zulu warriors. I felt like I could fly.

I got up in the ring full of energy. They had a female opera singer to do the national anthem and I bounced over to her and gave her a big kiss. Hoye was there, staring, trying to be intimidating. His trainer kept pointing at me and talking rubbish.

'We're coming for you, man! We're coming for you!' Lots of American bullshit like that. I just laughed at him.

'Cover up and move around,' Richard said. 'Keep moving. Box him, box him.'

They did the introductions and the ring cleared. The bell went. And that was it.

Round Five

HOYE comes out on the jab, I swallow it and rock him with a left hook. The punch seems to jar him back to life. He realises the fight is slipping away from him unless something changes.

He starts feinting on his way in and catches me with his best shot so far, a right hook that sends a spray of sweat careening off my head across the ring. He follows it up with a few more. Suddenly he fancies it again, then he tries to go for the body and hits me low for the third time.

The ref can barely believe it. Hoye gets a right telling off. He's narked me a bit as well. I keep that pot under control these days, but getting hit in the balls can wind you up. The crowd go mad as I rock him with four hooks, swaying to avoid his punches at the same time. Unbelievably, Hoye hits me low again. *What's wrong with this guy?* He loses another point and is threatened with disqualification.

All of a sudden, as the ref lays down the law, he looks confused, like a little boy. He ain't so scary now! What a nightmare this must be for him. So far from home, in the biggest fight of his career, *and everything going so wrong.*

You picked the wrong time and place to mess up, mate.

I move out of the corner, duck into range and unleash a barrage of hooks. Just like he did in round one, he starts to retreat. I'm not letting him off and bounce after him, catching him and catching him. I can't miss. Nothing is measured, it's all instinctive, but everything lands. I'm wobbling his head all over the place. He starts to look ragged.

I batter him from one side of the ring to the other. He half goes down, sags into the ropes, then rebounds back to his feet. He tries a two-fisted salvo to rescue himself but there's nothing on the shots. They are punches of sheer desperation. I catch them on my arms, tag him again and he's clinging to my waist.

He won't let go, like a toddler attached to his mum on the first day of nursery school. We stagger back together like drunken dance partners all the way across the ring. The ref has to pull him off me. As soon as I've got space, I land three more. He's folding, there's nothing coming back. I'm about to land another and then...

...it's over.

31

Not a nearly man anymore

I HAD a sense of unreality, like I was watching a film or having an out-of-body experience. There were no complaints from Hoye or his corner. They knew.

I went bonkers, jumped up on the ropes screaming. The noise in the venue was ear-bursting.

John Inverdale from the BBC shoved a microphone in Natalia's face at ringside.

'He's worked so hard for this,' she said. 'He really deserves it.'

Fans and friends, relatives, even people I didn't know, climbed in the ring to slap my back and hug me. It was pandemonium.

I looked across and saw Hoye, slumped and dejected in his corner. Sympathy spiked inside me. I knew what it was like to lose on an important night.

I squeezed my way through the forest of bodies to where he stood.

'Rico!' I said. He looked up. 'Hard luck, mate, you'll come again. Don't worry pal, I know exactly how you feel.'

'Thanks man,' he replied. 'Thanks.'

They were the only words we ever exchanged. I left him to his thoughts as security took a good five minutes to clear the canvas. Then the announcement was made.

'With Hoye in no position to defend himself, referee John-Lewis has stopped the contest at two minutes 59 seconds of round number five,' Mike Goodall bawled into the mike. 'Your winner and the new IBF light-heavyweight champion of the world, from Sheffield, Clinton Woods!' They gave me the belt and I stood there, holding it in the air, with this incredible wall of noise and cameras popping and flashing all around me. It was all I'd wanted for the last ten years. That moment was what everything had been about, what life is all about, I achieved something beyond myself, beyond normality, but then, like a rush of whizz, or an orgasm, it was over.

I walked back towards Dennis. The media wanted to interview us. An overwhelming sense of relief washed over me. Not joy, not excitement, but relief.

I'd proved all the naysayers wrong. They couldn't call me the nearly man anymore. I was champion of the fucking world.

Plaudits rolled in almost immediately. People at ringside were saying how great it was for British boxing. At the time, the UK only had three other world champions – Joe Calzaghe, Johnny Nelson and Scott Harrison, all of whom held the WBO belt, considered the weakest of the four main organisations. With the BBC pulling out of coverage and the sport's popularity on the wane, having a British IBF title holder could provide a massive boost.

They interviewed me sitting on the apron and I found it difficult to stay coherent. Adrenaline still coursed through my veins and I babbled some stuff about being under prepared in the past and how happy I was.

They tried to hook up a phone line to Joe Calzaghe to discuss a shot at my title, but Dennis poured cold water on that.

'Calzaghe can get in the queue,' he said. It was my moment and we didn't think it right that someone else should try to hijack it.

They asked me how happy I was and I blurted out about Natalia's pregnancy. My dad was standing next to her and looked shocked. We hadn't told anyone yet, but now I had announced it to the world.

'Bloody hell, my boss'll hear that,' Natalia said in my ear.

At last, all the hoopla was finished and we headed back to the changing room, where Dennis produced a few bottles of champagne and passed them around.

After a quick shower, everyone piled over to the Hilton for the victory party. There were people there who had watched me since my first fight at the Pinegrove and it was an emotional evening, as well as a drunken one. I remembered how I came back into boxing, ten years before, after my troubles with the law and the letter from Mam. I thought of Porty and how proud he would have been to see me just then. All those times on these sorts of nights, he shouted about me becoming British or European champion. I had even gone one better. The memories made me a little teary.

As we headed home in the small hours, I reflected on how perfect it had all been. The training, the preparation and then the fight itself. The way I felt that night, I don't think anyone could have beaten me.

A few days after the world title win, Dennis bought me a Rolex as a present. We didn't discuss business just yet. There was no need.

32

The right kind of champion

THERE'S an old saying in boxing that defending a title is harder than winning it. Throughout the sport's history, there were many guys who had one good night, picked up a world belt, then faded into obscurity. I didn't want to be one of those.

At the same time, I had no interest in a 'bum of the month' campaign and racking up a string of successful defences against third tier opposition. I always compared my situation to the two great super middleweights of the '90s, Nigel Benn and Chris Eubank. While Benn's reign was shorter, he took on and beat some of the very top Americans. Eubank, on the other hand, kept his title for several years by picking off low-risk opponents, one after the other. Benn had always been my favourite of the two.

Despite the fact I held the IBF title, one of the most prestigious, many pundits still placed me below the likes of Johnson and Tarver in the overall rankings. I hoped to cross swords with Johnson again one day, while there was lots of talk of a big money all-British match-up with super-middleweight Joe Calzaghe. Joe was a special fighter, but at light-heavyweight I was confident of giving him a run for his money.

Without knowing yet who my next opponent would be, I had the usual few weeks off then went back to the gym. Everything clicked into gear straight away and the team of John and Richard, with Dennis in the background, continued to work perfectly. Rather than chopping logs, I bought train sleepers which I swung an axe at.

I felt genuinely ready to take on anyone. Every fighter has a prime and this was mine. How long it lasts isn't always under your own control.

After about a month, while hitting the heavy bag, I noticed a steady and increasing pain in my elbows. I told John and we laid off bag work for a few days, but when I went back, it returned. It became one of those things that I had to grit my teeth and ignore. I didn't want to admit it to myself but it was possible, in my early thirties and after a decade of pro boxing, that my body was starting to show signs of wear and tear.

As Natalia's belly swelled and our excitement grew at the imminent birth of our child, news came through that my first defence would be the obvious one. The IBF nominated Julio Gonzalez, from Mexico, as my mandatory challenger. Gonzalez was the former WBO champion, had defeated Michalczewski and gone the distance with Jones in 2001, when Jones was still firing on all cylinders. He had also beaten Johnson, in 2003, something I had failed to do twice. Since losing the WBO belt in his first defence, he had racked up three straight wins, including one over Montell Griffin, in a final eliminator.

We knew he would be fit and we knew he would be tough as hell. Although they are more renowned for their prowess in the lower weight divisions, Mexican fighters are always hard as iron. We watched some tapes of Gonzalez and could see that he was always there, right up until the last second of the last round, but it looked as though he was stationary and easy to hit too. In particular, we studied his fight against Julian Letterlough, which was an insane battle. Gonzalez went down three times, Letterlough twice, but despite everything, the Mexican kept on coming and ground out a win. I knew my power had improved under the new regime with John, but I also knew it was extremely unlikely I could finish Gonzalez inside the distance. Up to that point, nobody had.

The fight was made for July at the Sheffield Arena and a broadcasting deal was made with Sky Sports. In contrast with the BBC, Sky were much keener on pre-fight build-up and when I met Gonzalez for some of the media stuff, I was struck by how fearsome he looked.

Taller than me, he had enormous shoulders and a face straight out of the *barrios*. He could have been the bad guy in a spaghetti western.

Gonzalez had that serious look about him. You could tell he was a man who had been through some tough times in his life and there was no pain I could dish out in a boxing ring that he had not experienced tenfold already. Despite that and like Hoye, his behaviour was gentlemanly, which I liked. Nobody thought it necessary to show disrespect or to start talking rubbish. Adam Smith, from Sky, called the fight 'as tough a mandatory as you could wish for'. No one could say I was doing things the easy way.

Opinion was pretty mixed and while some commentators gave me credit for my performance over Hoye and tipped me to win, others thought Gonzalez would be too battle hardened and would roll me over. He certainly wasn't fazed by the hostile atmosphere my Sheffield fanbase generated and as soon as the action began, I realised he was a better technical fighter than I anticipated.

On the videos, we had identified a big lump with balls the size of watermelons, but there was more to him than that. He had a very long reach and a deceptive feint in his movement. He had a knack of throwing hurtful shots to the body, where it looked like he was too far away. This was world-level boxing and everyone brought something to the table.

The early stages were close. He caught me a few times but I felt the cleaner shots came from me. About three or four rounds in, I twigged that Gonzalez was nowhere near as effective fighting off the back foot as the front. From then, I did all I could to apply pressure, which seemed to work. My hand and foot speed bewildered him at times. The bout was a gruelling war of attrition, but I took over as it wore on.

As I sat on my stool before round 12, Richard smeared Vaseline on my eyebrows and told me: 'Fast hands if you get a chance, Clinton, show them your quality. Show them who you are.' He was pretty much the only cornerman whose advice I had ever listened to.

I stayed on my toes, jabbed, tied him up when he got in close. He came after me, but there wasn't much left in his tank and I took a deserved unanimous decision. Afterwards, as I sat in the dressing room, almost every inch of me ached. What a battle. Gonzalez had been one tough character.

A month after my first defence, my son Jude was born. I held him in my hands at the Royal Hallamshire hospital and began to feel that I had finally grown up. I was 33 years old, earning decent money, although not the incredible sums some people think, and a father. The mayhem of my teenage years seemed a lifetime away.

I had a longer rest period after Gonzalez to help settle Jude in at home and also because the problems in my elbows flared up again. There were times I could barely pick up the baby, they were so inflamed and sore. Jude was a terrible sleeper, even by small baby standards, and for the first few months we were lucky if we got three hours at a time. Being a real father was going to take some getting used to.

Dennis kept himself busy in the meantime and managed to sign a deal with Ricky Hatton, a major coup. By that point, Hatton and me were the only Brits to hold 'proper' world championship belts. Since I won my title, he had become the IBF and WBA super lightweight champ and the biggest star in UK boxing.

Poxon started working with him as well. I didn't realise at the time, but this new deal would eventually destroy the dynamic of our team, which up to that point had worked so amazingly well. For the time being, though, things were still OK.

Dennis cued up a rematch with Jason DeLisle for my first voluntary defence. The Aussie was still ranked in the IBF's top ten and had given me a decent fight the first time, although I was always a level above him, really. Interest was phenomenally high. The affection in which I was held by the people of Sheffield really choked me up. I was featured regularly in the local papers and on TV programmes like *Calendar News*.

I would be walking the streets with my wife, the baby in a pushchair, and people I had never met would wander over.

'How're you doing, champ? Good luck in't next fight!'

'D'you mind if I get a photo wi' thi?'

'Could you sign this for my dad?'

Sometimes, if I was in a hurry or feeling tired, the attention could be a bit unwelcome, but I made it my business to respond as brightly as possible, no matter what. I truly appreciated the support I had had from my city and wanted people who met me to feel good about it.

'Where's tha livin' now?' they would sometimes ask. 'Are you movin' to London, or Hollywood?'

I used to find that hilarious. People really believed that someone in my position earned millions and rubbed shoulders with film stars, that I would therefore need to be somewhere glamorous. My answer was always the same.

'Listen pal, if they offered me a house in London for free, I wouldn't go. I love it around here!'

In truth, behind the scenes Dennis was chasing a trilogy fight with Johnson, or even a match-up with Tarver. I was universally recognised as being among the top three light-heavyweights in the world, but a win over either of them would give me a decent claim to being number one. The way my whole career had gone, starting off at 22 not expecting much, then picking up an area title, all the way through to a world championship, it seemed like a fitting way to end it.

Socially, they were quiet times, but occasionally I would head out with a couple of mates for a drink. By then, I would generally be on juice or water, but it was nice just to be out with them. About a month before the DeLisle rematch, I was out in Mosborough with some friends and a horrible kid with a scarred face spat on one of them.

'I fuckin' saw that,' I told him.

'Saw what?'

'That's fuckin' disgusting'

'Oh fuck off!' he hissed.

I didn't think anything of it at all. It was a typical pub stand-off, but when we left he was waiting for me outside. Immediately, he started walking towards me with one hand behind his back. Of course I knew he had a bottle.

It was a tricky moment. Did I whack him and risk damaging my hands or even being sued? Or did I just stand there and allow him to bottle me? The second one wasn't really an option, so as soon as he was close enough I slapped him across the face with an open palm. I figured that way it couldn't be claimed I was using my fists outside the ring.

'Put tha fuckin' bottle down,' I shouted.

The guy was drunk off his arse, staggered backwards, pulled the bottle out and slurred: 'I was only messing about, mate.'

Fortunately, that was the end of it. I never knew whether that incident happened because he knew who I was or because he didn't.

A week before I was due to fight DeLisle on 13 May, Dennis asked to speak to me. I sat down and he informed me he wouldn't be at the fight.

'How do you feel about that?' he asked.

'Well, it'll be reyt weird. You've always been there. But I'll be alreyt.'

It turned out Dennis was off to Vegas with Ricky Hatton, who was boxing Luis Collazo on the same night.

'That's a liberty,' a couple of my close friends said. 'Tha's been with him for years and now he fucks off wi'the golden boy?'

I didn't give it much thought, though. It genuinely didn't concern me and I had other problems. As my fight drew nearer, I started sleeping in the loft so as not to be woken by little Jude three or four times a night. There was no way I could afford to have that going on while training.

I boxed DeLisle at Ponds Forge and in Dennis' absence Poxon worked my corner with Mark Brooks. This time, I stopped the Australian in the sixth, backing him on to the ropes and finishing him with a perfect uppercut. In truth, I hammered him from the beginning and it was probably the best, most destructive performance of my career. Either I had grown as a fighter since our first meeting or he had diminished. Either way, at that time I still had that feeling. I was genuinely the best light-heavyweight on the planet.

33

As if you're big stars

DENNIS flew back from Vegas and we talked about my fight. He didn't apologise for missing it but I sensed there was a bit of unusual awkwardness there. Maybe he felt guilty. As far as I was concerned, it was no big deal. I wasn't upset, although some of my friends and family were.

With two defences to my name, I could consider myself an established champion and a month after DeLisle I got the news I was waiting for. I would be boxing Johnson again, in Bolton, in September. Bizarrely, Frank Warren won the purse bids.

Warren had nothing to do with myself or Johnson and had a deal with Sky at the time, but the bout was scheduled to be shown on ITV. Both Dennis and I believed that Calzaghe, who Warren managed, had to have something to do with it all.

Earlier in the year, the Welshman had put in a career-best performance, dominating the highly fancied Jeff Lacy over 12 rounds to become the unified WBO and IBF super middleweight champ. They were looking to push him into the American market. Becoming a two-weight world titlist would help with that.

Warren had a knack for hitting the right promotional buttons and the fight was billed 'For A Few Dollars More' on the posters. Dennis thought that was a little taunt at him, as Warren had won the purse bid by only a few dollars, and he was not best pleased about it.

I looked forward to seeing Johnson again, but disappointingly, at the press conference he seemed a different man to when we had last met. He turned up in a designer suit rather than his usual trackies and had developed an attitude. His wins over the likes of Jones and Tarver had clearly inflated his ego.

'No one's had it harder than me,' he said. 'I had to come from nothing. I have to fight for everything. I've been cheated all over the world, just like I was the first time I fought here against Woods. I'm the best. I know I'm the best. This time I'm going to knock him out. I won't rely on the judges.'

When my turn finally came and I tried to say a few words, Johnson and his team continued talking over the top of me.

'Why are you being so ignorant?' I asked. 'Show some respect. You've all come over here this time as if you're big stars.'

Johnson didn't like that and responded angrily. My pot heated up and we had a little argument. The TV people loved it. It was the first time I had done anything of that nature before the media, but at least it was genuine. We weren't pretending.

Training went great again, with exactly the same set-up as the previous two fights. The period in which I worked with Richard and John was definitely my best. The only negative was that my elbows continued to play up, especially when I threw hooks, more with the left hand than the right. It seemed to be one of those things that got a little worse with each training camp and John arranged for me to have some intensive physio to get me through to the fight.

Other than that, the camp went like clockwork. Yet despite the efficiency of our methods we found ourselves surprised at the weigh-in. Before Warren and all the cameras and journalists, it was announced that I was three pounds over. On our team, we all met the news with sheer disbelief. It didn't seem possible, but there was nothing else for it. I would have to go and sweat the weight off.

I shadow-boxed in a sauna for what was probably 45 minutes but felt like an eternity, until my legs were dead and my lungs scorched with every breath.

'Bloody hell,' I thought. 'I've drained myself here.'

When I went back, an hour later, I actually came in a pound light. There was no way I could have lost four pounds in that time.

213

There was no getting away from it, it looked suspicious. We believed there must have been something wrong the first time, maybe even some foul play from someone, trying to influence things in Johnson's favour. There was no way to prove anything, so we accepted it and carried on.

Our camp was calm as we waited backstage. We had experience of three successful world title fights by then and although we knew all about Johnson's strengths, we also knew I had improved since the last time I boxed him. The media told Johnson that I described myself as a new fighter. He found it funny.

'Wha ya mean?' he replied in his Jamaican accent. 'Am I boxing his twin brother?'

I had a lot to prove to everyone.

34

Woods v Johnson III

2 September 2006
Bolton Arena
IBF world light-heavyweight title

TRILOGY fights, eh? Boxing fans love them, as do writers. Ali-Frazier, Barrera-Morales, Leonard-Duran. What they mean, particularly when world titles are at stake, is that two men have found themselves so evenly matched over a number of years that their journeys become shared. The piece of human granite that was Glen Johnson, in many ways, defined my career.

I was ever so slightly uneasy as my theme music kicked in, 'Going Underground' by The Jam. I knew that if Johnson beat me again, there would be those who would question my elite credentials. They would talk down my wins over the likes of Hoye and Gonzalez and claim I never beat a true top-level fighter.

By the time this fight took place, Bernard Hopkins had stepped up to light-heavy and surprised a few people by outpointing Tarver. Johnson, on the other hand, was coming off a good win against Richard Hall.

The evening started with an argument over which dressing room we should have. Warren stitched us up with a small room, really little more than a cupboard. There was no space to shadow box or skip or anything and Dennis was having none of it. After a lot of shouting, posturing and preening of feathers, they moved us.

Despite the fact the show was in Bolton, the arena was still very much full of my people. A few thousand had made the 53-mile journey from Sheffield, with several organisations laying on coaches. I always received raucous receptions and this one was no different. It made my skin tingle.

Along with Poxon and Dennis, Ricky Hatton walked out with me, holding my belts. Hobson Promotions' two top boys, backing each other up. Dennis wanted to rub Frank's nose in it with a little show of strength.

In our previous fights Johnson always started well, so I made a point of taking centre ring from the start and sticking a stiff jab in his face. It only worked for about a minute. Soon, I found myself moving and backing off as he came after me, powering in his trademark hooks with both hands.

Johnson had this habit of growling as he threw each punch, a rough, throaty *woof,* like the bark of a dog. For some reason, I really noticed it in this fight, more than the previous two.

It pierced through the noise of the crowd as he attacked me. Every shot that bounced off my arms or thudded into my sides was punctuated with it. *Woof, woof, woof* as if I was in there with some kind of monster.

I established a rhythm by the third and from there it turned into yet another uncompromising war. Neither of us were the type to hide and both were too tough to falter. In all our rounds of boxing, the only time either of us hit the floor was when Johnson went down towards the end of our first meeting, although it was ruled a slip. It was just how we combined, me and him. Our styles collided. It was brutal.

During the middle rounds, I threw a hook that landed on his shoulder and immediately, it felt as though someone had poured scalding hot water on my arm. The raging adrenaline of confrontation helped me ignore the pain.

In the build-up, there had been a lot of pundit talk about Johnson 'defying father time' but at 38, as we headed into the eighth round, it was clear to me he was tiring. I had felt the pendulum swing in my favour for a while before then, but in that session he barely threw a punch. I jabbed and hooked away as he marched forwards, hands up, taking everything. The thought crossed my mind that maybe I could stop him. It was a foolish thought.

Maybe I was over confident and lost concentration, but Johnson sensed an opening in round nine and launched a vicious assault. He knocked me back against the ropes, I managed to escape, then he chased me all over the ring. For a while, I couldn't seem to divert his shots. Punch after punch rebounded off my skull and ribs. At the end of it, I slumped on my stool. Poxon and Hobson sounded panicked.

'Get your chin up, you're a champion!' Richard screamed.

'Let's believe!' said Dennis. 'Believe!'

The crowd became quieter too. I walked back out and stared across the ring, like I was searching for answers. *I hope he don't have another fucking round like that.*

Fortunately, it seemed my first thought had been right. Johnson was slow off his stool and I could tell by the way he came out that he was desperately tired. The big blowout in the ninth must have been a last-ditch attempt to get me out of there. It had drained him. He still threw shots, but less frequently. They were arm punches, mostly.

I've got you now. As I often did, I came into my own in the last three rounds. When I was right, fitness was never a problem. The crowd lifted me, as always. In the 12th he hung on, utterly exhausted. At the end, he didn't even have the strength to put his hands up.

We all felt I had got it, although it had been close and gruelling. Ironically, the two judges from across the Atlantic, Ramirez and Bays, both gave me the nod, while the British judge, Mickey Vann, scored it to Johnson by two rounds.

'Your winner by split decision...' the MC bellowed into the mike, followed by the obligatory five-second pause. I hopped from foot to foot, looking down at the canvas. Dennis massaged my shoulder anxiously.

'And still...'

The rest of the MC's words were drowned in noise as I was hoisted into the air then put back down. I couldn't hear, of course, but on the ITV commentary John Rawling said: 'Clinton Woods, by beating Glen Johnson, may just have proven that he is indeed the best light-heavyweight in the world.'

That was exactly how I felt.

Afterwards, once the scene in the ring had calmed enough, all the media interviews were done and we went back in our dressing room, our celebrations were interrupted by one of the security guards.

'Clinton,' he said. 'You should go downstairs to the press conference. I don't think they wanted you to be there.'

I shrugged, but Dennis was keen, so I threw a tracksuit on and we headed down. My elbow was agony by this point and I held it still, knowing I would have to get it looked at. When we arrived at the media room, Frank Warren was sat at the front table with a couple of officials from the IBF. He looked a bit sheepish.

Either side of his place, facing outwards, were two name badges. One said 'Glen Johnson, IBF light-heavyweight champion', the other said 'Joe Calzaghe'. Dennis pointed and laughed.

'What's all this, then, Frank?' he asked.

Warren looked up and smiled without humour.

'Shall I sit down?' I enquired.

'OK...err...yes,' he stammered.

It seemed he hadn't got the result he was looking for. The deal for Johnson v Calzaghe had already been made. But now it had been rendered meaningless.

The name badges were cleared away and Calzaghe never arrived, despite being at ringside. During the media questions, the prospect of a Woods v Calzaghe showdown was mooted repeatedly. Both Warren and Hobson made vague statements. I sidestepped the question when it came up.

In the days that followed, Dennis told me privately he thought that fight would definitely happen. He talked it up whenever he could, but maybe it's just as well it never did. In my prime, I'm sure I would have beaten Joe at light-heavy, but Calzaghe was clearly a class act.

In the same way that neither Ali nor Frazier were ever the same again after the 'Thrilla in Manila', I would soon realise that Johnson and I had taken a lot out of each other

35

Only one way to go

WHEN you reach the position of being arguably the best at your weight in the world (and it's always a matter of argument in modern boxing), it's tough to keep moving upwards. Naturally, Dennis began to look for money fights. While Calzaghe promised to be a huge UK event, at light-heavyweight the big American draws remained Tarver or Hopkins.

As Dennis worked the phones and harangued the right people as only he could, we moved out of our house to a new one at the bottom of Ridgeway, called Swallow Cottage. It's a beautiful place, in a rural setting, so far south of Sheffield that the address is actually in Derbyshire, but still just down the road from Mosborough.

It was only a stone's throw from Hobson's home and was one of the beautiful residences I used to walk past as a kid, on my way home from fishing trips. I had never truly believed I would be able to afford to live there and as we moved in I struggled to overcome my disbelief.

I was still by no means a rich man, but had earned five-figure purses consistently in my previous few fights. All the people who assumed as a world champion I made millions were way wide of the mark, but Natalia was pregnant again and it was important to me to provide as good a life for my young family as possible.

On doctor's orders, I rested my elbow and Dennis got busy trying to organise the fantasy fights, but the IBF soon got in touch with other ideas. It seemed the time had come around once more for me to meet their mandatory challenger. Unbelievably, it was Julio Cesar Gonzalez again.

Since losing to me the last time, he had got himself back into pole position by outpointing Jason DeLisle, then scoring a couple of impressive KO wins. We received notification and a deadline for the bout to take place.

We all accepted the news with good grace. We knew I would be able to beat Gonzalez, despite what a leathery, indestructible beast of a man he was. But we also knew it was likely to be another 12-round dogfight. Once I had got past it, we could chase after some of the big boys.

The fight was set for January in Vegas, as chief support to Ricky Hatton's IBF super lightweight title defence against Juan Urango. That bit of news absolutely made my day. To have come from where I started, at the age I started, and end up defending a world title in Vegas was a fairy story. I looked forward to it like a kid before Christmas.

But all was not well in camp Woods. I noticed the atmosphere between my team members had become tetchy. Arguments were frequent and there was something going on between Richard and Dennis that I didn't understand.

It was as if all the glory, glamour and extra money of world championship boxing had changed something. I noticed that Poxon started snapping at young lads in the gym, talking down to them. He had never been like that before.

The other issue was that almost as soon as training camp kicked in, the pain in my elbow returned. If anything, it was worse than ever. I was being sent over to a specialist in Manchester for acupuncture, but it was useless. Nothing helped.

Poxon brought in former world cruiserweight champ Johnny Nelson, by then retired, for sparring, which in my opinion, it was a ridiculous choice. Gonzalez, as we all knew, was an immovable lump who would get right in my face, refuse to budge and wage war. Nelson turned up and basically ran around the outside of the ring for three minutes at a time. Richard and I had our first argument since we started working together.

'What the fuck did you get Johnny Nelson in for?' I asked.

'He's quality.'

'But he's nowt like Gonzalez. It's a waste of time.'

'You leave the sparring partners to me.'

'This is bullshit!'

About two weeks before fight night, after I finished chasing Johnny around for half an hour, we ended our session with a pad workout. It might have been anger working its way out of my system, but I threw a big left hook with real power behind it. As my glove connected with the mitt, something internal snapped. The pain, which had been constant since camp began, erupted beyond belief. It was absolutely excruciating.

I threw my gloves off and charged into the dressing room. My arm felt like it was on fire. Almost in tears from the intensity of the pain, I knew there had to be something very wrong. Richard followed me in and found me with my head in my hands.

'That's it, my career's over,' I yelled. 'I've earned fuck all. I've hardly any money. How am I gonna live?'

Poxon sat down with me and calmly talked it over. It was clear I needed higher-level medical intervention than I had been receiving. We called Dennis in and explained there was no choice. We would have to cancel the fight.

Hobson was unimpressed, to say the least. It was an HBO and Sky pay-per-view show in Vegas and pulling out at such a late stage would create a very bad impression.

'If you want to work with these people, you don't let them down like this,' he said. 'Especially if you want to go over there for big money in future.'

'If he goes in with a fucked arm and loses, there'll be no big money fights anyway,' Poxon replied. He had a point.

I was booked in to see a sports specialist surgeon, who was flabbergasted at what he found. My elbow tendon had completely ripped off the joint.

'This must have been troubling you for years,' he said. 'How on earth did you manage to train and fight with an injury like this?'

He told me healing time would only be a couple of months, which was encouraging. Trying to make the best of things, I went over for the show anyway with my brothers and mates. Vegas didn't know what hit it.

In some ways, it was good to unwind, have a few drinks and forget about training and boxing for a while. Despite the surgery, the elbow still nagged at me and I knew there was no way I could throw my fists. The IBF gave us special dispensation, but if it didn't heal quick enough eventually my title would be stripped.

Three months after the operation, we suffered a setback when I had to go under the knife again. They had mistakenly attached a nerve to the tendon, which is why it was still so sore. That delay meant the overall healing process took about six months.

Once camp finally began again, I felt OK and trained hard. Yet something indefinable was missing. It was difficult to put my finger on it, but somehow the upper reaches of my highest gear weren't there. Was it the injuries? Was it my age? I was 35 by then. Or was it perhaps that events outside the ring had changed me as a person? I was a long way from the street-fighting kid I once had been.

I didn't know the answer and wished I did, but I knew that little edge was missing.

My daughter Lola was born in July '07, a couple of weeks into training for Gonzalez II. All of a sudden, I was a father to two young children, in his mid-thirties, with a large, expensive household to maintain. Maybe I had become too civilised. Maybe that old pot had stopped boiling.

The fight itself, held not in Vegas, but in a typically thunderous Sheffield Arena, took place just over a year after my bout with Johnson. Lots of people talked about ring rust, but the whole thing proved very similar to the first. The only real difference was that this time, Gonzalez weakened towards the end. For a short while, I thought I might achieve the impossible and stop him. I had him rubber legged in the tenth, caught him repeatedly in the 11th, nearly put him down, then continued battering him until a clash of heads broke the action in the 12th.

Overall, as we embraced at final bell, I felt a real kinship with Julio. The man was a proper *hombre*, although in all honesty I felt he was on the slide. He was a guy who only fought one way, but when every bout is a life-or-death battle, it's difficult to have too long a career. Each time he boxed, he took a lot of shots. That can take its toll. I also felt, compared to my fights against the likes of Hoye and Johnson, that I failed to hit the peaks. The bottom line was that neither of us were as good as we had been in 2005.

All boxers, they say, live out the four seasons of success. Winter can set in quickly. But after my fourth successful defence, the path was clear for Dennis to chase his big targets.

36

The Magic Man

AFTER winning the Gonzalez rematch, I could consider myself a well-established world champion. I had made four defences of one of the most prestigious titles, including two mandatories. Boxing fans all over the world recognised me as one of, if not the, best around.

In terms of my boxing career, I had reached a kind of mountaintop, but life outside the ring would quickly provide a reality check. A few days after the win, I got a phone call from Mam.

'Go and see our Shane,' she implored. 'He's threatened to kill himself.'

Immediately, I jumped in the car and bombed around to his house. The light was on in his kitchen, so I peered through the window.

Shane was sat on a stool doing the crossword. He always had a talent for crosswords. The song 'Love Me For A Reason' blared from the stereo. I shoved the door open and stepped inside.

'Hey up, Shane, what's tha' doin?' I shouted.

He looked at me with baleful eyes and said: 'You're too late.'

Two empty tablet boxes sat on the table in front of him. 'You're too late, Clinton,' he repeated. 'I've had enough.'

It turned out he had had a horrible row with his girlfriend and she had left him. I panicked, phoned an ambulance and tried to keep him talking until they arrived.

'He's tried to kill his sen,' I told them when they turned up with police in tow. They went into the kitchen. Shane looked very sick by then.

'Why didn't tha hang thi' sen?' one of the coppers said.

'Wha?' Shane's eyes were hooded.

'Those won't kill thi,' the copper chortled. 'You should have hanged thi' sen if you wanted to do it.'

I couldn't believe what I was hearing. They took us to the hospital and sat us on some seats outside the ward while they made the necessary preparations to pump his stomach. We had only been there five minutes when they brought a girl in too. She was quite attractive, in her mid-twenties. Shane turned to her.

'What are you here for, then?'

'I took tablets,' she replied.

He perked up.

'Have you, love? I've taken tablets too.'

'No way. Really?'

'I have, ar.'

The two of them started having a conversation, comparing how many pills they had taken and which kinds. Soon, they were both laughing their heads off.

'Come on,' Shane said after a while. She got up and he led her by the hand into a nearby disabled toilet. Soon, bumping and groaning could be heard from inside. After a while, the girl moaned with pleasure.

Shane came striding back out, laughing like mad and sat back down. She followed soon after, opened the door and collapsed, face down, on the floor. Doctors turned up and carried her away. In disbelief, I waited for Shane to be admitted to the ward then left him to it.

But two days after that, I had another phone call from Mam.

'Clinton, you'd better get down to the hospital again. Heath's been stabbed.'

It turned out two kids had walked into the Golden Keys, Heath's local, looking for someone. They approached Heath, who didn't like the look of them and told them to fuck off. An argument ensued, got out of hand, they pulled a knife and stabbed him in the leg. When I got there, Heath had lost some blood and was swearing revenge to anyone who would listen, but doctors said he would recover.

It hadn't exactly been the best post-fight week of my life, so with Heath and Shane both in hospital I arranged for a night out with some mates and my other brothers at a club called the Leadmill. It was a decent night with good music and I enjoyed myself until my mate Danny came running up to me at the bar.

'Clinton,' he shouted, grabbing my arm. 'Julian's getting dragged outside by a bunch of lads.'

I rushed to the door and saw Julian outside on the pavement, surrounded by five blokes. One of them cracked him and knocked him down, then another got on top of him and started hammering him. Blood streamed from his head.

'Oi!' I shouted and legged it out to the road. The lad on top of Julian, a typical shaven-headed bottle boy, stood up. No words, I just knocked him straight down like a bag of shit. All four of his mates came at me and I decked the lot of them, one by one. It was slapstick comedy, like something out of *Laurel and Hardy*. Once one went over, the next one would come. Then once I'd put them all on their arses, they started getting up and coming back at me.

It was like reliving my past, with punters watching from the doorway as I scrapped in the street. A girl ran up, blindsided me and raked her fingernails all the way down my cheek. I wheeled around and saw coppers arriving as she ran off.

'What's going on here, Clinton?' police asked.

I explained the situation and gestured at Julian's injuries.

'You have to be careful,' the copper said. He pointed up at a nearby lamp-post. 'There's cameras there.'

As a world champion, street brawling is frowned upon and they could have made life difficult for me if they wanted to. They spoke to some of the lads nearby to get their version of events.

Once the whole scene had calmed down, the first kid, the skinhead, wandered over.

'Look mate,' he said with a soft, apologetic look in his eyes. 'I'm really...'

Before he finished his sentence, he cheap-shotted me with a right hand and ran off. Little bastard split my lip as well. The coppers just looked at me and laughed.

I shrugged. 'What can you do?' I asked.

Soon, an ambulance arrived and my celebratory night out turned into yet another trip to the Northern General, this time to get Julian's head stitched. We didn't really do world championship glamour in the Woods family. Within a week of my fourth and most important title defence, three of my brothers had been admitted to hospital.

Still, our sights were now set across the Atlantic and with Hopkins looking likely to box Calzaghe, it left one major player – Antonio Tarver. He had made his name as the man who did the double over Roy Jones Jr, knocking him out in 2004, then outpointing him in 2005. While I continued my reign as IBF world champion, he took a break from real-life boxing to star alongside Sylvester Stallone as the bad guy in *Rocky Balboa*, filmed in early 2006.

Tarver's problem was that the film role entailed bulking up to heavyweight. It meant, like his old foe Jones, that he would have to shift a lot of poundage very quickly to regain shape. When he boxed Bernard Hopkins in June 2006, he still felt the effects of that, looked poor and lost a unanimous decision. But by the time I beat Gonzalez, he had rebuilt his reputation with a split decision win over highly touted Kosovan Elivir Muriqi and a four-round blow-out of fringe contender Danny Santiago. Tarver's stint in the movies ensured his profile was high and over Christmas Dennis informed me he was likely to be my next opponent.

I hoped for a Vegas slot but once the contractual details had been finalised, the bout was set for Tampa in Florida, Tarver's home town. On the same bill, my old nemesis Glen Johnson was boxing new champion Chad Dawson for the WBC belt. From my point of view, by any analysis it was a risky defence. Fighting at home was usually the champion's privilege, but we were handing that to Tarver to try to break the American market. In the back of our minds lurked the suspicion that if the fight was close, I would be unlikely to get the decision.

We started work, but Richard's attitude inside the gym began to get me down. He had been such a quiet, unassuming guy, but working with me during my best years elevated his standing. He was regarded as hot stuff, the young coach who had made me world champion. He didn't deal with it well and I would see him tearing strips off other fighters.

'If you're fuckin' two minutes late again, I'm never working another day with you,' he would say.

'You call that fuckin' bag work. I call it shite!'

It didn't suit him, as far as I was concerned. He also developed an issue with John. I have no idea what was at the heart of it. John was one of the nicest people you could wish to meet. But Richard began pulling me to one side.

'I think you should stop doing weights with John,' he would say.

'Why?'

'It's no good for you, Clint. We can work out a programme between us.'

Richard and Dennis were doing a lot of work with the Hattons as well and I got the feeling they had developed an attitude of being better than others around them. As the divisions in the team grew, the training suffered. It's not that we weren't working as hard as before, we just weren't working as well.

We clashed over styles too. Tarver was southpaw and a bloody good one. I had always struggled with southpaws, but had an idea I wanted to try. When I reversed my feet, I had an excellent southpaw jab. Maybe we could bring some southpaw work into my routine? Perhaps I could confuse Tarver by switch-hitting?

But Poxon was having none of it.

'No southpaw,' he insisted. 'You stay as you are.'

Early in the camp I felt sharp pain in my right elbow, just as I had before in my left. I could cope with it, but it was another sign that things were going downhill.

Tarver flew over to London in February for a head-to-head press conference, our first meeting. As usual, I expected to shake hands and discuss the fight like adults. But I would soon learn that wasn't Mr. Tarver's style.

'You an ordinary fighter,' he bellowed, standing up from his chair. 'I'm the magic man! I'm extraordinary! Don't you ever forget it.'

Dennis nudged me as if he wanted me to say something. I felt stupid.

'Oh shut up,' I replied.

'I know when you feel the heat, you gonna be in retreat. Man, you can't even carry my bag. You history on the 12th.'

He started banging his fist on the table.

'Every fucking thing I said I've backed up. You gonna get knocked out. You ain't never seen nobody like me.'

Dennis nudged me again. 'Err... you want to learn some manners, pal.' Was all I could think to say.

Dennis sat between us smiling as flashbulbs popped and cameras rolled. I would have felt daft trying to do what Tarver did. It wasn't my way and I didn't like it. He was like a less charismatic, less amusing version of Muhammad Ali. But of course, the press lapped it all up.

'What a horrible bloke,' I said in a solo TV interview afterwards. I meant it too. The boiling pot may have disappeared from my life but Tarver bugged the shit out of me. If there was one guy in boxing I desperately wanted to beat up, it was him.

Meeting him like that helped me return to training with new vigour. I ignored the pain in my right elbow and the cracks appearing in my team. I just wanted to focus on Tarver, so I could get in the ring and teach him a lesson.

First sparring partner of the camp was the familiar face of Lee Swaby, a great kid, but poor preparation for the sort of fight I had coming up. After Swaby, Richard booked in an American called Lou Del Valle who held the WBA title for eight months in 1997. On paper, he sounded decent.

I don't know if Del Valle was out of condition or semi-retired, but at 39 he was absolutely useless. Plus, he was short and compact – 5ft 10ins compared to Tarver's 6ft 2ins. Our sparring was uncompetitive and I had to hold back to stop myself hurting him. I raised it as an issue with Poxon and again he dug his heels in. We argued about it. Things were just not ticking along as they had before.

Three weeks before fight night, just a week before I was due to fly to America, I was winding down at the end of a session with John. We had completed a few circuits and I was squatting the Olympic bar, with no weight, just to loosen my legs and lower back.

'Two more,' John encouraged. 'Then that'll do for today.'

I lowered my backside down towards the floor and at the point when it reached the level of my knees, I felt a tightening somewhere around my spine.

'That was reyt weird,' I said, straightening back up.

'What was?'

'Just felt a twinge in my back.'

'OK mate,' he said. 'Better stop there.'

I showered, got changed and drove home without giving it a second thought. When I arrived, I gave Natalia a kiss and told her I was going upstairs for a hot bath, a good post-training habit for muscle relaxation and weight loss.

I lay in the bath probably for half an hour, alone with my thoughts, stewing on Tarver.

'I'm pretty as a girl,' he had kept shouting. God, I wanted to hurt him.

Once I'd had a good sweat and the water started to cool down, I decided it was time to get out. Placing my hands on the sides of the bath, I moved to sit up.

But I couldn't do it.

As soon as I tried to manoeuvre my back in any way, it racked with agony. Everything from my shoulders to my arse had set solid, in some kind of spasm.

'Natalia!' I screamed. 'Natalia!'

Frightened by the panic in my voice, she left the babies downstairs for a moment and came running up.

'I can't gerrout the fuckin' bath,' I told her as she appeared at the door. 'I've pulled my back or summat.'

With Natalia's help, howling and yelping, I managed to flop out of the bath, but the pain was so intense I couldn't get up or walk.

'What should I do?' Natalia asked.

'Fuck, I dunno, phone Daz!'

My mate, Daz Ashton, lived nearby. He worked as a builder and I knew he would have the strength to lift me. Fortunately, Daz was at home and arrived in about ten minutes. After a lot of huffing and puffing, Daz and Natalia managed to get me down the stairs and into the back of his van. I laid there like a corpse while he drove me down to Eccleshall Road to a physiotherapy centre.

Once they dragged me inside, the doctor put me on a table and twisted me one way, then another, while I screamed in agony. It was truly the worst pain of my life.

'Try and stand up,' he said. I couldn't.

'Listen, you've badly pulled your quadratus lumborum muscle. If you rest it, it should sort itself out in a month or two.'

'I've got a world title fight in three weeks,' I told him.

The doctor shook his head. 'The best I can do is get you moving, but without rest it won't heal by then.'

He continued the agonising manipulation of my arms, legs and back until I loosened up enough that I could stand. Still, every step I made and every movement sent shocks of pain up and down my back. When I got home, I phoned Dennis.

'Dennis,' I said, 'I'm sorry, my back's fucked. I'm gonna have to pull out of the fight.'

'What are you talkin' about?'

'I've pulled a deep muscle in my back doing squats. It's agony. I can't move.'

Dennis paused. I could hear him breathing. Then he spoke very quietly. 'Listen to me, Clint. There's no way you can pull out. This is a big Showtime TV event in the States. We pulled out of HBO last time. If we do this again, we'll never work over there, ever.'

'I can't fight, Dennis.'

'Clint, you have to,' And that was it. He put the phone down.

For the next week, I tried to rest as much as possible during what should have been the highest intensity period of camp. By the time I flew to America, two weeks before fight night, I was still only partly mobile.

I sucked it up and tried to get on with things as best as I could, but it meant I not only contended with problematic elbows, but a very stiff and sore back.

Poxon brought Swaby out to spar with me, of all people, probably because he was the cheapest option. It was all far from ideal. At least Daz came over to keep me company.

Dennis had sorted us out a lovely house to stay in and a little gym for training until the fight. Even in April, it was about 30 degrees in Tampa and when we arrived at the gym we found it a tiny, crowded place with a tin roof. Despite that, the guys in there were great and gave me a proper welcome.

'It's the champ,'

'You're the best light-heavyweight in the world, man! Respect!'

I tried gentle shadow boxing and found myself coated in thick sweat in about ten seconds. The place was like a sauna. It drained the life out of me.

A few days after arriving, on the pads with Poxon, I just dropped my hands and stopped. I had never done anything like that before, but felt so demoralised. My camp had been one problem after another and I felt like I was in the worst condition of my professional career.

'I in't doin' no more,' I shouted before walking away. 'I'm fucked.'

'One more round!' Poxon yelled. He looked rattled.

'I'm fucked.'

'One more round, I said!'

'Fuck that!' I screamed. 'I said I'm fucked.'

I sat down and refused to continue. Sweat streamed off my head and pooled on the floor at my feet. My team eyed me warily from across the gym. Dennis stormed out.

'Fuck the lot of you!' he shouted as he went. 'I'm fucking off back to England.'

Daz understood me. No one was happy, but I was the one who would have to go in the ring, in front of all those people. He came and sat next to me, then put an arm around my shoulder.

'Clint,' he whispered in my ear. 'Pull out, mate. Don't listen to nobody but yourself. You don't have to do this. I don't care what anyone says. You look terrible. You're in no state to box Tarver.'

'I can't,' I told him simply. In truth, I felt completely drained, empty and lost. More than anything, I wanted the whole thing over. I knew there were guys in the gym who were on speaking terms with Tarver. They would surely be reporting back to him. No doubt he would love what he heard.

That night, back at the house, Dennis arrived and asked to speak to all of us. He hadn't gone back to England in the end. Richard, John and Daz sat around in silence.

'All I've done,' Dennis said. 'All of it, every single thing, it's always been about moving you forwards. All the effort we made at building your career has brought us here. Look at where we've got to! We can't pull you out now. And why would we? I still believe you can win this fight. You're the champ, Clint. We all still believe you can win this fight.'

He looked around the room for validation. Everyone sat twiddling their thumbs, cracking their knuckles or pretending to check something on their phone. Undeterred, he carried on.

'And when you do, we're in the big league. I'm talking multi-millions! Come on! Where's your fighter's spirit?'

I mumbled something. We had worked together so long. The last thing I wanted was to let Dennis down.

Satisfied with the result of his inspirational pep talk, he left. I had a bit of dinner and went to bed.

And so, we limped on, towards the fight. Bickering among team members became a daily event and the injuries meant my training never picked up. Of course, in the background, Richard blamed John for everything, believing it was his routine that had caused my back problems. It became harder and harder to see those two working together in the future.

The one positive that did arise out of my outburst was that for the last week before the fight, Dennis paid for some air conditioning in the gym. There was a sort of massive shutter on one wall that could be rolled up and a van with a huge mounted air-conditioning unit was parked alongside it. It made being in the place more bearable.

I spoke to Natalia on the phone and told her I didn't want her to fly out. I knew how bad I looked and felt. No wife should see her husband like that. Natalia being Natalia, she came out anyway.

There were some more verbals at the weigh-in, which I didn't have the stomach for. Afterwards, I was interviewed by one of the Yorkshire radio newsmen.

'How are you feeling for the fight, Clinton?'

'Well, I'm feeling…' I couldn't get the words out. Suddenly, I found myself fighting back tears. He switched off the microphone.

'What's up?' he asked. I told him everything. He was respectful enough never to publicise what I said and I appreciated that. The truth was, for the first time in my professional life, I was scared. Not of Tarver, but of being embarrassed. I didn't want to go up there and make a fool of myself.

37

Woods v Tarver

IBF world light-heavyweight title
12 April 2008
St Pete Times Forum, Tampa, Florida

AS ever, a few hundred of the loyal Sheffield faithful made the journey out to America to support me, which made me feel guilty as hell. My passionate followers had spent money on tickets and airfares, even booked time off work, hoping to see me come away with a win, but I knew, barring a lucky punch, I would be unable to give them that.

Not only had Tarver got home advantage for the fight, he also insisted on coming out second, another usual champion's privilege. Walking to the ring, getting all sorts of abuse from the hometown crowd, I kept my face buried within my hood. There was no life in me. It was the only fight of my career where I knew I was going to lose before I started.

I tried to come out on the jab and threw it out a few times but it wasn't working properly. I found myself pawing with it, rather than chucking it from the shoulder, as Howard had shown me in my early days. My right hand stayed by my chin. I saw openings to throw it, but my body wouldn't react. As soon as I thought about what I was doing, the chances had gone. To work well, boxing has to be instinctive.

'You didn't show him one jab,' Richard implored at the end of the first. 'Just get it going.'

But I was a shadow of my old self. We knew that Tarver was good technically, but he tended to box at a slow pace. My best chance was to outwork him, keep him under constant pressure and throw him off his rhythm. That night, there was no way I could do that. Tarver fought exactly the fight we expected him to, but there was nothing I could do about it.

Round after round dragged by. Very little happened. In the seventh, the crowd started to boo. All I could do was plod after him while he picked me off, two or three punches at a time. Around the ninth round, tired beyond belief and getting bored myself, I remember actually wishing he would just knock me out so the whole thing would finish. Bit by bit, my right eye swelled and my lips ballooned. Rather than being in a fight, it just felt like slow torture.

When the last bell finally went, I leaned on the ropes and hung my head. I hadn't even been able to make the fight competitive. That was truly painful for me.

He won. I knew he had won and I didn't even see Hobson or Poxon afterwards. They never even came back to the dressing room and that told me something.

There's an old saying about seeing who stays by you in the bad times, not just the good. After Tarver was my worst time. Besides Natalia, who was there?

Out of all the hundreds of people who flew from Sheffield, one was Glyn Rhodes, my old trainer. He made his way backstage to see me. He could see I was upset.

'Never mind, Clinton,' he said. 'I'm still so proud of you, pal. We all know you're better than that. And listen, I believe if you want to, you can win a world title again.'

To me that was a measure of his character, that he took the time to do that, and I genuinely appreciated it. I thanked him, got changed quickly, went up to my hotel room with Natalia and closed the door. At times like that, one of the most important things to have is a door you can close. Inside, I laid on the bed, looked up at the ceiling and started thinking about life as an ex- champion.

38

Here we go again

ON the plane back to England, I reflected. I had never got going in the fight and knew why, but couldn't escape the fact that my biggest fear had come true. Lots of people, especially Americans, saw that performance and maybe thought it was the best I could do. I was embarrassed.

I didn't want to make excuses, so deliberately avoided talking about my injuries or all the problems in the camp during media interviews. I tried to be as mellow as possible, even though inside I was seething.

'Tarver was better than me on the night. I'm just a skinny boy from Sheffield,' I said.

Maybe it did me no favours. My modesty meant I took a proper hammering from the press. *The Guardian* wrote that I was 'woefully short of ideas'. *The Telegraph* said I had been 'outclassed and dominated, so severely'. All the other coverage made for similar reading.

To make matters worse, a week after my defeat, Calzaghe outpointed Hopkins in Vegas, meaning the blockbuster fight between the two of us would have been on, had I won. I could finally have made life-changing money and taken part in one of the biggest British nights of all time. Now that ship would sail on elsewhere.

After a couple of weeks back home Dennis called a meeting, where we all talked about what went wrong. It got pretty heated and by the time we went our separate ways, there was a finality about it. Nothing was said in so many words, but I knew if I decided to fight on, it would be with a new team, again.

I went through the all-too-familiar process of dealing with defeat. At first retirement looked a good choice, but when I thought about it coldly, a major issue jumped out. I had not made enough money from my career to be financially secure and if I stopped, I would have to get a job. The other factor was that when I thought about it, this felt most like the defeat to Starie, when I knew there were clear reasons why I had underperformed. Somehow, it didn't seem right to finish my career with a showing like that. I deserved better. Sheffield deserved better.

I kicked around the house, trimmed the hedges, mowed the lawn. All the while I knew that sooner or later I would have to bite the bullet, get a trainer and start again. The situation after the Tarver fight replayed in my mind. How Poxon had been nowhere in sight, but Glyn Rhodes tried to make me feel better. I phoned him up.

'Will you train me?' I asked.

'Of course I will,' he replied.

A month after the Tarver fight, I headed back to the Sheffield Boxing Centre on Burton Street for the first time in ten years. Glyn's gym was always busy and soon I was mixing it up with the pros, amateurs and keep-fitters that filled the place with life. I enjoyed getting back in there but even from the beginning, in quiet moments, I had to be honest with myself. The training was nowhere near the intensity I had become used to during the glory years with Richard and John.

In many ways, it was a return to how I had trained before, running, sparring, a bit of circuit stuff, but no specific weight training and no one supervising my diet. Glyn did a lot of pads with me, but with the rest I was left to my own devices. I tried to monitor myself and it's not as if I binged on junk food every day, but it's just not the same as having an expert sort it for you.

I would go for runs and instead of doing the hard uphill slogs of the old days, I would find myself gently jogging around. I kept promising myself to do one of my old hill sessions twice a week.

'Starting from next week,' I would think. 'I'll do hill sprints Tuesdays and Thursdays.' But every week, I found an excuse. I never did it. In the gym, I would do a few chin-ups, then stop when I felt like it. There was no one screaming in my ear to carry on until I could manage no more.

My elbows continued to play up. I just ignored them as best I could. There was no way I was prepared to shell out for sessions with a specialist.

I guess the reality was that my heart wasn't fully in it. Not in the way it needs to be to beat the likes of Rico Hoye, Glen Johnson and Julio Gonzalez. Day after day, I turned up at Glyn's and did what I was supposed to do, but I was just going through the motions.

After a few months, Dennis got in touch to say he had fixed up a fight with Kosovan New Yorker Elivir Muriqi in a sort of unofficial eliminator. After beating me, Tarver lost the title to Chad Dawson, but they were due to rematch. Myself and another American, Tavoris Cloud, were the favourites to take on the winner. That was provided I beat Muriqi, who had taken Tarver to a split decision in 2007.

The fight was made for Jersey in a beautiful venue, the Hotel de France, and I travelled over a couple of days beforehand with Dennis.

'This fight gets you right back into it,' he said. 'Win this and another title shot's around the corner.'

The night was done as a dinner show, with tablecloths and chandeliers. It was like boxing in The Ritz. In spite of the fact Muriqi had done so well against Tarver, the bout was an absolute doddle. In fact, it was so easy, it was boring. Muriqi never caught me. He kept throwing big, overhand rights that missed by miles and I outboxed him with ease.

I had expected a completely different fight and almost felt a bit let down. I puzzled as to how he had got himself so highly ranked. In truth, Muriqi was a very limited fighter.

Regardless, that put me back near the top of the IBF rankings, where I had been for most of my career since beating Yawe Davis in 2001. A couple of months later, Dawson beat Tarver again, then mysteriously relinquished the belt to take on Glen Johnson in a non-title contest. By then, Johnson was 40 years old and still plugging away.

All of that meant that my final IBF title fight came about in much the same way as my first. Just as Johnson had vacated to take on Tarver, leaving me and Hoye to box as the number one and number two contenders, so Dawson had left the spoils to myself and Tavoris

Cloud. Just as there had been with Johnson and Hoye, in 2005, there were rumours Dawson vacated to avoid Cloud, who he had boxed in the amateurs.

The fight was fixed for August 2009, by which time Cloud had been inactive for a full year. The last of his 19 straight wins had been an impressive tenth-round stoppage of Julio Gonzalez. Only one of Cloud's opponents to that point had heard the final bell and he was the first man to beat Julio inside the distance.

It looked a tough assignment, yet I looked forward to it without excitement or fear. I felt flat, like a man getting a train to the office. It was work for me, nothing more.

39

Woods v Cloud

**IBF light-heavyweight championship
of the world
Seminole Hard Rock Hotel and Casino,
Hollywood, Florida
28 August 2009**

I GOT hold of some tapes of Cloud and watched him knocking over opponent after opponent. But I still found motivation lacking. Glyn was great to be around and lots of fun on the pads, but other elements of my training remained half hearted. When I look back, I think I should probably have retired but something inside me wouldn't let me do it. I had to give it one last crack, even though at the same time I knew I wasn't preparing myself as well as I should.

I flew over to Florida and immediately reacquainted myself with the hot, damp Florida climate. Natalia came out a couple of nights before and left the kids with her mum. We stayed in a lovely hotel, but everywhere we went, a strange smell seemed to follow me around.

'Can you smell shit?' I asked Natalia in the hotel restaurant. She shook her head.

'You asked me that this morning in the room,' she replied. 'What's wrong with you?'

I shrugged. Other than that, it was the most relaxed I felt before any of my title fights. I guess I didn't really care.

By then, my frantic support had died down a little too. At 37, people probably sensed I had lost some ferocity and motivation. Sometimes I wondered if the pot had something to do with that. It had made me lose my temper at times, but it also drove me on. When I finally got myself under control, as an adult, the fire in my belly went out.

Altogether, maybe about 100 people made the journey from Sheffield, a fraction of the crowd I had taken to previous foreign fights. Just like the previous time in Florida, against Tarver, I took some abuse on the way into the ring.

'Just fight your fight,' Glyn told me. 'Fight your fight.'

The bell went and I found myself in for a surprise. I expected Cloud would charge out, get in my face and try to land a knockout shot. In reality, he punched away busily for about 20 seconds, but there was nothing hurtful in the shots at all. I began throwing out the jab and although it didn't snap out as it had in my prime, it still landed.

Fuck me, this is going to be a doddle.

In the second and third I began catching him, finding him easy to read. Cloud was a muscular kid, but small across the shoulders for a light-heavy, with fairly short arms. He was predictable in his movements too. I would block one of his, then fire back, jolt him and send him backwards.

I could tell he didn't like it either. Here was an unbeaten young fighter, ten years my junior, who had probably boxed mostly handpicked opponents. Against me, for the first time he wasn't getting things all his own way.

Despite that I knew my punches weren't hurting him as they should. My back didn't feel strong. My hands were a shade slower than four years before.

It became a strange fight, with Cloud bustling around and me feeling that he was technically nothing special, power-wise nothing special and psychologically nothing special, but not quite having the necessary devil to stick it on him.

Despite that, I felt the fight was close. Cloud missed with most of his punches. I threw fewer shots, but the majority landed. I felt a bit like I was sleepwalking, or fighting in a dream. I just did my thing, jabbed, moved, threw the right over, but I was detached from it all somehow. I wasn't in the moment, as I needed to be.

By the time we entered the last quarter of the fight, Cloud had learned that I was unlikely to hurt him. His youth and hunger made him brave. He began to come on strong. This wasn't educated pressure, or being blinded with science, as with Jones at his best. It was just an energetic kid going balls to the wall. I didn't have it in me anymore, that ability to take one, suck it up, spin him around and make him re-adjust.

Change your direction, change your level, change your distance.

My body wouldn't do it.

'USA, USA!' the crowd chanted.

In the tenth, he caught me with a left hook that sent canaries singing around my head. I waved him on. My intention was to tag him on the way in. But the punch never came. My hands stayed by my side. He caught me again.

'Get your fuckin' hands up!' Dennis screamed.

When I got back to the corner, I couldn't see. It was the first time that had happened to me. Everything was just a blur, like a washed-out watercolour painting.

That's when I really knew. As a fighter, I was done. Glyn Rhodes knew it too.

I was behind on the cards, so my only chance was a final-round knockout. But after the 11th, Glyn gave me some water and looked at me with kindly eyes.

'Listen to me,' he said. There was no urgency or desperation in his voice. 'It's the last round, Clinton. Just one to go. I don't want you to do anything stupid, OK? You keep your hands up and box. Just keep your hands up and it'll all be fine. We can have a drink and go home.'

Still, in the last round, I caught Cloud a few times and even then, I felt the old me would have won. But the old me wasn't there. At the end, the new me was just glad it was over.

It was nice the crowd appreciated me at the end. I suppose they were happy their man took it, but on the way back to my dressing room I got slapped on the back and cheered.

'Man, you're one tough bastard,' a guy in the front row said.

Backstage, I went over to Cloud's dressing room to congratulate him and maybe offer advice. I expected to find scenes of wild celebration, but when I opened the door he was sitting in the middle of the floor with his head in his hands. His trainer saw me and stood up.

'God-damn! You tough motherfucker!' he yelled. 'Look at my man. You fucked him up.'

Cloud didn't move. They told me that he had dehydrated badly during the fight and there had even been a conversation in the corner about pulling him out before the last round. It seemed that at 37, with my prime behind me, I still came within a whisker of being world champion again.

Despite myself, I couldn't help but wonder 'What if?' What if I had gone for it in the last three minutes instead of holding back? But then I looked at the relief in Natalia's eyes and stopped myself. There was no longer any point thinking like that.

40

And then?

ONCE we got back to my dressing room, Dennis and Natalia noticed I had green slime leaking from my right ear. It continued for the whole of the next day and smelled disgusting. Funnily enough, it smelled like shit, as I had kept mentioning before the fight. Natalia insisted I go to a hospital to get it looked at.

Once he had examined me, the doctor tutted, shook his head and made little faces.

'Have you found your balance affected?' he asked.

'No, I don't think so.'

'What about your hearing?'

'Fine.'

'Dizziness?'

'No, I just kept smelling a bad smell.'

'That's because you have a huge infection in your ear canal. It's completely blocked. There's no way you should have fought with this. You must have felt terrible.'

I shrugged.

He asked about my previous injuries and concluded that the damage caused by Mark Baker at Wembley all those years before had never properly healed. Since then, accumulated blows to the ear had obviously worsened it. Cloud had then re-perforated my eardrum, causing the infection to begin leaking out. As a precaution, he suggested I take some time out of the ring. I thanked him for the advice, but it was unnecessary. I didn't need to be told.

Since my best years in 2005 and 2006, both elbows had gone, my back had been disastrous and now my right ear was fucked. Those complaints could be listed alongside all the regular knocks that fighters don't even mention, like busted knuckles and broken noses. The reality was, as I headed towards the end of my thirties, that boxing was breaking my body down.

Without the desire to train flat out, I knew that true world level was beyond me. I wasn't a prodigy, like a Jones Jr or Muhammad Ali, someone whose sheer talent could carry them through. I was a guy who had to be at his very best to compete at the top. If I carried on, I would probably pick up more defeats, suffer more physical damage and end up as a gatekeeper, a name for young prospects to pick off as they fought their way through the ranks.

I knew a few who had gone on too long in boxing, guys like Meldrick Taylor. I never wanted to end up like them. Shuffling around, shaky hands, unclear speech. I thought of Jude and Lola, who by then were four and two years old. I wanted to be a proper father as they grew up, not an invalid and, for me, that meant the time was right to quit.

I told Natalia that night as we lay on the hotel bed. She could tell I meant it this time.

'It's the right thing to do,' she said.

But again, as we packed our bags and headed for the airport, I faced that familiar feeling. *What now?* The money I had cleared from the Muriqi and Cloud fights, along with some I had put away, could keep us going for two or three years, but then? Decades rolled ahead of us like an ocean. When we got home, we had a chat about the future.

'So other than boxing, what do you like doing?' Natalia asked.

'Gardening,' I replied. So that became option number one.

I went out and bought some gear, hedgecutters, strimmers, other bits. My first customer was Dennis, who lived just up from the road. His garden was so big that I had to use a sit-down mower to cut the grass.

Things went OK for a few months. Word of mouth built my client base and I ticked along. The money was poor, though. Unless you're doing landscaping or the more creative stuff, gardening is more or less a minimum wage gig.

By May 2010, I had taken on a job involving a bunch of trees that needed to be dug up. They were big old bastards too and it was murder. One day, it was boiling hot and I started thinking: 'What am I doing? What's this about? I'm killing myself for ninety quid a day.'

The more I thought about it, the more I realised I couldn't see myself sticking it out. I told Natalia. She accepted it philosophically.

'So what else do you like doing?' she asked.

'Plastering.' So that became option number two.

Just as with the gardening, jobs flew in pretty quickly and in no time I found myself busy, earning an average of £120 a day, a slight improvement. But again, I found the 38-year-old me didn't react to the work as well as I had 20 years before. I had such good memories of plastering, but I was a different Clinton.

After a couple of hectic months, I got a job for an old woman who needed her toilet ceiling done. The room was so tiny I could barely charge her anything. I ended up working in this miniscule space, too small to use a ladder, for £40. As often happens with those sort of jobs, although the area was small, it was devilishly tricky to work with. I plastered it by standing on the toilet and just as I was finishing, my foot went through the seat.

Of course, I had to go and buy her another one and it turned out the seat she wanted cost £45. I brought it back and fitted it, said my goodbyes and left. What a kick in the teeth.

For my very next job, I needed to skim an entire house. I had no labourer and did the job alone. On the last day, I had one ceiling left to finish and promised myself that when I got the job over with I would head out for a few beers with some mates. I needed some downtime. I put the first coat on, then ran downstairs to mix the plaster for the second coat on the driveway.

It was a freezing cold day and as I jogged from the house, towards the bucket, I slipped on some ice, went flying and skidded face-first for about ten feet across the tarmac. That was it.

I loaded up the car and drove straight to my brother Heath's house. He works as a plasterer. When he opened the door, I passed him all my gear.

'Here,' I said. 'Have the lot. I i'nt doing that shit again.'

Again, I went home and spoke to Natalia. She sighed. It seemed my days of manual work were behind me as much as my boxing. The unspoken issue was that I still received calls from Dennis and she knew it.

Hobson wasn't pressuring me at all, but sometimes he received offers from other promoters and let me know. Just before I gave up on plastering, he spoke about a potential contest with European cruiserweight champion Enzo Maccarinelli, from Swansea. The money was decent and, being honest, I was tempted. *One more can't hurt, surely?*

Natalia was dead against it. She even threatened divorce if I did it. Would she really go that far? I didn't think so.

'So gardening or plastering haven't worked out,' she said. 'What else is there?'

'Do you remember John, who used to do my weights and nutrition?'

'Yeah.'

'He's opened a gym and asked me to help him out.'

'Doing what?'

'He wants me to run a boxing class'

'Why not give it a go?' she said. 'You've nothing to lose.' So that became option number three.

I started boxing fitness classes on Saturday mornings at John's gym in the middle of 2010. To begin with, there were only five regular customers, but before long I built it up to 18-20 most weeks. As it developed I thought there could be a living in it, if I did it more often. The idea crossed my mind of opening my own place.

While I began discussing the idea with Natalia and John, I received a message from Dennis that absolutely thrilled me. He said Sheffield Council had been on the phone and they wanted to dedicate a star to me on the Sheffield Walk of Fame outside the town hall.

'Are you up for it?' Dennis asked.

'Course I am, ar.'

Known as *Sheffield Legends,* the star-shaped plaques are awarded to people from the city whose achievements are worthy of commemoration. Other names include actor and *Monty Python* star Michael Palin, Olympic gold medallist Sebastian Coe and rock legends Def Leppard. Only Brendan Ingle from the world of boxing had previously been awarded one.

I was invited to the town hall and had tea with the mayor before the ceremony was held. They asked me to make a little speech.

'I had a great career in boxing,' I said. 'And I never expected to achieve all that I achieved. I was always just a skinny boy from Sheffield!'

Photographers snapped pictures and the mayor shook my hand.

'Does this mean people have to call me Sir now?' I asked.

Once the presentation was over, we returned home and continued mulling over the gym idea. It made sense to get things started while my name was still in the public eye and it emerged there were premises available over the road from John's. With his help, I worked out a business plan. We reckoned with my own building I could do a mixture of morning and evening classes, along with one-to-ones in between.

The premises were council-owned, a former youth club that had fallen into disrepair. I met with the charity trust responsible for it and after a lot of wrangling, managed to pick it up, with the land around it, for about £130,000. That meant I had to make it work. It swallowed up pretty much all of my remaining money.

Once the 'Clinton Woods Boxing and Fitness Gym' opened later that year, one-to-one business kicked in quickly. People who could afford it loved the idea of personal training with a former world champion. The groups were slower to take off, but within a few months they were thriving too.

Most popular were the women-only sessions, where I regularly had 20-plus clients at a time. I charged customers five pounds each, which equated to £100 for an hour's work, decent going. But it was also highly stressful in its own way. Some of them would not stop moaning!

'It's too hot.'

'it's too cold.'

'It's too draughty.'

'It smells in here.'

But at my stage of life. I still preferred it to plastering or gardening.

Once things had started to roll along at the gym, I began to get interest from local pros looking for a trainer. Soon I had enough to run a session just for them. I went running with them in the mornings, then had them in the gym every day at 1pm. Among the boys I trained were super middleweight Lewis Taylor, super-lightweights Kas Hussein and Jamie Sampson and middleweight Reagan Denton.

I charged them just two pounds each per session because I know how tough it can be as young pro to make ends meet. They all wanted sparring as well, so I stepped in for that, too. But soon I found it was all becoming a bit much. Between working with the pros and all my private and group sessions, I barely had a minute all day to stop and eat. Weight was dropping off me. I became gaunt and ill-looking.

Soon, I realised that although I enjoyed running my gym and the craic with customers, training professionals wasn't for me. More than anything, I hated fight nights. Being in the corner frustrated me.

I would watch my lads train and feel they weren't putting enough of themselves into it. I could see the potential in some of them and found it upsetting. They complained of being skint, of not being able to pay their £2 subs.

'Just gerra fuckin' job,' I would say.

'No, can't do that, I'm looking for sponsors.'

That attitude annoyed me. I had always been a grafter and never asked for anything. No one sponsored me until I was Central Area champion. Why would someone want to sponsor a kid who's only had a handful of fights against journeymen?

When I had boxed at their level, I trained after work. I earned my money. But some of these boys seemed to feel the world owed them a living. It was a different attitude and after a while it began to bug me.

The straw that broke the camel's back was when one of the lads, who had a sponsor, had a fight booked in about a month's time. He approached me in the gym at the start of a session.

'Listen,' he said. 'Just between you and me, I'm pulling out of my fight.'

'Why?' I asked.

'I just don't feel like fighting. But please don't tell anyone. My sponsor's paying for my training and they'll stop my money if they know.'

I nodded and walked away. After the session finished and all the boys left, I sat on the canvas in the middle of my main ring and thought: 'Is this what pro boxing is now?'

Shortly after that I got them all together, told them I wasn't enjoying it and that they would need to find another trainer. It seemed to me that the professional game had lost all its soul. And I decided I wanted nothing to do with it.

41

The final piece
of the jigsaw

FORTUNATELY, I found myself able to make a living from the gym without the pros. I have a healthy client base, mixed between charity and white-collar boxers, keep-fitters and kids. I enjoy it and so do my customers, which is probably the main thing.

People want to leave my gym tired, so I give them that. Sometimes my punters have to crawl out of there. Parents value the discipline I give to the kids. I try to be old school, like Ray was with me, to teach them the basics, not let them get away with messing about. *No bleedin' fidget spinners, cheeky shite or bottle flipping in my gym!* Times are different now. Kids have phones and all kinds of distractions that we never had. A lot of those things just disconnect them from themselves. Most of them are so physically unfit. That makes places like boxing gyms more important than ever.

For a long while, I continued receiving offers to make a comeback. Matchroom wanted me to enter a *Prizefighter* tournament a few years back. Dennis remained convinced that a rematch with Roy Jones could be a moneyspinner. We even went over to Jersey in 2010 to meet him at an 'Evening with Roy Jones Jr' event. Tim Witherspoon was there too. It was nice to see him again.

'How about another fight between you and Clinton Woods?' someone in the audience asked Jones. I don't know if Dennis set the whole thing up. It wouldn't surprise me.

Roy turned to me. His face looked different, puffier cheeks, forehead carved up with lines, eyebrows swollen with scar tissue.

'How 'bout it Clinton?' he asked. I just shrugged.

The truth is I wouldn't want to fight him now. I don't think people would want to see it. I've seen clips of his recent bouts and they're sad to see. He looks sluggish and flat footed. He gets hammered by fighters unfit to lace his boots. I don't know if he's struggling for money, or just addicted, but I wish he would quit. I'm glad I avoided that ending.

As the years rolled on, the offers for comebacks slowly dried up. Heading towards my mid-forties, I don't expect to receive any more and in truth I wouldn't consider them if I did. Natalia would kill me, for a start.

My business at the gym has continued to grow and thrive, meaning I can look back on my career with a sense of achievement. Perhaps the most important thing was that I left the pro ring with my health intact. Not everyone can say that.

In 2012, I was humbled to receive another massive honour. An installation was planned for the Trans-Pennine trail, a walking route that crosses the city. Part of the installation would involve three steel statues and the Sheffield public were asked to vote for which figures to portray. It was one of the proudest moments of my life when I learned that I had been chosen.

Winning world titles is one thing, but being acclaimed by the people of your home city goes beyond that. I've always felt such a deep connection with Sheffield and the knowledge that I enjoy the respect of the city's people gives me more satisfaction than anything.

They are Sheffield.

I am Sheffield.

But Sheffield still sometimes shows me it's other side too. I guess I deal with it differently now, though. Only a couple of years ago, I received another of those panicked phone calls from Mam.

'Clinton, go down to the hospital. Your Heath's been stabbed.'

It turned out he had been knifed by his girlfriend, of all people, during a nasty domestic dispute. Both my parents were there in hospital reception when I arrived, white and shaking. A big drunk bloke stood in front of us, shouting at the receptionist, taking all the attention.

'Hey up, mate' I said, getting impatient. 'Gi' someone else a chance.' He turned around.

'I've been fuckin' assaulted!' he yelled.

'If tha' don't fuck off, you'll be assaulted again,' I told him.

He started walking my way, screwing his face up. In the old days, the pot would have boiled, but not now.

'Listen pal, don't fuck wi' me. I don't want to fight, but if I do I'll fuckin' ammer thi'. I'm in a bad mood.' I told him.

He walked off, so I started explaining to the receptionist what had happened. Thirty seconds later, the piss-artist returned.

'Listen mate,' I said. 'I telled thi. I in't speaking to ya. Don't come no closer.'

His face broke into a broad, inebriated smile.

'Tha looks a fit lad, don't tha,' he declared happily.

I couldn't help but laugh. He laughed back. The two of us stood there giggling. 'Oh, please fuck off,' I told him. He complied and fortunately, after a night of worrying, Heath came through that one too.

Funnily enough I ran into Howard Rainey not long ago, at a bonfire night event near my house. I don't know what he was doing there. They were charging a fiver to get in and he was standing around outside.

He looked terrible. He's lost a lot of weight. I asked him if he was coming in and he said: 'No, I'm staying out 'ere.'

I went in with my kids, turned around to look and he was still just loitering there. It seemed so strange. This guy was a really good trainer in his day, one of the top men in the country, and it slowly dawned on me that he wasn't coming in because he didn't have any money.

I went back out and got him, paid his entrance fee and bought him a drink. He didn't look right. I asked him how his inventions were going.

'I've got a buyer for one,' he said

'Oh yeah, who's that?'

'NASA!'

I was about to laugh but he was deadly serious.

'And how much are they are offering for it?'

'Six and a half million dollars.'

'Fuckin' hell, Howard,' I said. 'I hope you accepted it.'

He finished his drink and looked back at me. There was real anger on his face, like he might lash out.

'Fucking Yanks,' he spat. His cheeks had gone all blotchy. 'It needs to stay in this country.'

He threw his cup on the ground and walked off. It was the first time I'd seen him in years. So many ex-boxers end up losing it.

Yet despite the personal growth and satisfaction my career brought for me, something always nagged the back of mind. I tried to ignore it and had done for years, but it never left me. I felt it in my guts. I knew I would never be fully happy until it was sorted.

I dithered until 2014, considering advances, making excuses, when it was suddenly taken out of my hands. I was sitting in my lounge at Swallow Cottage, fiddling with my phone, when I received a Facebook friend request from Kyle. By then, he was 26 years old. I hadn't seen him since he was four. My heart thundered in my chest.

With shaky hands, I carried the phone into the kitchen.

'Natalia,' I said. 'Look at this.'

She took the phone, looked at the screen and burst straight into tears. Facially, as a young man, Kyle was a carbon copy of me.

'What should I do?' I asked.

'What do you want to do?'

'I need to see him.'

We became Facebook friends, as you do in the 21st century, swapped a few messages then arranged to meet at a pub.

'Look,' I told him. 'I know I can't be a fatha to thi. It's too late for that. But I'd like to be your friend.'

He was very quiet, a bit like myself. He accepted what I was saying without much comment.

'The thing is,' I went on. 'I were a little bastard when I were younger. I din't gi' a shit about nothing. I just wanted to drink and fuck about. It's not fair on you, but I can't change it. I'm sorry.'

We had a little talk and I really felt for the lad. He had had a tough life. His mum had difficulties with drink and drugs and he had been in care a few times. It choked me up and I wondered how it must have been for him, going through all that, knowing his estranged dad was a champion boxer. Somehow, he seemed able to forgive. We started again straight away.

Since that starting point, I've seen Kyle regularly. He comes to the house most weeks. Recently, he got married and had his first child, so I'm a grand-daddy now. So strange. It still haunts, though, how I abandoned him, still chokes me up. It's my one true regret in life. When I went to visit the baby, to hold my granddaughter for the first time, I looked over at him. He was staring back at me.

'I wonder if he's thinking how I was never there for him,' I thought.

Sometimes I sit in my garden, watching the hawks and buzzards flying overhead, seeing hares leap in the field. I can hear my kids playing inside the house and remember my days back on the Westfield, hungry, unable to pay bills. I recall the letter my Mam sent me.

My life could have gone in many directions but things worked out so well.

Natalia has been such a huge part of that. She put up with a lot and never nagged or belittled me. There were even times in the early days when she paid for both of us to live. She had to, as I had so little coming in. I can look back on all of that now, laugh and say I'm a happy man.

I'm not sure exactly how, but I found my way out of the woods.

Epilogue

12 November 2016

There are 20 or so punters moving around the heavy and medium bags hanging from the ceiling like ripe fruit. A spread of ages are present, both genders. Some are in shape. They move on the balls of their feet, lithe and swift. They look like proper fighters. Others sport beer bellies or arses as wide as the door. The air clouds with their sweat as a voice cuts through the music.

'Now uppercuts, come on! Faster.'

'Ten seconds! Jab, jab, move!'

'Harder, harder, come on!'

They walked or drove here, through Saturday-morning drizzle to exert their bodies. But they have also been drawn by something else.

One by one, the shouting man takes them on the pads. Youthful, decrepit, muscular, flabby, it doesn't matter. They dance on the floor next to the ring. Seamless, he adjusts to the level of each, feet working in circles, hands carving arcs in the air. He is gentle. He smiles. They smile back.

Glowing, they return to their bag work, each having boxed a world champion. The subtle magic of that lifts them, from domestic or professional routine. From work, bills and *setterdy neet dahn tahn*.

Away from the murky world of the prize ring, where he was never as appreciated as he deserved to be, this is what Clinton Woods now does.

He offers escape.

And it works.